PUTTING QUALITY INTO PRACTICE

Other titles by the author and published by
Stanley Thornes (Publishers) Ltd
The Assessment of Performance and
Competence
Instructional Techniques and Practice
Teaching and Learning in Further
and Adult Education

PUTTING QUALITY INTO PRACTICE

L. Walklin

Stanley Thornes (Publishers) Ltd

First published in 1992 by:
Stanley Thornes (Publishers) Ltd
Old Station Drive
Leckhampton
CHELTENHAM GL53 0DN
England

British Library Cataloguing in Publication Data

Walklin, L.
    Putting quality into practice. – (Further education teachers' books)
    I. Title   II. Series
    378.1

    ISBN 0-7487-1360-3

Typeset by Tech-Set, Gateshead, Tyne & Wear.
Printed and bound in Great Britain at The Bath Press, Avon.

CONTENTS

Acknowledgements   vii

How to use this book   ix

Introduction   xi

1 Planning for Quality – Mission and Strategy   1

2 Introducing Change   38

3 TQM – Concept Development and Implementation   51

4 TQM – Putting the Customer First   70

5 TQM and BS 5750 in Education and Training   85

6 Service Design   108

7 Service Delivery   130

8 Service Results   154

9 Monitoring and Evaluating the Service Provision   178

10 Audits and Probes   189

11 The Curriculum Audit   231

Bibliography   259

Index   262

ACKNOWLEDGEMENTS

The author and publishers are grateful to the following for permission to reproduce copyright material:

The British Standards Institution (BSI) for permission to reproduce the BSI definition of 'quality audit' given in BS 7229, p. 6, para. 4.2, and of 'nonconformity' given in BS 4778: Part 1 (1987), p. 9, para. 3.20; Figure 3.1 'Increasing quality awareness and improvement activities' taken from BS 6143: Part 2 (1990), p. 2; the definition of 'method study' given in BS 3138:1979, p. 2, para. no. 10003; Figure 5.9 'Cross reference of quality system elements' given in Appendix A of BS 5750: Part 4 (1990) p. 12; and reference to 'Guidance notes for application of BS 5750/ISO 9000/ EN 29000 to education and training' (Sixth draft), BSI Quality Assurance, Milton Keynes January 1991.

The Employment Group – Training Enterprise and Education Directorate (TEED) for numerous references to the content of its publications.

The Dorset Training and Enterprise Council (TEC) and the Coventry and Warwickshire Training and Enterprise Council (TEC) for references reproduced from their respective versions of the *Training Provider Quality Survey Manual.*

The Further Education Unit (FEU) for quotations taken from *Towards a Framework for Curriculum Entitlement*; Figure 6.1 from *Strategy and Processes,* 1986; and for numerous other references to the content of its publications.

William Collins Sons & Co Ltd, for many references to terms given in the Collins English Dictionary.

The Institute of Personnel Management for permission to reproduce Figure 7.1 'Training cycle' and a definition of 'planned training' taken from J. Kenney and M. Reid, *Training Interventions,* 1986.

The Principal, The Bournemouth and Poole College of Further Education for permission to reproduce quality flow charts and other documentation designed by the author and drafted by Brian Snape, College Media and Information Co-ordinator, and Dawn Whelan, Graphic Designer.

Stan Turner, Vice Principal Planning and Resources, The Bournemouth and Poole College of Further Education for suggesting the tentative agenda framework for accountability, quality assurance and institutional evaluation given in Figure 10.7.

Andrew Furphy, Managing Director, J. Furphy & Sons Pty Ltd of Shepparton, Victoria 3630, Australia, for generously providing information about the company's quality policy and also for permission to reproduce data concerning the history and development of the business and a photograph of the original Furphy Farm Water Cart. Thanks are also due to Ken Barber, Supervisor, North Pine Country Park, Queensland and Reg Hodgson of the Queensland Steam and Vintage Machinery Society for assistance in tracing the origin of a particular vintage water cart.

Antoinette Brandi, Staff Development Manager, North Point College of TAFE, Bracken Ridge, Queensland 4017, and the College Director, for providing information concerning the college organisational structure.

Bob Cowdrey, Dorset Skills Training (DST) Quality Assurance Manager, for providing information regarding documentation and records. In addition, for working closely with the author in developing quality procedures for DST within the Bournemouth and Poole College of Further Education.

Every attempt has been made to contact copyright holders, but we apologise if any have been overlooked.

Disclaimer

HOW TO USE THIS BOOK

What is written is based upon the author's practical experience backed by literature searches, reference to current British Standards and involvement in designing flow charts and quality procedures. This work is presented in the hope that readers as practitioners and others interested in quality matters will be able to make immediate use of the content.

Putting Quality into Practice may be read from cover to cover or used for spot reference. A list of topics is given at the front of each chapter and this is intended to help readers form an overview of the coverage.

Relevant complementary and underpinning knowledge is outlined, as are methods of dealing with a range of quality functions. Embedded in the text are important considerations for the chain of internal suppliers and customers, together with criteria for action relating to the roles of service provider, supplier and quality auditor. Factors to bear in mind are inset in heavy type, as are suggestions for improving the service in order to meet consistently customer expectations.

A number of different style flow charts have been included to guide readers when planning their own procedures and audit trails. One type lists the sequence of events comprising a given procedure and specifies the records associated with each stage. Another type, that could be used when planning procedures and for audit purposes, lists a sequence of questions and, where necessary, directs the provider to a corrective procedure designed to satisfy requirements.

Quality probes comprising questions that could be asked by teams establishing current status when looking into quality requirements have been included throughout the text. The probes are intended only to trigger the readers' ideas for monitoring their own provision and effecting internal audits. They are not intended to be definitive. Although the words 'must' and 'will' are frequently used, rather than softer words like 'should' or 'may' there is in general little legislation or rigid requirement to be enforced. The words are used to suggest that when and if documented quality procedures have been approved they must be implemented rather than leaving it up to individuals to please themselves whether or not to operate according to accepted systems.

Satisfying customer entitlement and meeting required standards when planning, preparing, delivering, monitoring and evaluating a service can only be achieved when quality procedures are fully implemented, regularly reviewed and corrected as necessary.

Although the text is focused on training and education the concept and much of the content is readily transferable to the entire service occupational area.

INTRODUCTION

Looking back over the years it occurs to me that I have been involved with quality-related matters for longer than I care to remember. I first became interested in quality assurance and the control of quality while working for Gillette, initially as assistant to a very capable engineering manager named Norman Brown, and later as a development engineer. Our work involved the design and development of high-speed, mass production systems, processes and machinery that operated to exacting specifications. With the aid of a team of highly-skilled toolmakers and precision fitters we were then required to introduce and perfect the innovation, and train production staff to operate the systems efficiently and effectively to Gillette's self-imposed, high quality standards.

Gillette has from its inception insisted on meeting customer expectations and requirements and going just that bit further in search of excellence at the least cost. For me it was a baptism of fire and it was then that I began to understand the quality concept and what it may be about.

Since those days I have endeavoured to learn more about making a commitment to quality and taking account of the value to management of a total quality philosophy underpinned by systems such as BS 5750.

I consider myself fortunate in that I have, over a number of years, been able to observe and participate in attempts to introduce a total quality approach in a number of different working environments. Having spent some time working for a major electrical retailer as a salesman, installation engineer, bad debt collector and delivery man; as a civil engineering plant fitter; and as an express coach driver in the UK and driver/courier on continental tours, my observations of customer behaviour, needs and requirements have been, to say the least, very revealing.

Perhaps the secret to success in meeting customer requirements lies within an amalgam of approaches advocated by leading quality gurus. So, with this suggestion in mind, I have attempted to integrate what I have learned from their work with my experiences, gained formerly as a practising engineer and more recently as a staff developer and trainer in education and industry.

As the reader will see, an attempt has been made to relate the total quality concept to formal quality assurance systems, procedures, probes and audits that hopefully will work in education, training and service industries.

Some will argue that there are significant differences between training and education, but since we are dealing with a quality systems approach throughout the text, the term training is meant to apply equally to education. When interpreting the requirements of BS 5750 and in particular when identifying certain quality system elements within education and training there may be some difficulty in making direct comparisons, but the reader will no doubt be able to make suitable connections.

Products and outcomes include training programme content and service delivered to users, qualifications, competence achieved and customer satisfaction. Customers include sponsors, employers, trainers, trainees, internal or external clients and any other end-user that obtains services from the supplier or provider.

Les Walklin
1992

CHAPTER ONE

Planning for Quality – Mission and Strategy

Chapter coverage

Quality culture
    Mission statements
    Organisational charts
    Typical management structures
Quality management systems
    The need for competent staff
    Management responsibility
    Quality policy
    Quality manuals
    Quality planning
    Quality procedures
    Achieving BS 5750 certification
    Responsibility and authority
    The management representative
    Management review
The quality system organisation
    The quality plan
    Strategic planning
Quality audits
    Audits defined
    Audit objectives and responsibilities
    Preparing for audit
    Arranging audits
    Internal quality probes

1

Health and safety in the learning environment
    The Health and Safety at Work Act 1974
    Basic obligations of employers
    Basic obligations of employees
    Laboratory safety
    Fire hazards
    Promoting a positive attitude
    Health and safety while training
    Accident procedures

Quality culture

In order to fulfil profitably their business objectives, many enlightened organisations are urgently promoting strategies that will result in a more responsive and effective service to customers. The need to maintain a competitive edge over other providers and to assure consistent quality of provision is reinforced by the requirement to survive. This provides an exciting conceptual framework for the corporate inspiration and continuous quality development that has proved to be so rewarding to world-class businesses following the American and Japanese traditions.

In order to attain quality goals, the latent potential to bring about enhanced performance at all levels must be realised. This will require that quality management systems involving everyone, backed by user-friendly information systems, are brought into play. Putting quality concepts into practice can result in sought-after improvement in service reliability and perceived quality, together with a reduction in quality costs. However, the notion of total quality can only be realised when the hearts and minds of all employees are committed to the pursuit of quality within a corporate culture where customer requirements come first.

This culture entails building quality communities with uniform notions of quality and shared values. Each member of a community will have common ownership of parts of the service provided and will form an important link in the quality chain within the organisation. Each employee will be responsible for supplying a quality service. Responsibility, accountability and commitment to quality will be delegated to individuals who must seek to fulfil effectively their role as a supplier to others.

There is no universally recommended approach to assuring quality although some form of quality initiative is required in order to benefit from the pursuit of continuous quality development. Initiatives that can contribute to achievement of enhanced quality include: using audits and probes; the adoption of systems such as BS 5750, ISO 9000 and EN 29000; total quality management; and investing in people and strategic quality management.

Mission statements

Customers have at least one thing in common – they expect to get value for money. They will judge a supplier on the quality of service received and the extent to which their requirements are consistently met. Continued success in the service business will depend upon the supplier's ability to deliver products and services that are fit for their intended purpose and satisfy users' needs. Today there is no place for the *caveat emptor* principle. The concept, 'Let the buyer beware', has been replaced by the warning, 'Let the supplier beware'.

Today, the notion of total quality and the introduction of systems of quality assurance affect every person employed in an organisation, as does the duty to strive continually to satisfy customers' requirements.

Recognising the need to provide a comprehensive and, where necessary, integrated range of services of the highest quality to meet clients' needs is implicit within the now widely-used mission statements and strategic service visions.

A **mission statement** defines the philosophy that underpins a supplier's business operations. The statement expresses in the broadest way the philosophy's objectives, direction and underlying purposes. Related organisational **objectives** tend to be rather more specific and are statements of intent concerning goals for the whole business. However, each department will have its own **unit objectives** and probably different sets of **course team targets**.

Today, training providers are expected to meet successfully the demands of both business and individual customers. They need to organise themselves around quality-assured procedures and make a heavy commitment to providing modern vocational training as well as long-established, traditional education work.

The supplier's mission statement may be included in the **quality manual** which is a policy document for the business. The policy document will be supported by detailed codes of practice and organisational charts. Sample statements describing the missions of typical education and training providers are given in Figures 1.1 and 1.2.

A corporate mission statement is intended to focus every employee's attention on organisational policies and their individual and collective responsibilities in the pursuit of quality standards and in meeting

---

Mission

We are committed to creating an enduring training provision and we aim to be a leader in our occupational area.

Our training expertise and customer service are key to establishing a reputation as a caring training provider. Learning achievement and satisfaction of our customers' needs are measures of our success. It is this that provides a reward for our stakeholders and secures our long-term future.

We serve our customers.

We take a pride in imaginatively anticipating and responding to national, regional and local training initiatives and matching these to our customers' needs. We will provide them with a wide choice of high-quality training and education opportunities, and excellent value, in an attractive and welcoming learning environment.

We value our people.

We will create an atmosphere in which our people can develop their talents and contribute as part of an energetic and enthusiastic team. We will invest in staff development training. We will reward their professional application of knowledge and skills.

We work in partnership with our contractors.

We share a common interest with our contractors and suppliers in meeting customers' needs. We will be fair in all our dealings, respect contractual agreements and aim to develop long-term relationships of mutual respect with them.

We support the community.

We will make a positive and responsible contribution to the lives of the community in which we live and work, and we will be recognised as good neighbours.

We support our occupational area.

We are proud of the training business in which we are involved. We shall work continuously to improve efficiency and standards, to manage our resources effectively and to assure quality of provision.

Figure 1.1 Mission statement – training provider

Mission

- To satisfy local, regional and national employment needs for staff educated and trained to various levels of creative sensibility and technical competence to carry out work-related activities in a variety of occupations dependent upon the particular area of specialisation.
- To provide each customer with an accurate and realistic insight into work-related employment opportunities, requirements and prospects.
- To structure learning opportunities so as to provide the educational and professional experiences necessary to enhance customers' employment prospects.
- To develop customers' creative, intellectual and craft skills to a high level, and to aid personal development and the ability to adapt to changing circumstances.
- To provide encouragement, advice and assessment in order to help each customer fully realise individual potential.

Figure 1.2 Strategic service vision – vocational college

customers' needs. This concept is not new, as is illustrated by the example provided by J. Furphy and Sons Pty Ltd.[1] The company mission role dating from the nineteenth century was reproduced in a message in raised letters on the end castings of the water cart shown in Figure 1.3. The inscription reads:

Good, better, best
Never let it rest
Till your good is better
And your better best.

Figure 1.3 J. Furphy water cart[2]

While mission statements are intended to harness creative energy it is individual quality standards that really count. The mission alone would amount to nothing more than a collection of words without the support and commitment of the people who are the business. Quality is a moving target and this is confirmed in a note to the author from Andrew Furphy, Managing Director of J. Furphy & Sons Pty Ltd:

After 120 years we are still trying for the 'best'. Just when you think you are there you realise it's a race with no finish line. But we enjoy competing.

Organisational charts

An **organisational chart** gives information at a glance about the management structure and framework within which the quality assurance system will operate. The total quality management function is influenced by the inputs and outputs of each element of the business, and the contribution made by internal suppliers and customers. In order to achieve organisational objectives a major management operation is demanded, so that resources, both human and physical, may be effectively and efficiently utilised in the pursuit of excellence in a chosen field.

Organisational charts take many forms, two of which are shown in Figures 1.4 and 1.5. The 'concentric circle type' illustrates the structure of a training provider while the 'family tree' shows how a large art and design college may be structured.

Figure 1.4 Circular organisation chart

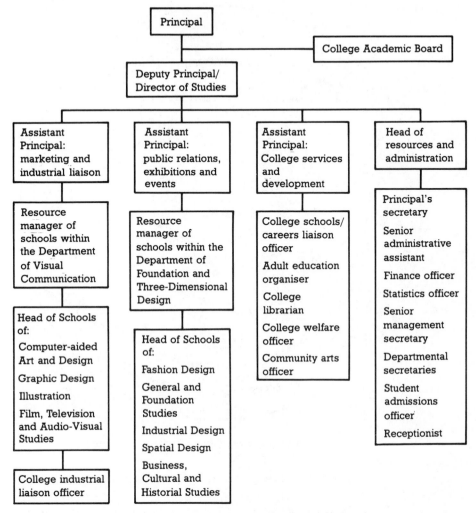

Figure 1.5 Structure of a college of art and design

The organisational chart shown in Figure 1.6 overleaf represents a modern concept of an operational structure. This type of organisation will not operate in a prescribed format. Units may be put together for a particular task or function; when the task is completed they are disbanded.

Some basic theories relating to such an organisation that need to be understood include the following:

- Traditional hierarchical structures and associated procedures are considered totally inappropriate in such an environment and should be ignored.
- Decisions will be made by the person best equipped to make that decision, e.g. a gardener will make decisions about the garden.

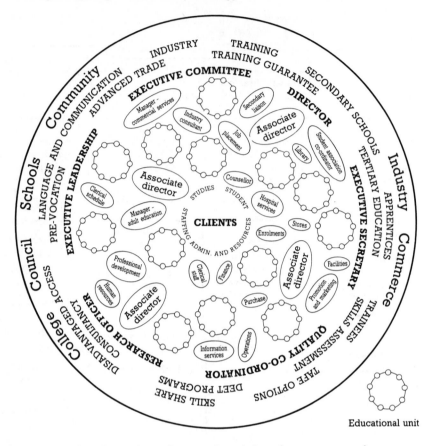

Educational unit

'Quality education and training for everyone'

Figure 1.6 North Point College organisational structure[3]

- Each staff member will be encouraged to communicate directly with the person who can provide assistance. Others will be involved on a 'courtesy' or 'need-to-know' basis.
- Small self-managed teams (preferably heterogeneous) are considered to be the most productive units of operation.
- A flexible and open organisation may function quite differently on successive days. For example, corporate goals may be achieved by using many different strategies.
- Everyone will have specific responsibilities but will also be encouraged to acquire additional skills, allowing them to contribute as the need arises.
- The success of this type of organisational structure will be evident when all staff are totally committed to it. Everyone has to be involved. Everyone has a say.[4]

Quality management systems

A total commitment to product quality and performance will go a long way to ensuring that an organisation will play an important role as a leading education and training provider in modern competitive markets.

Future growth will depend to some extent on achieving quality throughout the entire organisation. Therefore, in any total quality organisation there will be a commitment to the continual improvement of the service provided. To achieve this objective competent staff need to be employed or the support of existing staff obtained. This idea is reflected in the statement of The North Point Way shown in Figure 1.7.

Providers may be thought of as being fully integrated businesses involved in the design and delivery of training. Continued profitable expansion (or at least retention of market share) now, more than ever before, requires qualified people to strengthen the senior management teams now in place in successful **human resources** training organisations. Forward momentum cannot be maintained without employing high-calibre, technically sound professionals.

THE NORTH POINT WAY

Our way is the way of excellence and quality of service to our clients.

Whilst up-to-date equipment, modern buildings and spacious grounds help, it is only our people who can produce this outcome.

So our way will create an environment in which each of us will experience the opportunity to contribute our best in pursuit of these goals.

We believe that all the staff of North Point have the ability to make decisions, to contribute to the professional health and wealth of the college, to work single-mindedly towards serving our students excellently and to seek better ways of achieving these outcomes.

Our way will be the way of total quality management (TQM) in all aspects of our operation. The processes of TQM will be embedded into our organisational processes.

Our way is being flexible to needs and demands of our clients. We need these attitudes to address the changing environment of the next decade and the next century. We need a very flexible organisation that can create and recreate itself as needs be. We cannot build by controlling, only by creating.

WE ARE TOO GOOD NOT TO BE BETTER

Figure 1.7 The North Point Way[5]

The need for competent staff

Responsibility for ensuring that deadlines are met and that outcomes are efficiently achieved, which are consistent with challenging cost, quality and customer need, rests with course leaders or project managers, and their teams. An autonomous role is called for where the manager is encouraged (and allowed) to take responsibility for the day-to-day running of his or her area of provision.

Accountability for enhancing overall service in terms of performance and profitability of staff employed within a given area of provision will rest with team managers. Their organisational skills and ability to lead and motivate other staff will be important factors in achieving performance targets. But their key role will be to initiate, investigate, develop and implement innovative ideas and methods aimed at improving training processes. To do this they must have an open-minded approach with good analytical skills and be able to succeed under pressure or when encountering resistance. If they are successful, a total quality improvement culture will start to develop which will, hopefully, spread across the organisation.

Developing novel and cost-effective methods of working, with improved productivity in terms of delegate throughput or measurable achievements, is always on the agenda. Return on capital employed will be an important measure of a successful operation and profit is not now universally regarded as a dirty word among people employed in educational establishments. Many grades of college staff have come to realise that they need to work within budgets and generate income whenever and wherever possible. As in fully-costed work, the aim is to create profit or at least ensure survival.

All aspects of resources management must be handled effectively and efficiently. This will call for innovative control systems to be devised and installed. Extensive use of control and resource applications, modelled on those utilised in modern flexible manufacturing systems, such as material requirements planning (MRP) and just in time (JIT), will go some way to increasing productivity and economy in the usage of staff time and expendable materials. In this way, financial savings may be made in the amount of resources held at any time.

Nowadays, a full-time or part-time management accountant or cost accountant may be found working for more of the smaller providers. This function is regarded by some as an expensive luxury, but when an organisation is undergoing growth or dynamic change the right accountant will be able to help management meet inherent challenges. The person appointed will provide the financial management accounting input needed to advise the management information system. Examples of tasks performed include:

- estimating and controlling costs relating to new provision;
- creating financial plans;
- assessing funding and capital investment needs;
- preparing budgets and operating plans;
- preparing revenue reports;
- financial modelling;
- liaising with funding providers and bidding for TEC (Training & Enterprise Council) contracts and other work;
- setting up and using computer-based accounting systems;
- monitoring market share, penetration and growth.

In order to take the provider through the nineties and beyond, the aim must be to develop the best financial and performance information systems that can be afforded. State-of-the-art systems will impact on virtually every aspect of training provision, giving vital support to decision-making processes.

If a provider does not happen to have a system in place it is likely that competitors will. Control of costs and maintenance of cash flow will determine whether or not a business survives and prospers. No one is rewarded for effort alone, it is effective management and efficient working that yields the results that count. Working efficiently to do the wrong things is a waste of resources. A system that is closely focused on the drivers of profitability will go some way to providing the information needed to make the best decisions.

When seeking to introduce new learning opportunities for customers, to maintain market share or for continued expansion, an imaginative public relations person or press officer can prove indispensable. An under-standing of media and advertising, backed by knowledge of print, production and the benefit of good press relations, combined with the ability to write promotional material, is an important need for any marketing person.

Having someone on the staff who is able to create and manage news events and write press releases to support the organisation's activities will be a great asset.

Seasoned managers and competent staff with proven abilities who can demonstrate substantial work experience in a number of the areas discussed above may not be easy to recruit. To meet the need, existing staff will probably fit the bill, provided they are committed to take on the responsibility for meeting fundamental changes in quality standards and the increased emphasis placed on customer care.

Management responsibility

The training provider will need to operate a quality management system that is defined by a **quality policy**. The management team is charged with the responsibility of formally documenting and publicising the provider's quality intentions.

The management will need to produce a manual that clearly details quality systems and appoint a management representative to oversee quality functions. The quality management system must include documented methods of applying, recording and auditing quality assurance and improvement programmes.

Quality probe – management responsibility

- Is there a quality policy?
- Is the quality policy an integrated element of the corporate policy?
- Is the policy documented and has it been authorised by top management?

Quality policy

Quality policy should relate to the provider's **mission statement** and embrace quality aspects of its strategy and operational plans (see Figure 1.8). The policy must set achievable targets and aim to make the most effective use of the human and material resources available to foster a climate of continual quality improvement. Outcomes in terms of consistently meeting customers' needs and expectations must be foremost in the minds of all employees operating quality systems. A staff development and training policy would ensure that new employees are inducted into a quality-oriented approach to their work and all other employees are trained to work competently, with total commitment to the achievement of quality criteria.

In order to keep policy up-to-date, objectives, implementation and staff responsibilities must be kept under review.

COLLEGE POLICY

The objective of the management of Charlton Marshall College is to provide education and training opportunities which are competitive in price, reliable in service and conform to the customer's contractual requirements.

In order to achieve this objective it is the policy of Charlton Marshall College to establish and maintain an effective and efficient quality management system.

The governors of Charlton Marshall College will ensure that staff at all levels within the organisation are acquainted with and experienced in applying company quality objectives.

Service design, resourcing, process, delivery and communications will be fully controlled. Resources, administration and operations will be consistently improved to produce results conforming to the optimum of customer requirements and expectations of the service provided.

The quality assurance manager is authorised to implement and maintain the quality management system of Charlton Marshall College. All managers are responsible for the quality system and quality of provision in their own departments.

All members of the management, teaching and support staff are responsible for the quality of their own work.

Compliance with the College's quality management system is compulsory for all staff in order to ensure that current and prospective customer requirements are consistently achieved and sustained.

The quality management system of Charlton Marshall College is based upon the requirements of BS 5750: Parts 1 and 2 (1987), and ISO 9001 and ISO 9002 (1987).

S. G. Weber-Brown
Chairman
Board of Governors
June 1992

Figure 1.8 Policy document

Quality probe – quality policy

- Is the quality policy understood, implemented and maintained at all levels?
- Are all full-time and part-time teaching staff and trainers, subcontractors and consultants, technicians, administrators and other support staff fully conversant with policy content and competent in its implementation?
- Has the quality policy been signed by the management representative having responsibility for quality assurance?
- Do senior managers demonstrate commitment to quality policies?

Quality manuals

A **quality manual** is produced for the use of individual businesses. The manual belongs to a particular company and it lays down exclusive quality policy and practices that are essential to satisfying customer requirements. It contains continuously-updated quality assurance procedures, specifying responsible persons and describing how quality functions will be effected. It also serves as a reference for quality control systems, quality reviews and audits.

The manual may comprise several parts, including a widely-circulated quality policy and details of organisational structure, communication links, documented quality assurance procedures and quality plans. **Work instructions** detailing how resources will be used and how the service will be delivered, monitored, evaluated and quality controlled will facilitate departmental functioning.

It may be necessary to produce a quality manual that relates to, and covers, key elements given in the appropriate parts of BS 5750 or international standards, such as the ISO 9000 series or the Australian 3900 series.

Documented **procedures** are required so as to ensure only one possible interpretation of processes and work instructions. These clear instructions are essential to ensure consistent performance in accordance with the contract and to eliminate ambiguity, misunderstandings and mistakes.

The quality manual will serve as a policy document but must be sufficiently detailed to be used to audit the systems in use. It will be backed up with codes of practice that define processes, procedures, activities and specifications by which the organisation will satisfy its policy and mission.

Each manual will be unique in that it will refer to the systems in use in a given organisation and how they operate. It will contain an index of easy-to-follow operating procedures that describe how an activity is required to be performed and by whom. It will also include an organisation chart with clearly defined responsibilities. Having a comprehensive quality procedures manual is critical to the maintenance of service provided at the right quality.

Summary of quality manual content:

- statement of quality policy
- confirmation of a quality commitment
- brief history of company
- organisational chart
- quality objectives
- quality operating procedures
- summary of scope and responsibility for each procedure
- documented work instructions
- implementation guide
- record of amendments
- audit and review procedures, frequency and auditor details
- printed forms and documentation.

Quality probe – quality manual

- Documented systems procedures?
- Details of what is controlled?
- Concise statements of the meaning of technical or subject-specific terms relating to procedures?
- Details of scope, purpose, applicability and relevance of procedure?
- Details of process and activities carried out by staff involved in the procedure?
- Details of controls and audits and when applied?
- Name and job title of person responsible?
- Action to be taken in the event of change or non-conformance?
- Full set of systems documentation?

Is the manual written in a user-friendly form and is the content concise, relevant and valid?

Quality planning

A quality management system is the bedrock on which total quality is built. It is a documented system that exists to ensure customer requirements are satisfied. It aims to remove the causes of error and non-conformance and provides for corrective action to be taken if necessary. It requires that a **quality plan** be written for the provision.

Where a large-scale operation with differing inputs and resources is concerned, each department will need a plan that can be integrated into an overall quality plan. This requires everyone in the operation to work systematically to documented procedures and to generate specified records while operating the procedures.

Planning involves:

- analysing service requirements;
- developing performance criteria and action plans to enable standards to be achieved;
- documenting systems and control procedures and defining responsibilities;
- resourcing and delivering the service;
- monitoring, auditing and reviewing the effectiveness of implementation and operating a quality improvement programme where non-compliance is revealed by audit.

Quality probe – quality planning

Does the plan:
- identify customer requirements and contingencies?
- facilitate feasibility studies of ability to meet identified customer requirement?
- identify and specify the provision of necessary resources?
- correlate customer needs with the service provision?
- provide for compatibility checks between customer needs and the provision?
- link programme development with product quality requirements?
- cover deployment of resources needed to meet service requirements?
- specify assessment and testing procedures, methods of recording outcomes and certification processes?
- provide for corrective action where necessary?
- provide for feedback of results to the management information system?

Quality procedures

Written documentation will specify the scope of the provider's procedure – what has to be done, the manner of doing it, who does it and who is responsible for it.

Procedures that define the provider's activities are normally filed in ring binders with each procedure numbered within a sub-division of the file.

Each procedure will be approved by the process owner, head of department or responsible manager, and the quality manager. Sample documentation is shown in Figures 8.6, 8.7 and 8.8 and 8.9a and b on pages 170–4.

The flow of recorded information and copies of reports, records and standardised documentation will be charted and there will be named job holders who will be responsible for controlling inputs at specified stages. Process inputs will be monitored and records will be created as work progresses. Contracts will normally be reviewed prior to acceptance in order to determine precisely what is needed and to check whether the provider has the capability to meet contract specifications.

Procedural instructions

Documented instructions for training activities and associated routines must contain specifications and procedures that cover all stages from the curriculum design to delivering the training programme or supplying the end product.

Instructions must contain well-defined criteria that adequately describe acceptable quality standards. Standards must be achievable and assessment and test procedures employed to confirm conformance must be compatible with the specified criteria. Procedures for corrective action must be included.

Proper use must be made of the instructions which must be regularly and systematically reviewed.

Where provision requires the provider to have special skills or competences, detailed specifications of staff development and training programmes must be documented.

Original copies of any instructional handouts, assessment papers or other resources must be held by the named individual responsible for the procedure. Any changes or additional paperwork must pass through that individual's hands. This will ensure that appropriate approval for changes will be obtained, obsolete documents will be withdrawn and the process kept under control. Major changes are usually authorised by the chief executive or principal.

Where a procedure reflects the content of similar written procedures, generated by a number of other stakeholders or standard setting agencies, the procedure numbers must be cross-referenced on a chart to be included in the provider's procedures file (see Figure 1.9 overleaf).

A decimalised numbering system would be applied to groups of procedures.

Work instructions

Clear, precise and complete written work instructions must be available for use by trainers and support staff wherever the need arises. This is particularly important where quality could suffer from lack of sufficient or complete instructions. Where necessary, margin notes and cross references will be included to aid clarity and understanding. The need for comprehensive and readily-understandable work instructions is high-lighted in the following extract taken from BS 4891.

> Work instructions should be developed and maintained to prescribe the performance of all work that would adversely be affected by lack of such instructions. These written instructions should not only be created and brought to a satisfactory state and put into use, but should also be subject to continuing evaluation for effectiveness and adjusted as necessary. They provide a basis for control, evaluation and review and without them, differences in policy and procedures can arise and variation in practice may occur resulting in confusion and uncertainty. Further to this, they provide means for delineating work to be done and for delegating authority and responsibility.[6]

Charlton Marshall College	BS 5750	Local TEC
1	9	4
2	4	8

Note: The numbers given in the columns are procedure numbers relative to each stakeholder

Figure 1.9 Cross-referencing procedures

Achieving BS 5750 certification

When third-party certification is sought, documentation must be sent to the contracted assessment body. The appointed assessor then compares and evaluates the quality system described against requirements of BS 5750.

The assessor then visits the organisation and checks that what is claimed to be done is actually implemented. After external assessment and accreditation, regular audits of the quality systems are conducted in order to validate system activities.

A possible approach to gaining BS 5750 accreditation is given in Figure 1.10.

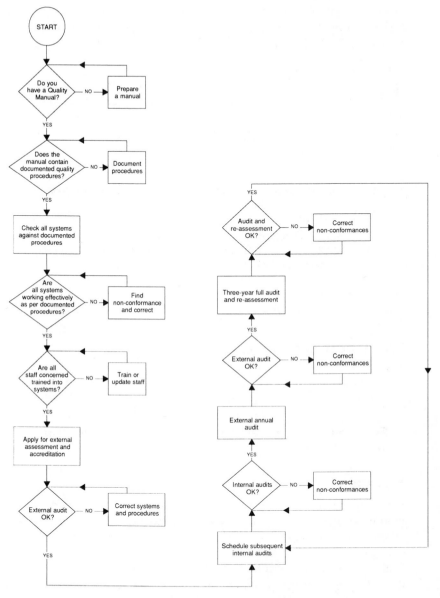

Figure 1.10 Going for BS 5750 accreditation

Responsibility and authority

Roles must be allocated and defined and responsibilities for implementing quality policies and procedures must be specified. Authority must be given to those charged with making decisions and taking action to stop, correct or initiate processes impeding the achievement of policy objectives. All too often people are given the responsibility for operating systems or processes without having the executive authority necessary to perform effectively.

Making decisions without thinking about the consequences for others is not to be recommended in a total quality context. Poor communication can play havoc in a system, resulting in loss of control of quality. The corrective actions taken must be effective and that is why the inter-relationship between role holders must be clearly documented and understood by all concerned.

Quality probe – responsibility and authority

- Has the responsibility and authority of all staff whose actions may affect quality been documented?
- Are such duties described, documented and recorded within the quality system manual or elsewhere?
- Is the document available for inspection by internal auditors and external assessors?

The management representative

A **management representative** having an appropriate level of responsibility for implementing and maintaining quality functions, and with the level of authority and ability needed to execute the role, must be appointed.

There must be an appointed deputy to the management representative.

Management review

A management review of the quality system must be carried out by a nominated responsible person, either the quality assurance manager or other senior management representative. Details of the frequency and timing of reviews, and the form and structure of the report, are given in the quality manual. An analysis and evaluation of quality policy implementation, system documentation, purchaser (student/trainee/sponsor) satisfaction, qualifications achieved and other performance indicators, and continuous improvement activities, would be undertaken.

The quality system organisation

The training provider must establish a formal system of quality management that incorporates the procedures and supporting documentation needed to achieve quality assurance objectives. The quality system must not stand in isolation. It should be blended into the provider's total management information system. Feedback concerning quality matters can then be used to inform other parts of the organisation, since TQM is intended to assure that provider's and customer's interests and expectations are met fully and economically.

> Documented procedures and instructions must be sufficiently detailed to enable staff to understand the required actions, responsibilities and authorities.[7]

The quality plan

The **quality plan** identifies the key elements necessary to provide the level of quality desired and defines the ways and means by which their achievement will be assessed.

It is recommended that a **quality plan**, in the form of a flow chart, be devised for each training product or service to be offered. The flow charts, together with any notes on quality assurance interventions, would be equivalent to codes of practice for a product – from design, through delivery to monitoring and evaluation of outcomes.

Where **trainer-centred monitoring** is used, a prerequisite will be adequate training in the selection, identification and use of resources, assignments, assessments and other teaching and learning inputs.

Training documentation must give clear and comprehensive information that will enable learners to perform according to the scheme of work and the units, elements and performance criteria specified. In order that they may do this, resources and training interventions must be compatible with the processes and procedures written into the quality plan.

The Education Reform Act 1988

Probably the most influential agent associated with further and adult education institutions has, until recently, been the local authority. In future, the Government's Education Reform Act 1988 will give colleges more freedom to manage their own day-to-day affairs in terms of the provision of Local Authority maintained Further Education than was the case up to 1989. Having lost direct control over colleges (local management of schools and colleges (LMS)), Local Education Authorities (LEAs) will probably operate as planners and advisers at a strategic level. Inspectors will also ensure, by evaluating performance, that education and training is provided at the right quality levels.

In the main, colleges that provide courses of Advanced Further Education (AFE) were removed from Local Education Authority (LEA) control altogether by 1 April 1989, while further education colleges that provide relatively little AFE remained under bureaucratic LEA influence in terms of procedures and policy making. It may well be that the TECs will operate non-advanced further education (NAFE) budgets and negotiate contracts directly with colleges and other training providers.

Financial powers are delegated to Further Education (FE) colleges and they are now governed by formula-funding arrangements, while performance indicators are used to assess their efficiency (see *Managing Colleges Efficiently*, DES 1987).

Governing bodies were reformed and colleges are now required to manage their own financial and human resources. Governing bodies, of 20 to 25 members, have greater powers to appoint and dismiss staff, to decide staffing grades and levels, and more independence within the LEA strategic framework.

The 1988 Act is about greater choice, competition and freedom from traditional constraint; giving increased customer power over college principals and lecturers and helping to shape a responsive educational provision. The modern adult education service is market-oriented. It is not, as some think, simply a provider of courses designed to fill leisure time. It is a service whose curriculum seeks to complement and supplement mainstream education; to meet the demands of adults with needs relating to literacy and basic skills; to work with the unemployed; to provide opportunities for open learning; to set up information technology centres; and to provide a high-class, educational information and guidance service.

Strategic planning

Training providers will need to adopt strategic planning in order to anticipate and meet customer requirements and maintain market share. In the case of further education, income will derive from planned student numbers and enrolling the 'right' categories of student. Income will be sought from increased activity in a marketplace vying for consultancy, 'fully costed' work, and from tapping sources, such as the European Social Fund, Mutual Development Fund (MDF), the Employment Department Group – Training Enterprise and Education Directorate (TEED), TECs, Scottish LECs (Local Enterprise Companies), the Department of Education and Science (DES) and any other sources from which funding may be available.

With the considerable freedom to manage their own affairs comes the need for colleges to exercise greater accountability than was sometimes the case.

Quality audits

Audits defined

An **audit** is an extremely thorough check or inspection in order to find out whether or not implementation of the system or process being examined conforms to specified requirements.

The term **quality audit** is used to describe the independent examination of quality to provide information. However, BSI suggest that as and when appropriate more specific terms should be used, such as product quality audit, process quality audit, service quality audit or quality systems audit.

A more detailed definition of a quality audit is:

> A systematic and independent examination to determine whether quality activities and related results comply with planned arrangements and whether these arrangements are implemented effectively and are suitable to achieve objectives.[8]

The process of questioning, revising and writing audit objectives leading finally to their implementation is shown in Figure 1.11 overleaf.

Audit objectives and responsibilities

Audits will be used to establish the suitability of a supplier, such as a work placement provider, in terms of contractual requirements and to ensure that the user's needs are being met. Where contracts have already been established, audits will be used to verify that quality systems continue to be implemented according to approved documented procedures. Audit programmes will allow for follow-up visits, during which any corrective action resulting from previous audits needed to establish conformance to standards will be verified.

Audits will be carried out by trained staff. A **lead auditor** will be responsible for managing all aspects of the quality system audit (see Figure 1.12 overleaf), and will have the authority to decide how the audit shall be conducted. The **client** will initiate the audit, define its scope and receive audit reports. The **auditee** will be responsible for providing access to resources and evidence needed for the audit, communicating the scope and objectives of the audit to employees, appointing a responsible person to accompany the audit team, reviewing audit findings, implementing corrective action and ensuring the co-operation of those concerned.[9]

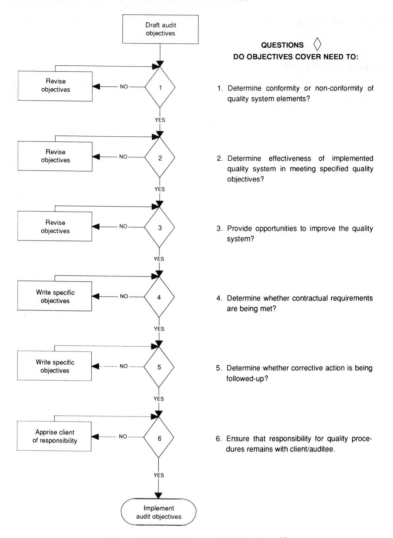

Figure 1.11 Writing audit objectives[10]

The auditor should be responsible for:

- complying with audit requirements and standards;
- planning and implementing audits;
- maintaining his/her independence from the auditee;
- recording observations and (if possible) causes of non-conformity;
- analysing the evidence gathered;
- maintaining security and confidentiality of audit/client documentation and records;
- reporting audit outcomes.

Figure 1.12 Auditor responsibilities[11]

The results of audits must be documented and brought to the attention of the persons responsible for the processes audited. They will take timely action on non-conformances and improvements needed.

Preparing for audit

When clients (suppliers or training providers) and auditees (provider's employees) are preparing for a quality audit based on BS 5750, it will be necessary to check that they have written policies and procedures covering up to 20 quality system requirements. These include the requirement to carry out a comprehensive system of planned and documented internal audits, scheduled on a basis of the status and importance of the activity.

> In order to ensure that the product or service conforms to specified requirements, the provider (as supplier) must establish, implement and maintain a quality system comprising documented quality policy, procedures and work instructions.

The audit preparation process is shown in Figure 1.13. overleaf

In order to meet system requirements it will also be necessary to identify, prepare and keep essential quality records.

> The provider must establish and maintain procedures for identifying, collecting, indexing, filing, distributing, storing and retrieving records.

Arranging audits

Plans will include details of responsible persons, a description of the **scope and depth** of the audit, and show how to meet specific audit requirements relating to purpose, importance of the activity, urgency of need, and availability of time and resources.

> The client or sponsor will specify what is to be reviewed, together with associated procedures, standards and documentation.

The lead auditor, together with the client, will prepare a structure for the audit.[13] This will include: an opening meeting to introduce representatives and agree communication links and the audit schedule; identifying the need for any specialists, for example, covering COSHH (Control of Substances Hazardous to Health), HSE or information technology, to support the audit team; examining the process, audit trails, means of gathering evidence, the review and evaluation; a closing meeting with the auditee; and the preparation of an audit report.

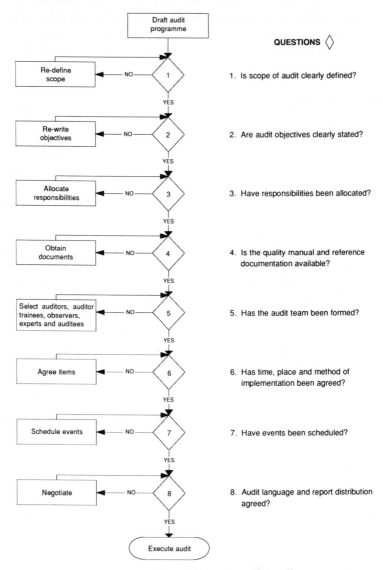

Figure 1.13 Audit preparation[12]

When the need for process improvement and verification of corrective action is noted in the audit report the auditee will complete the specified actions and then initiate a *verification audit*.

Working documents
Auditors will need to use several types of document during the audit, while observing processes and challenging the authenticating evidence.

The documents include:

- a quality manual with organisation chart, flow charts, documented procedures and work instructions;
- a checklist relating to quality system elements;
- prepared questions;
- a list of records to be examined;
- non-conformance notes and report sheets.

Lead auditors will produce a summary of findings, and assessment of results of the audit. They will agree corrective actions needed, subsequent monitoring and follow-up arrangements.

Internal quality probes

It can be seen from what has been discussed above that the preparation of a quality manual, policies and written procedures forms an essential part of the quality chain. Each policy must cover the need to monitor, review and evaluate systems performance regularly and continuously update aims, objectives, quality procedures, implementation, staff responsibilities and other appropriate quality elements.

Writing and documenting procedures can be very off-putting to staff who are thrown in at the deep end without any form of training or awareness raising. Some will view the task with suspicion and try to avoid the work involved. Others will be inclined to write whole new procedures setting themselves and their colleagues unnecessary and unrealistic targets. The resulting documented procedures will be difficult to interpret and more complex than is necessary to meet contract requirements.

It has been suggested that a better way is to keep things simple, documenting only that needed to meet the client's requirements and the provider's house standards.

A suggested starting point for writing procedures is to record where the provider is now and then to consider where the provider needs to be in order to meet BS 5750 requirements or that of other clients, such as TECs.

It may be helpful to consider how quality probes as a diagnostic tool might be used to question and establish the current status of a process before writing the procedure. A number of flow diagrams and quality probes have been introduced throughout this book and they are intended to stimulate thought about the kind of things that will need to be considered before commencing formal internal audits. In some instances, the content of probes may go well beyond the minimum standards acceptable to certain clients.

Self-assessment checklists, such as the one shown in Figure 1.14 overleaf, may also be helpful when preparing for an audit.

Audits and probes are discussed further in Chapter 10. The remainder of this chapter is devoted to a possible approach to the examination of current existing health and safety policies and procedures.

QUALITY ASSURANCE SELF-ASSESSMENT CHECKLIST

Purpose

This Self-Assessment Checklist is designed to ensure that information required to fulfil the Quality Assurance (QA) System is provided and maintained and that employees have access to the information.

In answering these questions please note that you will be required to demonstrate the procedures or requirements to internal and external auditors.

Checklist Format

The questions are formatted to require a YES or NO answer. YES means that you believe that your answer is satisfactory and that you are in compliance with the standard. NO means that you believe you have a risk of non-compliance to the standard or that you have not understood what is required (Please tick the appropriate box in answering the questions.)

Checklist – Management Responsibility   **YES**   **NO**

1. Can you demonstrate that you know your responsibility to ensure that the QA policy is understood, implemented and maintained within your department? ☐ ☐

2. Can you show an up-to-date list of programmes you and your department are responsible for delivering? ☐ ☐

3. Can you demonstrate that you and your staff understand the organisation of responsibility and authority within your department? ☐ ☐

4. Do you know who the QA Manager is? ☐ ☐

5. Can you and all your staff demonstrate ability to access documentation relating to the QA system? ☐ ☐

6. Do you have access to the documented procedures relating to the QA system? ☐ ☐

7. Can you demonstrate that all the required procedures are in place, up-to-date and accurate? ☐ ☐

8. Would you and your staff be able to demonstrate these procedures to internal and external auditors and other appropriate customers? ☐ ☐

9. Are you fully conversant with the content of the Quality Survey Manual? ☐ ☐

10. Can you and all your staff demonstrate the controls for documentation? ☐ ☐

11. Can you show internal and external auditors and other authorised persons samples of documents controlled according to the QA System requirement? ☐ ☐

12. Can you demonstrate the documented procedure for removal of obsolete documentation? ☐ ☐

13. Can you demonstrate corrective action procedures for instances of nonconformity? ☐ ☐

14. Have you a training records system for all your staff? ☐ ☐

Figure 1.14 Quality assurance self-assessment checklist[14]

Health and safety in the learning environment

A TQM policy requires that the management will consider how best to promote in themselves and the staff, trainees and work providers a positive and enduring attitude towards the duties of employers, employees and customers in terms of section 7 of the Health and Safety at Work Act 1974.

Quality probe – health and safety policy

- Are documented procedures that define the provider's health and safety responsibilities available?
- Are procedures consistently implemented?
- Is there evidence that all staff, trainees and sub-contractors understand their responsibilities under the Health and Safety at Work Act 1974, provide a safe environment and demonstrate safe working practices, as appropriate?
- Where incidents or accidents have occurred, has action been taken to reduce risk, remove hazards and prevent recurrences?
- Is there evidence that regular monitoring of safety policies and procedures takes place?
- Is health and safety training and updating provided?
- Are procedures followed to the letter and is there evidence of continuous improvement?

Some important aspects of the Act and how quality probes may be used to assess awareness and implementation of safety in the learning environment are outlined below.

The Health and Safety at Work Act 1974

The Health and Safety at Work Act received the Royal Assent on 31 July 1974. It provides a comprehensive system of law covering the health and safety of all at work.

The Act comprises four main parts:

- Part 1 is concerned with health, safety and welfare in relation to work.
- Part 2 relates to the Employment Medical Advisory Service (EMAS).
- Part 3 amends the law relating to building regulations.
- Part 4 deals with various and general provisions.

Since the Act was introduced, training and support staff have been affected by its implications, and the legislative framework provided by the Act has had considerable influence and effect on the day-to-day operations of training providers.

The Act covers all staff employed by the provider, trainees, visitors and contractors, and it gives statutory protection to anyone who is present on the site.

The Act is concerned with:

- Securing the health, safety and welfare of persons at work as described in Part 1 of the Act.
- Protecting persons other than persons at work against the risks to health or safety arising out of, or in connection with, the activities of persons at work.
- Controlling the keeping and use of explosives or highly inflammable or dangerous substances, and preventing people acquiring, possessing or illegally using such substances.
- Controlling the emission of noxious or offensive substances from any area.

Basic obligations of employers

Employers (including LEAs, colleges and training providers) have a duty to ensure that their activities do not endanger anyone. Employers are required to provide (so far as is reasonably practicable) for employees and other persons a healthy and safe environment. **Probes** may be used to examine and test the quality of provision and implementation of a safe working environment.

Quality probe – employer's responsibilities

Are employers providing for employees and other persons, so far as is reasonably practicable:

- healthy and safe systems of work with safe plant and machinery?
- equipment and appliances, all of which are maintained in good working order?
- safe methods for use, handling, storing and transporting materials, articles or substances?
- healthy and safe working environments, including premises with adequate amenities?
- adequate instruction and training for employees, including such information and supervision by competent personnel as is necessary to ensure the health and safety at work of employees?

Basic obligations of employees

Quite apart from any specific responsibilities that may be delegated to them, trainers have a legal obligation under section 7 of the Health and

Safety at Work Act 1974, to take care of their own health and safety as well as that of trainees and of any person who may be affected by their acts or omissions. This obligation applies to all employees in industry, commerce or elsewhere (except domestic service).

Quality probe – employee's responsibilities

Are employees:

- co-operating with their employers so far as is necessary to perform any duty or comply with any requirements imposed as a result of any law that may be in force?
- making themselves familiar with and conforming to any statement of safety policy or safe code of practice issued by principals or governing bodies?
- avoiding the possibility of committing criminal offences due to putting the health and safety of themselves or other persons at risk?
- conforming to safety instructions issued by principals or governing bodies and sharing their responsibility for safety, health and welfare?
- reporting any hazard, accident or dangerous occurrence to their immediate superior and to their safety representative, whether or not physical injury has occurred?
- using and ensuring that trainees use the appropriate protective clothing, equipment and safety devices at all times, and ensuring that any such equipment or devices are maintained in a safe working condition?
- complying with improvement notices or prohibition notices that may have been served on them as employees?
- complying with the duty not to interfere with or misuse things provided, pursuant to any of the relevant statutory provisions?
- setting a good example to trainees, colleagues and the public in their approach to health and safety matters?

Duties and responsibilities of teachers and trainers in the training environment

A trainer must ensure that learners are carefully briefed about safety arrangements when in unfamiliar surroundings. Examples of such situations might be when new starters begin training programmes, or if they are transferred to another annex or site, or when practical or laboratory work commences, or in any other novel situation.

It is essential that the trainees should know:

- the fire exit route;
- the location of the nearest first aid box;
- the location, uses and methods of operation of fire extinguishers in the vicinity;

- the content and application of accident and fire regulations;
- what to do in the event of an emergency.

When trainees are on the register the trainer is in charge and must accept responsibility for all aspects of safety and control of the environment in which work is taking place. Any activities that the trainer is expected to supervise must be inherently safe. If a situation arises where any aspect of the work is judged to be hazardous to the health or welfare of trainees, such work must stop immediately and a report be made in writing to the provider's management.

Since the trainer is in charge in a workshop or laboratory, support staff such as technicians and caretakers, whilst being helpful, can only offer advice to the trainer or trainees. The 'buck' stops with the trainer in the learning environment. It is the trainer who is responsible for ensuring that trainees are properly instructed and it is the trainer who is responsible for trainees operating machinery or processes safely, not the technician. Likewise it is the trainer who must ensure that no request is made of trainees or technicians to undertake operations that are or may be hazardous.

Burden of proof

In any proceedings for an offence under any of the statutory provisions consisting of a failure to comply with a duty or requirement, section 40 of the Act lays the burden of proof on the accused. It is usually the employer who will be required to prove that it was not reasonably practicable to do more than was done to safeguard employees or other persons injured or otherwise disadvantaged by a contravention of the Act.

Laboratory safety

Trainers working in laboratories will be aware of all the potentially hazardous conditions and dangers that may exist. Over a period of time, materials will have been accumulating that may not be in regular use; large stocks of little-used resources may be held; quantities of flammable chemicals may exceed the permitted allocation or be incorrectly stored; and incompatible materials, poisons, gases or other dangerous chemicals may be stored unsafely. All these elements promote a potentially dangerous environment.

Disposal of chemical waste will present problems when waste is washed down sinks, or disposed of by burial, burning or other methods. Practical work in laboratories will always be subject to physical hazards, and hazards associated with chemical, electrical and mechanical processes, and the use of power tools and appliances.

Quality probe – laboratory safety

Reports are heard of the bad state and organisation of some laboratories and the contravention of regulations. As a training provider you will have tacitly accepted responsibility for all aspects of safety relating to your training operation.

How safe are workshops and laboratories in your business? Carry out a comprehensive check of your working environment, bearing in mind some of the points made above, and confirm whether or not it is free of hazards by repeatedly asking the question 'Is it safe?'

Fire hazards

Unwanted fires can break out because someone has carelessly added fuel to the two other ingredients required to ensure combustion; heat and air. Any combination of these three ingredients will result in fire.

Fire prevention must be a high priority for all teachers and trainers and particularly when electrical power and flammable liquids, gases, wood, paper, and other combustible materials are handled during training. Even when care is taken, volatile materials, heat sources, powders and appliances can start fires, while negligence, discarded cigarette ends and thoughtless behaviour can add unnecessary risk. Everyone must be ready to react to fires.

Quality probe – fires

Despite all reasonable precautions having been taken a fire breaks out. What action must staff take when:

- the fire alarm is sounded?
- a fire occurs in their vicinity?
- called to the scene of a fire?
- asked to classify and report a fire?
- asked to supervise the evacuation of an area?

State what staff must know about fire fighting equipment and other facts relating to fires including:

- alarms
- blankets
- buckets
- classification
- doors
- drill

- escape notices
- escapes
- exits
- extinguishers
- hazards
- prevention.

> Make a plan of your establishment and note on the plan all references to fire precautions and fire-fighting equipment and escape routes.
>
> Check that all the equipment is serviceable and that staff are competent to use it?
>
> Make sure your staff and trainees know the drill and practice before a fire occurs.

Promoting a positive attitude

Basic obligations of employees under section 7 of the Health and Safety at Work Act 1974 are that they must act in the course of their employment with due care for the health and safety of themselves, other workers and the general public.

Employees must also observe the provisions of the Act wherever applicable to them or to matters within their control. They must co-operate with employers so far as is necessary to perform any duty or comply with any requirements imposed as a result of any law that may be in force. They must not put at risk the health and safety of themselves or others.

An important duty of a trainer is to encourage maximum learner participation in the creation, implementation and monitoring of health and safety policies, practices and activities, both within the training provider's establishment and at the workplace.

Health and safety while training

Reducing the probability of injury or accident while training must be an important item in the minds of every teacher or trainer. Every kind of activity has inherent risks and it will never be possible to remove every aspect of danger from the material and physical requirements of training.

Competition and the intrinsic motivator, challenge, may drive people further than their ability dictates. As a result, trainers may also have to cope with learners' self-imposed dangers.

Quality probe – risks and dangers

Assess the range of resources and equipment that you use including the chemicals or preparations associated with the work. Carry out a COSHH assessment.

Survey the risks and dangers associated with your resources and trainees. Review your methods and facilities with a view to confirming that you are not exposing people to unnecessary risk, and produce an action plan for continually reducing dangers and improving safety aspects of your operation.

Accident procedures

The sample questions given in the following quality probe and the suggested procedure for notifying and investigating an accident (see Figure 1.15) are meant to stimulate thoughts about how the reader might attempt to carry out staff awareness audit of accident procedures in-house.

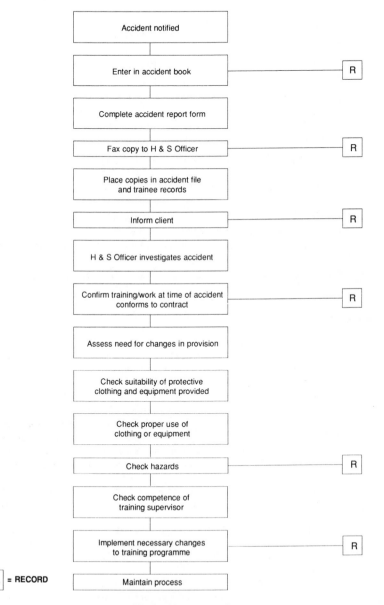

Figure 1.15 Accident procedure

They are not intended to cover every aspect of a possible quality probe, but may help when preparing a schedule of actions that staff would need to take to respond efficiently and effectively to an emergency in your own establishment.

Quality probe – accident procedures

Sample questions to ask:
If there were an accident in your location would you know what to do? Would your trainees be competent enough to take appropriate action? If the answer is 'Yes' please confirm by responding to the following:

- How would you set about calling an ambulance?
- How would you get hold of a qualified first-aider?
- Specify the locations of first aid boxes and the nearest sick room.
- Should you leave the patient alone? Manipulate the patient into the recovery position? Cover the patient? What if the patient has received an electric shock and is still in contact with the power source?
- Where can a phone connected to an outside line be found in the evening?
- If you intended to report the accident by phone or runner, what information would you give?
- How would you manage to contact a parent, guardian, relative or friend?

Notes

1   J. Furphy and Sons Pty Ltd is an Australian company specialising in structural, mechanical and agricultural engineering. John Furphy, the company founder, was born on 17 June 1842 at Moonee Ponds in Victoria.

In 1873 there were about 13 families living in and around the Shepparton area. John Furphy, then aged 31, bought 10 acres of land (now prime city space) in Shepparton and quickly set up a blacksmith and wheelwright shop.

He soon added a steam works and was able to progress from light smithing and engineering to heavier work. In about 1878, a cupola furnace was installed and the iron foundry business began. The implement and foundry business flourished and by 1880 there were 38 staff on the payroll; by 1888 it was the largest business in Northern Victoria.

In 1906, the business moved to a site opposite the railway station, the plant was modernised and J. Furphy and Sons was one of the few electrically-powered factories in Victoria at the time.

John Furphy showed a flair for public speaking and writing that was reflected in his advertising. An example being: 'The stripper which I exhibited at the Centennial is now on view at my factory. It is the best I know how to make and only modesty prevents my adding – the best in the world.'

Quality has always been Furphy's watchword and it is neither by accident nor luck that the Company has 120 years of experience as engineers with the ability to provide the skills and service needed to meet their customers' requirements.

2   Probably the most distinctive product to carry the Furphy brand is the water cart used to carry water to the troops in Europe and the Middle East during the First World War. No similar vehicle was used at the time and the method of carting water in those days was confined to horse-drawn wooden casks placed on a skid or sledge. John Furphy employed the method of shrinking an iron band on the end casting to hold and tightly seal the body of the tank.

   In 1895 the end castings carried the message: 'Good, better, best – Never let it rest – Till your good is better – And your better best.' In 1910, a Pitman's shorthand inscription was added which when translated reads: 'Water is the gift of God, but beer and whisky are concoctions of the devil, come and have a drink of water.'

3   *North Point Training and Further Education College Organisational Handbook*, p. 3. Provided by Antoinette Brandi, Staff Development Manager, North Point TAFE College, 157 Norris Road, Bracken Ridge, Queensland 4017, Australia.

4   Ibid. p. 4.

5   Ibid. p. 1.

6   BS 4891:1972 *A guide to quality assurance*, p. 15, para. 11.2.

7   *Guidance notes for application of BS 5750/ISO 9000/EN 29000 to education and training*, sixth draft, p. 6 para. 4.2. BSI Quality Assurance, Milton Keynes, January 1991.

8   BS 7229:1989 *British Standard Guide to Quality Systems Auditing* p. 2. BSI, London, 1989.

9   BS 7229:1989 provides guidance on auditing quality systems. It provides audit principles, criteria and requirements for audit practice and assists in the establishment, planning and execution of audits of quality systems. The guidance given in the British Standard can be equally applied to any one of the following three specific and differing auditing activities: a 'first party' quality systems audit carried out by a company on its own systems for the purpose of giving assurance to the management that its quality systems are effectively achieving the planned quality objectives; a 'second party' audit carried out by one organisation on another, with whom they either have a contract to purchase goods or services or intend to do so; 'third party' audits carried out by independent agencies that may be accredited using national or international standards, such as BS 5750 Parts 1, 2 and 3, ISO 9001/2/3 and European Standards EN 29001/2/3, to provide assurance on the effectiveness of quality systems.

10   Ibid. p. 3.

11   Ibid. pp. 3–4.

12   Ibid. p. 4.

13   See note 9.

14   Source of table is Bob Cowdrey, Quality Assurance Manager, Dorset Skills Training.

CHAPTER TWO

Introducing Change

Chapter coverage

Introducing total quality management (TQM)
    Resistance to change
    Organisational culture
    The challenge of change and product development
    Responding quickly
    Force field analysis
    Managing change
Embedding NVQs in the training provision
    The background to NVQs
    The need for new policies and procedures
    Planning
    Organisational aims – meeting the challenge
Modularisation
    Developing a modular programme
    Suggested aims
    Innovation/implementation

Introducing total quality management (TQM)

Long-term investment in, and commitment to, total quality yields positive results. Quality is clearly appreciated world-wide by major and smaller companies alike. An experienced manager who has learned the hard way how to control costs will ensure that waste is rooted out of a system by instituting procedures that will assure active implementation of a quality assurance policy. Much can be accomplished to change things for the better within an organisation by using existing staff and services to meet particular objectives. Quality assurance systems work best when managers, governors, principals, head teachers, training providers and their staff are committed to a common interest and work as a team to that end.

Even so, a visionary approach to putting people first and corporate culture change does not in practice always result in a smooth transition. Disputes over ends and means will often occur, since different groups within the organisation may have dramatically varying interests and values. Where objectives are not clear cut or have been introduced without adequate negotiation and agreement with staff, the ingredients for conflict will be in place. Staff may suffer from the resulting culture shock.

Some managers fully committed to providing a quality, cost-effective service will go for the quick kill. They will get down to business straight away. Departmental managers will wish to link provision with their customers and ensure that staff deliver a responsive service. They will state their views, confront problems and argue their case hoping to reach the conclusion they have in mind as quickly as possible. Time and the face-to-face contact needed to arrive at a win–win outcome is often underestimated and once negative murmurings begin these are rapidly taken up by all and sundry. Before long there may be unanimous agreement that the organisation 'ought to do this' or 'do that' instead of what was originally proposed. Arguments geared to reinventing the wheel or salvaging existing make-do non-systems may take precedence over the need to sell the proposed total quality concept.

One manager's investment for the future in the form of introducing quality assurance systems may be perceived by another person as a waste of time and money resources. So when planning to introduce change the programme must be kept simple and readily understandable to everyone involved. It must be sold on its own merits as perceived by staff.

A quantum leap in improving the quality of customer service can only come from seeking to foster supportive attitudes throughout the entire organisation. An environment which encourages innovation and both individuality and teamwork, together with potential for personal development, can be a prerequisite for success. Setting this up takes time and a lot of effort.

With this in mind, a better way may be to obtain consensus and harmony by adopting a serious but courteous attitude. A longer-term view may need to be taken. A relationship of trust needs to be established before attempting to introduce the proposed quality assurance systems. Potential differences must be addressed in a constructive manner. In this way no one loses face and difficulties are ultimately overcome.

Resistance to change

Whenever there is a move by management to innovate, to introduce new policies or to change priorities, some individuals will eagerly grab any opportunities presented while others will resist and opt for the status quo. Some will refrain from any form of discussion and will stand firm against the proposed change. Others will strongly oppose the move and may even refuse to accept or comply with the change that is imposed. For the latter category, only a threat to the organisation that cannot be ignored or a risk to their own security or well-being will promote a positive response.

Colleges are thought of by some as large institutions that have been founded for a particular purpose. As such they are cumbersome and difficult to change due to their size and complexity. Long-serving staff may have themselves become conditioned to institutional routine and will avoid any opportunities to negotiate and collaborate. When people feel uncomfortable, conflict will almost certainly result.

The way forward will be to neutralise feelings of hostility and facilitate a collaborative approach to managing the change. This is easier said than done, but if ways can be found to cause individual and organisational goals and needs to converge they will eventually meet at a common point. A satisfactory conclusion will be the reduction of conflict and a consensus in the shape of widespread acceptance of a decision by those who propose the change and by those who will be affected by it.

During a seminar, when delegates feel very strongly about an emotive concept, it has been found helpful to record comments about each individual's feelings on a flip chart placed well away from the seminar leader. This is thought to dissociate the leader from the intense emotional attitudes that delegates may hold about the topic, while still allowing the problem to be confronted. Similarly, when conflict arises it may be productive to use the guidelines for management of conflict by collaboration suggested by Robert Fisher and William Ury:

> Separate the people from the problem, focus on interests not positions, generate a variety of possibilities before deciding what to do and insist that the result be based on some objective criteria.[1]

Organisational culture

Organisational culture may be thought of as reflecting the total range of established ideas, beliefs, values, knowledge and shared traditions which constitute the bases of organisational behaviour. It is maintained and transmitted by the workforce; and attitudes held by people will be influenced by the respect and regard they feel toward the business or alternatively by the degree of enforced compliance they experience.

Introducing a quality-oriented approach to the way people work may call for change in thinking, behaviour and in working procedures. For some, this can result in culture shock, giving rise to feelings of isolation and inability to cope with the change. For these people perhaps the promotion by management of one of the 14 points embraced by the Deming philosophy of quality, 'Reduce fear throughout the organisation by encouraging open two-way communications', would prove helpful. But for others, the proposed change will be seen as an opportunity for personal empowerment, for demonstrating a commitment to the quality policy and to improving customer service.

Staff development and training programmes can significantly assist with the implementation of organisational strategies by offering relevant learning opportunities that will support the proposed change. But, organisation-wide cultural change cannot be achieved overnight. It is well known that while individual delegates may immediately benefit from learning new things after attending a seminar, organisational change is longer-term and achieved by the 'ripple-effect'. The process of 'cascading learning' from consultant to individuals or small teams often progresses slowly through groups, departments and eventually across the organisation. Effective management of the initial stages of implementation of the learned behaviour in the workplace is critical to how its relevance, value and utility is perceived throughout the organisation.

The challenge of change and product development

One of the hallmarks of a successful training provider's rise to prominence is the eagerness with which the management has been able to grasp new opportunities, together with their ability to adapt quickly to change.

Every new product, every change in training-related law, every fresh TEC or government-sponsored training initiative, or unexpected opportunity to bid for externally-sourced funding has an immediate impact on management thinking. The spotlight is focused on existing systems, policies and procedures. The implication of change in relation to current operations is evaluated. Requirements are analysed so that practical solutions for maintaining market share, organic growth or the ability to capitalise by acquisition or co-operation becomes a possibility that may be converted into reality. A fast-moving, customer-led organisation responds positively to challenge and that is how they become leaders in their field.

The staff concerned will need to be able to accept the challenge that inevitably accompanies the imperative for rapid change. People with an instinct for excellence will need to shape innovative systems and solutions that will drive the business forward. In order to do this they will need to demonstrate key qualities, such as tenacity, flexibility, initiative and the ability to apply creative problem-solving skills. The role of agent of change will call upon staff to respond to change almost as a matter of course and proactively look ahead at potential scenarios, to contribute to forward planning, to plan for contingencies and to participate in decision making.

The people described above can be found within any organisation. They are there but their full potential may not have been recognised to date. They may need a hand from time to time and will need someone to lead rather than boss them. But their unrealised energy and strengths can be released giving them the chance to prove themselves. When staff own a problem they are more likely to come up with a good answer – provided that it is acknowledged that they own the solution too.

Neither moaning about the competition and hoping that the threat they pose will go away, nor being complacent, is to be recommended. It is too late to shut the gate after the horse has bolted.

The growth of National Vocational Qualifications (NVQs) presents an irresistible challenge to the status quo for many training providers. Rising standards and customer expectations highlight an urgent need for some businesses to innovate as a prerequisite for survival. Considerable change can be accomplished when a need, such as introducing NVQs and embedding associated processes and procedures, is acknowledged. (A possible approach to embedding NVQs is discussed later in this chapter.)

Responding quickly

A quick response to change, demanding urgent and essential action, may be called for. To maximise opportunities we may need to carry out audits of one or more of the five Ms: money, materials, machinery, methods and manpower (both male and female).

A staff audit involves looking at what people in the business are doing and what they are capable of doing when adequately trained. In the first place, only innovators, such as principals, managing directors and the like, together with willing staff should be involved. Their expertise may then be drawn upon and any work to be done shared out. When once the accepted approach of involving everyone in an awareness-raising programme, stimulating interest and actively engaging opinion leaders in initial training and piloting has been effected, progress and attitudes can be evaluated.

People at the top of an organisation should maintain a high profile and be seen to be supporting and valuing what is going on while encouraging, where appropriate, a bottom-up strategy for policy making, planning, decision making and implementation. Delegation by senior staff to others is to be applauded, but to delegate without giving proper ongoing support is unforgivable and will surely lead to loss of drive and low morale. Poor outcomes can result from withholding available resources or indecision by those who hold the power to make decisions. People look to senior management for leadership and become quite frustrated when little or no initiative is forthcoming when it is so urgently needed.

Opposing forces are almost always present in times of change. There will be driving forces that tend to move the business forward in the direction of desired change and restraining forces that tend to maintain the existing state of affairs. When these forces are in equilibrium no movement may be perceived.

For something to happen, the restraining forces must either be overcome, their line of action changed or they must be removed. Alternatively, the driving forces may be increased, but this should only be used where a reduction of opposing forces cannot be achieved in the time available. It is for the innovators and their supporters to resolve the problem of opposing forces. A device often used to gain a clearer picture of the disposition of forces is a force field analysis (see Figure 2.1).

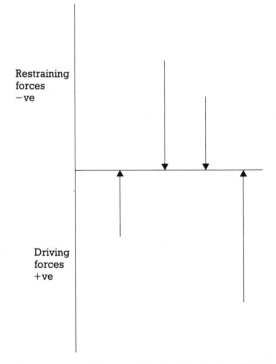

Note: Length of line could indicate 'strength of force'

Figure 2.1 Force field analysis

Lines of force relating to factors favourable to the proposed change are located on one side of the datum line; those concerning present position on the opposite side.

The analysis is carried out during the early stages of an assessment of what people's attitudes and reactions will be toward a proposed change. It can be seen that the length of the lines of force drawn on a particular diagram are proportional to the perceived importance of opposing factors. These factors are identified during an analysis of how people profess to feel about the change after careful explanation and discussion of what is involved.

Attention and resources may be targeted after identifying the main concerns and problems that have to be overcome, and priority given to the solution of each.

Managing change

Managing organisational change and continuous improvement called for in quality assured services is a priority task for effective managers.

As suggested in BS 5750, a system is needed for the control of change. In a formal co-ordinated system, appropriate documentation is available and any changes are authorised by the originator of the document. With innovation, however, change is a dynamic process and not an event. Change takes place in a social environment where those involved in a changing situation interact and are themselves changed during the process.

The need for change may be entered into willingly and perceived as a process of natural evolution and growth of a business; on the other hand change may be thrust upon the provider. Plans may be made to accommodate the change imposed. Planning to meet the needs of a modified provision may be fairly straightforward, but it is the implementation of change that often causes most of the problems. Just waving the magic wand will not do since effective implementation will involve a process of adjustment by agents of change and the target user group.

Quality probe – managing change

- Is the climate right for change?
- Is the change required clearly defined?
- Is there a plan for introducing the change?
- Is there a planned, staff awareness-raising programme?
- Can staff openly state views?
- Do staff have the necessary knowledge, skills and understanding required to facilitate change?
- Can staff cope with any extra workload?
- Can the business cope with the changes?
- Are adequate resources available?
- How will change be monitored and evaluated?
- What are the barriers to change?

A successful innovation relies on its value and relevance to the user group, its relative simplicity, its flexibility, its feasibility and cost in resource terms, and its implications for those affected.

A successfully implemented innovation depends on:

- high staff morale;
- commitment of all concerned to the innovation;
- backing by senior management;
- active and supportive leadership;
- teamwork;
- setting a large number of lower priority attainable goals together with fewer high priority and more demanding goals;
- a timetable for implementation;
- readily available information and guidance on how to go about the tasks involved;
- support of consultants where appropriate;
- effective feedback and continuous planning;
- participants 'owning' the innovation.

Balancing needs
Change involves the need for managers to take account of people-related factors as well as the problems and tasks generated due to the proposed change. The approach taken by managers will affect results. Consider two circular beer mats, one marked 'people factors' and the other 'problem or task' (see Figure 2.2). Place one on top of the other so that only one can be read. To an observer it would appear that the other does not exist.

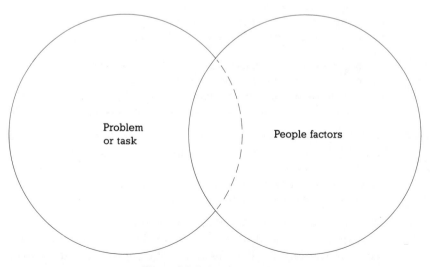

Figure 2.2 Balancing needs

This is what can happen during change. People must not be forgetten. If the manager focuses attention and resources only on the problem there will be little chance of effective implementation of the proposed change. In order to be successful, the needs of the problem and people involved must be balanced and the degree of overlapping will depend upon individual circumstances and the dynamics of the change process.

Quality probe – promoting change

In order to bring about change have you:
- justified the need for change?
- mapped the current position?
- defined the target position?
- carried out a force field analysis?
- identified key factors for and against change?
- prioritised facilitating objectives?
- prepared an action plan?
- allocated resources to overcome problems and implement change?
- arranged for monitoring of progress?
- arranged to evaluate outcomes?
- arranged regular post-implementation reviews?

Have you also:
- checked that functions of proposed change will be covered by the quality system?
- appointed a management representative to be responsible for implementation of change?
- documented each element of the change process?
- got a system of communication and document control?
- appointed staff to service change?
- organised any related staff training?
- considered the benefits and rewards to agents of change and those affected by it?
- got contingency plans for dealing with blockages?
- plans in hand to set up systems and provide resources needed to maintain the changed processes and procedures?

Quality probes, such as the examples given here, can be used when auditing the arrangements for promoting and managing change. It is often found that one set of questions results in many more questions being raised. This is not a bad thing when working through a checklist and establishing an action plan for change.

An important innovation that will continue to affect a good many providers is the need to deliver competence-based training leading to effective learning, the demonstration of competence and achievement of NVQs.

Some of the issues concerned with embedding NVQs, modularisation and the provision of opportunities leading to achievement of competence are discussed below.

Embedding NVQs in the training provision

The background to NVQs

Prompted by recognition of the importance of training to economic growth and the low take-up of training opportunities nationally, the government set up a Review of Vocational Qualifications in March 1985. The White Paper *Working Together*[2] advocated the setting up of the National Council for Vocational Qualifications (NCVQ) to oversee the development of a new national framework for vocational training. This framework was to be broad in scope and content, and easily understood. It would rationalise the plethora of qualifications available, making them flexible and relevant to the world of work.

The key features of NVQ awards as they evolve are that they are employment-led, work-based and performance-related, with open access for training, and assessment which allows the on-going development of competence. Based on units, elements and performance criteria they allow for progression to higher levels of experience and qualification.

The need for new policies and procedures

There is a need to have in place policies and procedures that will adequately match the rapidly increasing demand for NVQs over the next ten years.

Policy will call for strategic and operational planning needed to address the key features of provision, such as:

- learner support services;
- open-access facilities;
- induction and initial assessment;
- learner entitlement;
- open and flexible attendance and study patterns;
- unspecified period of study;
- competence-based, employment-related training;
- assessment procedure for prior learning, academic and occupational competence;
- credit accumulation and transfer;
- recording achievements;
- framework for NVQ training to various levels;
- keeping up-to-date with change;
- routines and systems needed for operating assessment centres;

- maintaining coherent teaching and learning opportunities that may be linked with education and training in the wider community;
- quality assurance systems.

Planning

It is recognised that the plans of some Local Education Authorities, colleges and training providers lack a coherent strategy for planning, delivering and accrediting NVQs. This shortcoming will need to be urgently addressed and a comprehensive staff development programme will need to be implemented, in order to achieve the necessary quality of service to clients.

Throwing money and staff time at the problem will not alone suffice. A planning-led approach is called for, based upon hard facts derived from an internal audit of where the organisation is now, where it needs to be and how to get there.

A list of suggested aims for an in-house survey that would help management and staff working together to establish what needs to be done and how to best to meet the challenge is given in Figure 2.3.

Staff appointed to work on the survey would undertake an examination of current practice within the organisation, identify good practice outside the organisation and make recommendations regarding changes in resourcing, delivery, assessment and accreditation.

---

1. To get up-to-date with national developments in NVQs and in particular with strategies for:
   diagnostic assessment and admissions procedures;
   accreditation of prior learning and achievement;
   induction;
   safe working;
   delivering underpinning knowledge;
   coaching;
   assessing performance;
   recording achievement;
   accrediting competence and certification.

2. To investigate the implications of competence-based skills testing including the provision of assessment on demand, in line with NVQ proposals.

3. To investigate current provision and to make recommendations about the resource implications of embedding and delivering NVQs, and implementing assessment and recording systems.

4. To devise staff development strategies aimed at supporting staff who will be planning, resourcing and delivering NVQs. Training is to include updating in modularisation, off-the-job and work-based training, learning and assessment, recording achievement and certification.

Figure 2.3 Organisational aims – meeting the challenge

Modularisation

Developing a modular programme

Preparing for work on modularisation of education and training provision will entail allocating physical resources and staff to do the work, and writing the aims and a plan of activity.

Suggested aims

- To develop modular programmes of study which will be compatible with developments in NVQ and take account of subsequent changes in content imposed by industry lead bodies. Modules will link with requisite units of competence and cover the necessary underpinning knowledge and understanding.
- To produce appropriate learning materials suitable for a range of attendance patterns and delivery modes.
- To incorporate into the structure: features of individual learning plans; flexible entry procedures; and methods of aligning assessment with other modes of recording and assessment that will allow for credit accumulation and transfer.
- To development assessment procedures in line with NVQ requirements and to provide accreditation of prior achievement and ongoing recording of achievement.
- To pilot modules produced within those training opportunities which fall within the orbit of NVQ awards.

Innovation/implementation

Within most organisations there will be innovators and opinion leaders or early adopters who will be thinking ahead and making an effort to do something about the impending change from the traditional course provision to modularised learning opportunities. There are also those who adopt an unplanned approach or doctrine of unrestricted freedom, sometimes known as 'professional laissez-faire', where committed individuals take upon their shoulders the task of 'being prepared' when the day comes. There will be others, the laggards, who will avoid the pressure for change and keep their heads below the parapet.

What is needed is a combination of all types bonded together using a teamwork approach to the task. A good leader will be able to harness the goodwill of innovators, early adopters and opinion leaders to the latent potential of adequately motivated laggards. Willing hands are needed. Pressed people are of little value to the team, although it is a great pity that relatively few innovators often carry the large majority. Managers will know that in far too many organisations there are a few keen and committed staff who always seem to end up doing the bulk of the innovative work. The same names keep cropping up and spring readily to the manager's mind whenever something needs to be done well.

A suggested approach to carrying out modularisation might be to:

- Establish a planning team that will design and steer activities.
- Examine current practices and carry out a survey of recent developments in other organisations. (Existing training content may be analysed and synthesised into a modular format, which will be competence-based and will conform to NVQ specifications.)
- Identify a separate team of subject specialists who will write learning materials and put more specific detail into modules.
- Focus team effort onto developing course materials and reviewing assessment systems, including accreditation of prior learning and work-based achievement of competences.

Outcomes of work undertaken may be used to develop guidelines for future modularisation programmes. Additionally, the experience gained by staff involved may be shared with colleagues across the organisation.

Notes

1   Robert Fisher and William Ury, *Getting to Yes: Negotiating Agreement without Giving In*, p. 11, Hutchinson, London, 1983.
    See Brian J. Caldwell and Jim M. Spinks, *The Self-Managing School*, pp. 192, 200–1, The Falmer Press, Lewes, 1988.

2   *Education and Training*, July 1986, MCB University Press Ltd.

CHAPTER THREE

TQM – Concept Development and Implementation

Chapter coverage

The concept of TQM
  Total quality defined
  Quality gurus
  Quality of work, products and processes
  Features of TQM
  Quality assurance
  Quality chains
  Quality costs
  The quality costs model
TQM benefits
  Benefits to the provider
  Benefits to staff
  Developing TQM
  Team building and teamwork
  Motivation
  Leadership
Reviewing the provision
  Selecting areas for improvement
  Method study (SOCDIM)
Implementing TQM
  Steering groups

Managing activities
    People as a valuable resource
    Involving everyone
    Forming positive attitudes
    Delegation
    Roles and responsibilities
    Suggestions and ideas
    Monitoring improvements
Quality circles
    Setting up circles
    Management support
Training
    Awareness raising
    Staff trainers and supervisors
    Educating the workforce
    Personal development opportunities
    Cascading principles and practices
    Diagnosing need

The concept of TQM

Total quality defined

TQM (total quality management) is a senior management-led, company-wide initiative intended to improve effectiveness and to build quality into the service delivered. Involvement of the whole workforce and a commitment to doing the right things correctly is emphasised. The principles apply equally to manufacturing industries and to training providers, although practices may differ.

Words like 'commitment' seem to crop up everywhere these days. But staff are not always ready to pledge their support to what they do not fully understand. They may be sceptical at what they perceive as being the latest flavour or instant remedy for all ills. Their support may be hard to win without carefully promoting a teamwork approach to a lasting, organisational total quality climate.

However, if quality is assured within the training organisation then its competitiveness will be increased. Sponsors, such as the TECs, will be reassured and will confidently award contracts.

Organisational quality, driven by the need to put customers first and meet their requirements, may lead the provider along the road to full BS 5750 status.

Quality gurus

A guru may be thought of as a teacher or leader of a movement. Whereas a religious teacher gives spiritual guidance to disciples, quality gurus serve as theoreticians and practitioners, guiding providers in their search for strategies that lead to the attainment of total quality. Knowledge of the work of one or more quality guru will influence our attitude toward making a commitment to a total quality philosophy and adopting a company-wide approach to quality improvement.[1]

Quality of work, products and processes

'Fitness for purpose and safe in use' and 'satisfying customer requirements at least cost', are two definitions of quality. The concept of quality is abstract and difficult to put in a concise form but there are a number of characteristic essential features that may be identified. These include:

- conformance to requirements;
- meeting the customer requirements;
- fitness for intended purpose of a product or service;
- satisfying stated or implied needs;
- excellence achieved by responding to market-led forces;
- providing an efficient and effective service to customers;
- preventing things from going wrong and getting everything right first time, every time;
- involving everyone concerned from conception to after-sales service.

Features of TQM

For some people, the concept of total quality is based upon little more than a personal outlook or view of what they believe to be requirements imposed by external agencies and powerful stakeholders. For others, some system of total quality management is seen as being desirable in order to ensure that every person and every resource employed work properly together. Whichever view is taken, there is a need to satisfy customer requirements in order to become successful or stay in business.

TQM acts as an agent of change involving all staff. It calls for positive attitudes toward achieving the appropriate level of quality. It aims at making the provision of a company-wide quality service everyone's responsibility. Meeting this aim calls for the operation of a system of documented procedures that will promote a 'zero defect' approach and the achievement of a quality operation. Competent performance by everyone then eliminates the risk of errors and prevents problems occurring.

Responsibility for quality rests with those who control resources and carry out work. Continuous improvement replaces the, 'That's near enough. It'll do.' attitude.

Quality assurance

Quality assurance is a term that is used to describe activities taken to prevent non-conformance and to remove doubt about meeting customers' requirements. Quality assurance incorporates procedures for planning, establishing, monitoring, auditing and evaluating management systems. The object is to provide consistent quality of service and remove any possibilities of failure to meet customer expectations.

> Quality assurance systems preserve the quality of the service provided and generally result in improvements and reduction in total quality costs.

Quality chains

Every member of staff is a supplier with a customer for their service or product. Trainers are suppliers for trainees and employers, and are customers of the support staff. The idea of a quality chain applies both to internal and external suppliers, and each must know who their customer is and what their expectations are. Suppliers must aim to satisfy their customers' requirements. Everyone who supplies a service to another is charged with the responsibility to monitor and maintain the quality of their own work. Non-conformance to standards breaks the quality chain and generates customer complaints. Failures that go undetected result in bigger problems later.

> Strategic planning, involving doing the right things and doing them right the first time (getting training and learning provision right), may be reinforced by analysing the reasons for any failures, rectifying these at source and preventing them from happening again.

Quality costs

Quality costs are an indicator of success. If they are low then there is a high probability that quality assurance systems and procedures are working well. If they are substantial then there is a need to bring things under control. Customer needs – that is, the needs of trainees, sponsors and employers, and internal customers – should be satisfied at the least cost.

Poor quality costs money. Conversely, quality costs can be considerable but add nothing to the value of the service provided. Errors tend to multiply and may disrupt products and services in other parts of the provision. The philosophy should be one of prevention not detection. Time and money are spent on finding out why things have gone wrong or checking up on everyone to make sure that things will not go wrong. Such wasted effort is made at the cost of undertaking profitable work.

No system is perfect. Everything can be improved. When you think you have got it right probe it from different viewpoints. Aim for continuous improvement. The guideline should be to review continuously training provision and trainee progress; and to assess, monitor and apply remedial action to assure quality of achievement.

The quality costs model

Quality related costs generally fall within three main headings: failure costs, appraisal costs and prevention costs. The summation of these costs is known as the **total quality-related cost** and there will be a combination of costs that gives an economic balance. This will occur at a point where the total costs are at a minimum.

The effect of increasing quality awareness and continuously improving prevention of failure and non-conformance is shown in Figure 3.1.

Failure costs are those costs incurred by failing to achieve specified quality standards relating to customer needs and requirements, complaints and the cost of putting matters right. Failure costs include the costs incurred in investigating under-achievement, reviewing candidates' post-programme complaints, redesigning and reteaching, resits and the need to retest and reassess candidates, loss of goodwill and business; the administrative costs of liaising with dissatisfied customers; and associated handling costs.

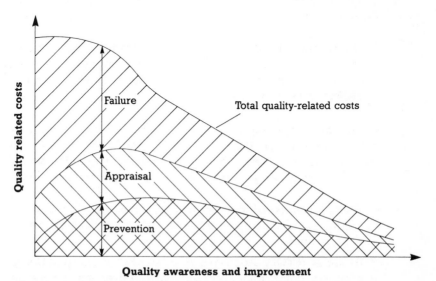

Figure 3.1 Increasing quality awareness and improvement activities[2]

If a quality management system based upon BS 5750, together with a TQM philosophy, is working well then quality-related failure costs should be minimal.

Appraisal costs are the costs of assessing quality achieved before the training programme commences, during delivery and upon its completion. Proposed training provision should be verified against NVQ units or programme specifications and learner achievement should be monitored. All software and resources bought in or produced in-house should be checked. Monitoring and evaluation (M&E) forms, questionnaires and other evaluative instruments should be analysed to establish whether or not client quality requirements and internal customers' expectations have been met.

Quality surveillance is carried out in order to verify that procedures and all specified requirements of service provision are being met.

Corrective action must be taken where the subsequent evaluation of outcomes of surveillance indicate deterioration.

Prevention costs are the costs of preventing or reducing the incidence of non-conformance and investigating causes of failure. These are the costs directed towards reducing or avoiding instances of the non-fulfilment of specified customer requirements. By taking precautionary action quality is maintained. Mistakes are anticipated and therefore prevented.

By maintaining a formal training programme for sub-contractors (consultants and other suppliers) and part-time staff, as well as full-timers, the chances of meeting the requisite service standard can be enhanced.

Quality auditing before and during programme implementation is an effective activity that is used when appraising the quality assurance system used by the provider. These costs may be classified as prevention costs.

Failure and appraisal costs may be reduced by carefully planning procedures relating to the service to be rendered. Written procedures and work instructions given in the quality manual, if adhered to, should assure the achievement of the appropriate level of customer requirement.

There is now considerable movement towards a process control model that is concerned with the costs of conformance and non-conformance.[3]

Associated TQM processes directed toward assuring the quality of inputs, continuous improvement and preventing poor performance will tend to reduce quality costs and result in benefits.

TQM benefits

Considerable benefit may derive from implementing principles of total quality management in the provision of education and training. In businesses a good deal of effort can be expended on correcting errors, rework and rectification. This is also true to some extent in the service industry but 'working smarter' and making sure things are done correctly first time, every time, can result in benefits. Greater efficiency and effectiveness, reduced waste, lower unit costs, enhanced reputation and more business can be achieved through TQM. This all adds up to improved quality of service for internal and external customers.

For the training provider, TQM will result in increased responsiveness, flexibility and greater competitiveness.

Benefits to the provider

Effectiveness
The purpose of the TQM system is to improve the effectiveness of the organisation in achieving targets and continuously to improve the quality of the provision and client satisfaction.

Evaluations of effectiveness may be made against specific criteria or by using comparisons, such as in-house versus sub-contracted work. Measures of effective working could include quality cost savings, unit costs, the break-even point for programmes, profits, the degree of customer satisfaction and survival.

Efficiency
Efficiency is the ratio of output to input. In training, a higher efficiency ratio can be obtained by improving the quality of resources, training inputs and learning outputs, without increasing capital, volume or effort.

Significant improvements in return on capital employed within the training provision can be attained by the improved utilisation of resources and systems. This does not necessarily mean working harder; it does mean 'optimising the process' by continually improving methods, monitoring the effect of changes implemented, improving productivity and reducing costs.

Benefits to staff
Wherever TQM operates, staff should be actively involved in managing quality and playing an important part in management decision making. Without staff involvement and support TQM will become ineffective and will grind to a halt.

The delegation of power and authority to influence the way in which training provision is organised and facilitated encourages staff to set their own quality goals. These self-imposed goals are often challenging and set at higher levels than those that autocratic managers could hope to achieve. Staff concerned perceive this sharing of responsibility as an intrinsic reward and benefit from the experience.

When quality targets are negotiated by management, staff and customers together, objectives will be better understood by all concerned and there will be less chance of confusion and non-conformance. Creative thinking will be promoted as the process of continuous improvement takes hold and this will stimulate co-operation and teamwork. In turn, this will contribute to job enrichment.

Developing TQM

Investing in people is a concept that is aimed at helping senior management tackle staff development and training matters. In order to develop TQM there is a need to have in place a team of competent staff conversant with all aspects of quality management and implementation.

A collection of staff may or may not make an effective team that is willing and able to involve itself in the process of problem solving and improving quality. With this in mind there is a need, as Deming suggests, to break down barriers between departments and to encourage open, two-way communications. Some hierarchical managements that operate the 'do what you're told' style of control and impose rigid rules and regulations may not be compatible with the 'do what you think best' and listening to staff lobby.

> Recall that for some it is hard to say thank you and easy to tell people when they are wrong. If you are one of these people then perhaps the time has come to examine the strengths and weaknesses of such a strategy.

Open communication and comment can only happen if people are not afraid of expressing their opinions. Of what use is a mission statement and a declared management commitment to TQM if staff are concerned about what the principal will think or do, were they to actually say what they really think or believe? TQM must be company-wide and it must start at the top. It tests the credibility of the management and establishes whether or not it is serious about committing resources to quality assurance systems. Staff can pick up attitudes, and depending upon how they perceive their manager's intent to put the customer first, will take their cue from his or her approach.

If senior managers demonstrate commitment to TQM and by their attitudes show that quality assurance is important to them and to their employer, then hopefully everyone will accept the need to prevent failure. All will be accountable for attaining the quality of service that will meet their own customers' expectations.

Total quality assurance is everyone's responsibility and effective teams committed to a quality philosophy have to evolve. This will involve the need to provide general learning opportunities for the entire workforce, bringing long-term benefits to the provider, customers and the staff themselves. Team members will need the active support of managers in achieving short-term operational objectives and longer-term strategic quality goals.

Paying lip service will not do. Neither will hype that uses exaggerated or intensive publicity either in-house or when marketing the service. Customers will be quick to see through the deception of effective promotional material and presentable 'front men' when they realise that actual services or products do not match the hype.

Team building and teamwork

Team building in TQM

Teamwork has been found to benefit business situations where it has been encouraged. When working co-operatively, outcomes are often better than when individuals are working in isolation. When several staff are involved in making a decision, members will be committed to carrying it out; where individual contributions are recognised and rewarded, even greater effort will be made.

The function of the team leader will be to negotiate group objectives, plan, brief, control and support members, inform, review progress and evaluate outcomes.

The action-centred leadership theory suggests three sets of needs that overlap and interact in any teamwork activity:

- needs relating to the task;
- individual team member's needs;
- overall team maintenance needs.

The need to accomplish the task set will clearly affect each of the other two sets of needs. Each individual's needs must somehow be satisfied and supportive leadership is essential to success. Team maintenance will be reinforced by making good progress with the task and keeping up team morale. A delicate balance between the three sets of needs must be maintained in order to get the task completed without losing group cohesion or individual support.

By using a teamwork approach a favourable attitude to developing TQM can be promoted by:

- creating a co-operative attitude among the team and subsequently right across the organisation;
- clarifying the success criteria for individuals, team and workforce as a whole;
- allocating responsibilities to the people best suited to carrying them out;
- making sure that everyone knows what they are required to do;
- utilising individual talents;
- collectively setting objectives and regularly reviewing progress;
- encouraging effective communication within the team.

Apathy and lack of effort are not simply a matter of laziness. Often, they are healthy reactions by normal people to an unhealthy environment – created all too commonly by unsound leadership practices and policies. When operating as a team, loyalty, co-operation and morale will improve, and people will undoubtedly function more effectively and achieve higher attainments than could otherwise be expected.

> **Management attitudes and behaviour affect rank-and-file motivation in business; the same is true in education and training. The TQM supervisor must be careful not to have an adverse effect on staff attitudes towards implementing both quality management and quality assurance.**

Working together

A favourable attitude to TQM can be promoted by working co-operatively with all other staff to achieve quality goals. When people work as a team, motivation increases and individual talents are utilised for the benefit of the group. Any tendency to destructive behaviour and lack of support is replaced by positive and helpful effort, leading to a responsible attitude and the will to succeed.

Results of teamwork are normally much better than the sum of individual efforts. Personal satisfaction is gained from helping one another to master tasks confronting the whole group. Some quality managers have succeeded by communicating well, showing an understanding and caring attitude, setting a good example and involving and encouraging their people right from the start.

Effective managers have a high level of 'people skills' that contributes to the success of a project. Owning such skills helps when developing teams, individuals and managing in order to enhance quality performance.

Quality probe – teamwork

Motivating the team

Is there provision for:

- improving morale and effectiveness?
- setting targets?
- encouraging the team to decide work methods?
- allocating team and individual responsibilities?
- giving recognition and praise, and saying thank you?

Leadership

Is there a commitment to:

- establishing and maintaining trust and supporting the team?
- forging an honest and constructive relationship?
- creating effective working relationships?
- communicating and consulting?
- encouraging ideas and suggestions?
- identifying and minimising conflict within the team?
- maintaining standards?
- counselling and support?

Reviewing the provision

Selecting areas for improvement

Method study is defined as 'the systematic recording and critical examination of ways of doing things in order to make improvements'.[4] Method study techniques are used to examine departmental layouts, laboratories, drop-in centres, assessment centres, work-stations and learning resource centre operations. Materials handling, support service activities and physical and human resources also come under scrutiny. In addition, teaching and learning methods, curriculum design and quality standards fall within the scope of method study.

Managers could use method study as a means of finding out the best way of operating the existing service, considering how present methods can be improved and entirely new ones devised.

Method study (SOCDIM)

Method study (see Figure 3.2) involves:

Selecting a particular area of operation for study;
Observing what is happening and recording all relevant facts about the operation;
Critically examining data gathered;
Developing improvements;
Introducing and installing changes; and
Monitoring and maintaining the changed process or procedure.

Key matters for attention and study might include:

- service design
- service delivery
- service results
- administration
- communication
- curriculum audit
- learning environment
- external affairs
- data initiation, recording and analysis
- management information system
- feedback and control systems
- implementation of legislation
- housekeeping
- hygiene.

The method study procedure involves six main stages:

- **Select** – identify for study the individual job, department or specific provision, or whole organisation.
- **Observe and record** – the location of the training event or other activity, the sequence of activities, and the movements of staff, trainees, materials, aids and resources.
- **Critically examine** – analyse what is happening by getting a clear picture of the present position and obtaining all the facts.
- **Devise and develop improvement** – review each piece of information obtained from the examination of content. Check for non-conformances. Justify the retention of key elements. Cut out unnecessary work. Redesign or modify then take corrective action. Compare with plans or specifications and record changes.
- **Install and implement** – introduce and establish the new method. Record and check that the design specification complies with agreed customer requirements and is compatible with the provider's strategy and objectives.
- **Monitor and maintain** – continuously review and evaluate new methods. Verify that the content and procedures conform to specifications defining the product or service. Seek sources of improvement.

Figure 3.2 SOCDIM

Implementing TQM

As in all management strategies, commitment and support is a pre-requisite for the successful implementation of TQM. Commitment starts from the top – from the principal, chairperson or chief executive. It is likely that this person, together with senior managers, will be directed and supported by governors or the board, and monitored by TECs, contractors representatives, LEAs and the like. Leadership, enthusiasm and drive will need to be perceived by the workforce and every member of staff will need to follow the example set.

Poor leadership results in little or no commitment from the workforce.

Steering groups

Achieving a reputation for providing a quality service takes time and hard work. Energetic people cannot make it on their own. They need to adopt a planned approach based on fully-documented systems and procedures. They need a lot of support from management and guidance provided by a steering group that can focus and direct its effort towards key result areas. A list of possible target areas for improvement could include:

- promoting awareness of the importance of customers;
- forming project or action teams;
- involving everyone in planning and implementing a total quality philosophy;
- devising a strategy for change in attitudes towards working to new systems and procedures;
- training in quality procedures, problem-solving, leadership and teamwork;
- evaluating ways of reducing quality costs.

Quality circle facilitators and quality co-ordinators report developments to the steering group.

Managing activities

People as a valuable resource

The most important resources within an organisation are the people who make up the workforce. They provide the know-how, creativity and skills, willingness and commitment, and the energy to make things happen. They are the engine that drives the organisation. It is they who make the quality assurance system work effectively.

Involving everyone

All staff should be involved in a continuous process of improving quality. Course team leaders and tutors should be encouraged to demonstrate leadership and help their colleagues deliver a better service. 'Easier said than done', some will say as they rush about chasing paper, answering phone calls and snatching messages off their desktops. Besides that, there will be reluctance of some staff to expose their shortcomings to others. Some will prefer to keep their heads below the parapet and carry out avoidance behaviour, rather than to do anything other than talk about improving the service.

Forming positive attitudes

Deming stresses the importance of driving out fear so that staff may concentrate on working effectively for the organisation. Fear gives rise to feelings of distress. When people are affected by low morale and feelings of apprehension it is difficult for them to apply themselves effectively to their work.

Appraisals and evaluations of performance by others are an important source of anxiety for many. Staff perceive appraisal as a management device that can be used to make life unpleasant for them, rather than as a means of continuously reviewing staff development needs and enhancing the quality of performance.

> Managers need to break down barriers and promote the concept of training for change. Self-assessment and self-improvement opportunities should be afforded staff so that they may update themselves and take on board new competences.

There is a difference in opinion about whether decision making should follow a 'bottom up' or 'top down' approach. Some prefer the consensus model where general or widespread agreement among the staff is sought. This follows the belief that ownership of initiatives, projects and decisions will secure commitment and goodwill. Others prefer to be told what to do, like to follow guidelines or instructions and automatically tend to avoid taking responsibility for any decision.

> Staff may need to learn how to deal with change and managers may need to think about how to handle the 'tell or sell' dilemma.

Delegation

The art of delegation (rather than lumbering anyone who will take on work) is neither universally understood nor practised, in many cases. Confidence in subordinates – who as often as not have ill-defined responsibilities – may be lacking in terms of their ability to clarify objectives, supervise projects, review and monitor performance and know when criteria have been achieved. Opportunities should be sought to delegate authority and decision making to responsible persons and to involve everyone in the process of operating a total quality policy. This will help them to understand better and support what the quality manager and other key staff are attempting to do on the quality front.

> Delegation of authority and responsibility for decision making and taking action should be recorded in a job description and be entered in the quality manual.

Roles and responsibilities

When operating a TQM policy the roles, responsibilities and activities of key people should be defined and those accepting roles should be fully briefed as to how they will be involved in planning and implementing policies.

Suggestions and ideas

Every effort should be made to communicate the importance of quality and to welcome suggestions as to how improvements may be made. Suggestion schemes and competitions where prizes are awarded for ideas that result in savings in quality-related costs and better service to customers can create considerable motivation. Other means of generating interest include: staff meetings with quality on the agenda; inclusion of the importance of quality in induction programmes for trainees and new starters; staff circulars, posters and news sheets; and using DTI and commercially-produced videos.

Monitoring improvements

Monitoring improvements may take the form of financial audits or customers' perceptions of the product or service. The gathering and selection of evidence to be analysed and used to evaluate progress will help to determine the measure of success in implementing customer care and quality assurance procedures. These measures will vary according to the criteria that define whether or not the TQM process is operating as planned.

Quality circles

A **quality circle** is a small group of volunteers drawn from the same department or curriculum area. Members of the group assemble regularly to identify, analyse and solve their own work-related problems. Its brief would cover matters relating to the provision of the service including curriculum planning, resourcing, delivery and quality of training.

The work of quality circles may be regulated by a facilitator or cross-college co-ordinator trained in communicating, problem-solving and team-working, backed by group leaders for each circle. The co-ordinator collates circle actions and reports developments to the steering group or management representative responsible for implementing and maintaining quality functions. Proposed solutions to specific problems are communicated to the person responsible for the process under investigation.

Setting up circles

The work of quality circles in an education and training context differs in some ways from that of circles operating in manufacturing industries. Training providers will, in the main, be dealing with people rather than products. Whereas a production line may be started at 8 a.m. and shut down at 5 p.m., with staff at their work stations throughout the day, the situation is different in education and training.

Training is very labour-intensive with flexible timetables and cross-site working patterns. Teams may find it difficult to agree a mutually acceptable time to meet. The diversity of subjects taught, delivery modes and curriculum content further compound the problems of course-based activities and specialisms that lack coherence.

Common ground may be difficult to find. With this in mind, it may be necessary to restrict quality circle activity to projects that involve implementing changes in policy, systems and procedures rather than exploring problems concerning specific products and services. Alternatively, course teams could double as quality circle members and focus on departmental matters with cross-college teams handling items with wider applications.

> **The work of quality circles should have the backing and active support of the senior management team.**

Training

Awareness raising

Cultivating and nurturing a constructive attitude towards the organisation's quality assurance programme and philosophy of total quality management is necessary.

> **Awareness raising and targeted training should form an integral part of the provider's quality strategy.**

Staff trainers and supervisors

Staff trainers should have a clear understanding of TQM principles and practice, and be committed to organisational quality policies. Training should not be labelled as a bolt-on, non-productive activity but should be promoted vigorously and backed by senior management. Unwilling people are not an asset and only those with positive attitudes should be recruited to facilitate the staff development programme. Trainers, acting as catalysts and agents of change, who maintain a continuous dialogue about individual staff training needs and expectations tend to get co-operation and results. Those who are respected by their colleagues will be able to establish rapport and achieve positive outcomes, but those inexperienced in developing their staff lack credibility and will soon come unstuck. Staff are quick to spot the incompetent.

> The relationship between the quality initiative and senior management, staff and staff trainers should be established early in the planning cycle.

Educating the workforce

When discussing staff development needs with managers and their staff they will nod their heads and agree that training is needed – but not for them, just the others. However, with TQM, training is for everyone in the organisation.

Personal development opportunities

People who are ordered to attend, sent along, nominated without negotiation or briefing, or who have been bullied into attending a training event are not likely to learn much. When they get back to their departments they will spread the bad news, rubbish the trainers and alienate others. A better way is to secure commitment well before the training session and allow staff to discuss what is in it for them as well as for the organisation.

> Training should be based upon identified training needs.

Learning may be achieved using learning materials derived from many sources including written study guides and case studies, backed by video products. Supported self-study and distance learning conducted by groups or individuals, either on site or outside the workplace is now replacing much of the formal teaching that many have previously experienced. Support comes in the form of tutors and facilitators from the company itself, local colleges, training providers and consultants.

Cascading principles and practices

Every employee needs to understand the procedures of a practical quality assurance system. They need to be able to handle the technical language and content of BS 5750-modelled and approved systems, and to operate effectively within a company-wide quality framework with each playing their part.

An effective way of achieving widespread understanding of TQM and knowledge about its application within the organisation is by the **cascade model** of staff development. Trainers attend tailor-made courses that meet organisational specifications and return to share their newly-acquired knowledge and attitudes with others. This can be a very effective way of raising awareness, promoting interest and gaining commitment.

Quality probe – diagnosing need

When conducting staff interviews and reviews:

- are strengths and weaknesses of the team identified and compared with tasks and requirements, such as their roles, technical skills and interpersonal skills?
- are current competences, potential future competence and career aspirations matched with needs?
- all are invited to participate in an evaluation of team development needs and to help in planning and delivering appropriate training?
- are staff encouraged to take responsibility for achieving their own objectives?
- are mismatches between team members reduced or eliminated?
- are development objectives achievable, realistic and challenging, and do they relate to results to be produced and quality standards to be met?
- are the objectives negotiated and agreed with team members applicable?
- are formal, informal and work-related activities specified in any development plan?
- are existing resources utilised where possible?
- are training plans and outcomes reviewed and changed as necessary?
- are development plans assessed and constructively criticised using objective feedback and is the learning progress self-evaluated where possible?

Notes

1   A brief outline of the work of some leading gurus is given in an Enterprise Initiative booklet forming part of the DTI's 'Managing into the 1990s' programme. (See *The Quality Gurus – What can they do for your company?*, prepared by Professor Tony Bendell of Nottingham Polytechnic on behalf of Services Ltd for the DTI, London, (undated).

The text refers to the work of people such as W. Edwards Deming, Joseph M. Juran, Shigeo Shingo, Bill Conway, Philip B. Crosby, Armand V. Feigenbaum, Dr Kaoru Ishikawa, Dr Genichi Taguchi and Claus Moller.

2   BS 6143: Part 2 (1990), *Guide to the economics of quality – Part 2 Prevention, appraisal and failure model,* p. 2.

3   The 1990 revised edition of BS 6143: Part 2 replaces BS 6143:1981, *Guide to the determination and use of quality related costs,* which is withdrawn.

   In the Forword to BS 6143:Part 2, BSI say that Part 1 of the standard (the process cost model) 'sets out a method for applying quality costing to any process or service. It recognizes the importance of process measurement and process ownership. The categories of quality costs have been rationalized to the cost of conformance and the cost of non-conformance. This serves to simplify classification. The method depends on the use of process modelling and the standard gives guidelines on useful techniques. The application of the process control model is compatible within the concept of total quality management.'

4   BS 3138:1979, *Glossary of terms used in work study and organization and methods (O & M),* p. 2.

CHAPTER FOUR

TQM – Putting the Customer First

Chapter coverage

Putting the customer first
  Why bother?
  An organisation's image
Customer care in training and continuing education
  Suggested management objectives
  Marketing the provision
  Customer relations
Infrastructure and staffing
  Improving the provision
  Customer requirements
Everyone's a customer
  Customer charters
  Customer satisfaction
  Customer services and liaison
Access and initial assessment
  The role of student services
  Complaints and their resolution
  Governors and board members
First impressions count

Putting the customer first

Why bother?

Customers are important. They have the ultimate choice when it comes to buying products and services and their requirements must be satisfied. Forget this and you will soon lose your customer base. Customers' needs are of prime importance both to themselves and to the prospective supplier. If they have a training problem they will seek help from a provider. They will look for a speedy and effective response. If they do not get the kind of quality and service they are entitled to they will vote with their feet and will not return; and do not expect any recommendations. But when customers receive a courteous, efficient and effective service they come back for more and recommend your products and services to contacts.

An organisation's image

In order to gain and retain customers an organisation must operate to acceptable standards and present a positive image. Its standing in market segments will depend upon its customers' awareness of the quality of products, processes and services it provides.

The corporate image will be reflected in its policies and commitment to quality systems that work. The way an organisation is perceived by contractors and the public at large will influence the number of contracts it is awarded and the amount of business that may be won.

> A successful organisation is one that knows how well it is meeting internal and external customer requirements, and transmits the right signals about its people, processes and products.

Customer care in training and continuing education

Customer care is a term which has appeared fairly recently within continuing education having been previously almost unheard-of. Competition for adult returners, people needing retraining and updating, and school-leavers, in times of falling rolls, has changed things. Spoiled for choice and with expectations of a better deal than was offered in the past these customers are now in a position to force the pace of change. The necessity to react quickly and favourably to enquiries from prospective customers and then to meet their needs with quality service creates an urgent requirement for increased responsiveness. Improved efficiency and effectiveness is now a vital pre-requisite for survival.

Putting the customer first together with the need for suitably targeted marketing is now becoming an established and accepted function of management (see Figure 4.1). Developing a culture that embraces a range of ideas and activities that will lead to a tradition of good customer relations is an essential part of any marketing strategy.

- To cause all staff to be aware of the need to market the provision effectively.
- To identify areas of good practice in customer relations within the organisation and areas which could be improved.
- To establish targets, priorities, standards and action plans that will facilitate the achievement of identified improvements.
- To establish and maintain good customer relations that are essential to the success of the organisation.

Figure 4.1 Suggested management objectives

Marketing the provision

Effective marketing is important. Marketing the organisation will involve all those well-known activities that are essential to doing it right the first time. That is providing our customers with the right learning opportunity at the right price, in the right place and at the right time.

Activities comprise:

- Market research planned to discover those factors influencing customer behaviour and to analyse market characteristics.
- Creating a corporate identity underpinned with quality of service.
- Resourcing and developing the teaching and learning provision in order to provide better programmes and services.
- Creating consumer demand by honestly convincing customers of the potential worth of your service.
- Effectively costing, pricing, advertising, promoting and selling the service and products.
- Continuously promoting good customer relations.
- Implementing exit surveys and an efficient post-training, after-sales service.
- Targeting improvements and implementing suggestions according to a planned timescale.

Marketing plans should include schedules for surveying marketing and promotional arrangements. The following guide for assessment has been suggested.

'The provider plans all promotional and marketing arrangements, monitors external perceptions of their programmes, regularly evaluates their arrangements and there is evidence that evaluation positively informs subsequent activity.'[1]

Quality probe – marketing function

- Is there a direct marketing link between the supplier and customer? If so, is the market perception of services provided fed back through prescribed channels and evaluated? Where necessary is recommended corrective action taken?
- Is marketing information that has been gathered utilised to:
    Aid further promotion of existing products and services?
    Identify additional customer needs?
    Develop new products and services?
- Does feedback obtained confirm the provider's ability to satisfy customer requirements at the contracted quality level?

Customer relations

A **customer** is commonly thought of as someone who buys something. However, a customer can be any person who receives a service or product from a supplier. From this idea stems that of internal or external customers and suppliers.

> An aim covering the training supplier's intentions might be to provide customers with services available from the organisation that meet their individual requirements and to foster good relations with local industry, commerce, public authorities and the community at large.

Typical examples of customer relations activities might include:

- Reviewing the market by contacting people in public places, support and referral agencies, employers' and other providers' businesses; and finding out their training requirements.
- Preparing training and developing learning opportunities to meet the demand-led needs of individuals and groups, such as returners to education and people seeking professional and commercial updating and retraining.
- Enhancing the design and presentation of a user-friendly and readable prospectus, and other advertising and promotional material.
- Using testimonials, thank you letters and success stories reported by former learners. These tell how the provider helped individuals achieve their targets and gain the competences needed to get where they are today within their chosen occupational area.
- Discovering who the customers are and why they are important to the business. Asking why customers' needs are important to them individually. Realising that survival depends upon customers enrolling with your organisation rather than with competitors.

- Discovering why prospective customers did not come to your organisation and how providers are supplying what your organisation could not.
- Looking for new markets, new products and new customers who are seeking learning opportunities, and finding ways of responding to the customers' perceived needs.
- Seeking to better serve adult clients and those with special learning difficulties and other special needs. Working with customers and helping them to make important decisions about their training and education.
- Providing access to customers in such a way that greater flexibility and professionalism results. Recognising that all staff, including non-teaching and support staff, know and accept their important role in customer relations.
- Satisfying customers as competition increases and providing facilities, service and personal skills that are of the right quality.

Infrastructure and staffing

The **infrastructure** is the basic fabric or structure of an organisation and includes premises and the systems by which training provision is made available to customers.

A **survey of premises and equipment** would result in the assessment of overall quality on a continuum ranging from, at the low end, 'evidence that the premises are unsuitable for the use being made of them', to, at the high end, evidence that 'premises are well planned, maintained and continuously reviewed and updated to provide optimum support to the programmes provided'.[2]

Systems and staffing surveys would establish whether or not the implementation of quality procedures and the design and delivery of training programmes were meeting customer requirements.

> The learning environment influences quality of service provided and learning opportunities perceived by learners. The provider will need to satisfy both customer requirements and organisational needs.

First impressions count. As media advertisements pronounce 'You never get a second chance to make a good first impression.' With this thought in mind readers may care to have a good look at the infrastructure of their workplace. How will customers tend to view it? If they phone in how long will it take before someone on the other end answers the call? When intending to make a personal visit will they be able to find the organisation? If they do will they get a 'No-parking' sticker on their windscreen within minutes of leaving their car on the campus? (That is if they can find anywhere to park.) Will there be a welcoming atmosphere when they enter the building? Will they be able to find reception or the place where they need to be? Will there be someone on hand to attend to them? If so, will that person stop what they are doing and listen carefully to what has the customer has to say? Or will they be so pushed and stressed that they will transmit their anxieties to the customer and terminate the conversation before getting a clear picture of what is needed.

Will customers benefit from an efficient appointments system, or will they be sent off to run the maze or be directed from one person to another until they admit defeat, abandon hope of finding the person they need to see and clear off? If it is information on provision the customer is seeking will copies of a current prospectus be available ? Will there be a computerised database of availability? Or will these customers be sent off to run the maze? Will customers have to join a long queue to get a cup of coffee, need to clear rubbish from the table when they do and brush filth off a chair before sitting down? Will they appreciate the so-called, fast-food service with its limited menu, microwaved preparation and recycled chips? Will the food be cold by the time they leave the queue at the checkout till? Will they find somewhere to sit down to eat the meal? Will they sit shivering? Will they be able to see across a smoke-filled room and will they be able to find a clean toilet?

> It is likely that the reader would be able to add to the list quite a lot more features of a 'take it or leave it' attitude to customers. If so, then the need to do something about it must be getting quite urgent!

Customers' enquiries should not be viewed as an interruption to our work. The customer is important to survival and continued expansion; they have needs and expectations that must be satisfied. We are therefore dependent upon them giving us their business. With this in mind and in order to retain existing customers and attract new customers:

- Provide clear signposts that show ways into the organisation and others that indicate where to park, and the locations of reception, conveniences, facilities and main areas. Provide large-scale plans of the site in the reception area and at other strategic locations.
- Provide clean, comfortable surroundings, reception area, refectory facilities and other material things that help to provide a reasonable level of comfort for customers.
- Reassure customers that staff are there to help and support them in any way appropriate to the role of vocational education and training provider.

- Inform, up-date and communicate with customers so as to give and obtain that feedback essential to the provision of an efficient and effective service.
- Provide a fast response to customer enquiries, doubts and initiatives, thereby ensuring a user-friendly service.
- Maintain a personalised, warm, friendly and welcoming atmosphere supported by an interested and committed workforce.

Improving the provision

In order to enhance customer relations the following proposals could be implemented or further enhanced in order to improve existing provisions:

- Improve advertising and publicity and other promotional matters. Sell the benefits that the organisation can offer. Improve information flows. Consider standardising all advertisements using a corporate identity and appointing one person in the organisation to handle all advertisements. Provide what is offered at the quality that will satisfy customer requirements.
- Develop a customer service centre (student services) or an assessment centre staffed with qualified people experienced in handling initial enquiries. Introduce an appointment system for people seeking advice, guidance or counselling. Ensure that appointments are honoured and that the right person meets with the customer.
- Improve strategies and operational planning. Where possible, avoid creating chaos, muddle, making eleventh-hour decisions and 'flying by the seat of one's pants'.
- Improve communications between trainers and support staff. Foster an awareness in all staff of the content of other's jobs and the problems that these people solve or overcome, and the difficulties and matters that they deal with daily in their normal course of work.
- Modularise college provision and, if necessary, offer education and training at module, unit and element level, backed by an accreditation system and record of achievement process. Take into account perceived needs of individual learners, employers and the community at large.
- Promote the need and opportunity to gather often together in small teams so that review and mutual support may result in a more acceptable and effective provision. A quality circles approach may be appropriate.
- Utilise to better effect existing accommodation and refurbish sub-standard rooms.
- Implement academic and administrative cover throughout vacations so that the public will not be deprived of the service that they may be seeking.
- Identify features of existing customer relations where the organisation performs well and also areas where things could be done better.

- Appoint a person to be responsible for customer care in the organisation and a team to work out what should be done to improve matters. Create an action plan for implementing the changes.
- Instigate an extensive staff development programme designed around matters needing improvement and those needs and suggestions outlined above.

Customer requirements

Putting customers first means ensuring that all that the provider does is directed towards delivering the service the customer expects and the desired end result, every time. Customer-driven, total quality policy depends upon the maintenance of internal quality by ongoing employee-centred quality improvement processes.

Internal quality is achieved by embedding throughout the organisation a fundamental approach that serves as a basis for assuring quality from design to delivery of the service to the customer.

If this policy is adopted, the proposition that everyone's a customer, whether they be internal or external customers, can become a reality. This then leads to the strategy of forming a continuous chain of customers from those who conceive of the product or service to those who buy it.

Everyone's a customer

The philosophy and practice of operating a quality customer service applies both to external and internal customers.

External customers include buyers and **end users**, such as employers who sponsor training, students and trainees paying for education and training, tax payers, purchasers and users of other products or services, and the community at large who in some way contribute to or participate in the service provided.

Internal customers include all who receive or make use of products or services provided by other staff in-house, sub-contractors or outside suppliers of resources. Every person involved in the organisation will at some time be an internal supplier who will be expected to meet the needs and expectations of other staff. They in turn will be customers of other internal suppliers and will have needs and expectations of their own that should be satisfied.

In every department and course team there will be chains of suppliers and customers with each link needing to meet the requirements of the next in the chain. Customer requirements can only be met when their specific needs are communicated and correctly perceived by suppliers. It is therefore important to learn to listen so as to get a clear picture of what the customer wants rather than what the supplier thinks they want. Customers are generally only interested in what the supplier can do for them personally. They expect to get what they want and do not wish to hear reasons why the supplier cannot meet their requests.

> Having the capability to meet the requirements and supplying at the right quality at the supplier/customer interface ensures conformance to standard. This can prevent problems cropping up later and will go a long way toward managing quality and giving a value-for-money service.

Customer orientation is the act of aligning oneself and the processes and resources one controls with the needs and expectations of the customer. In order to do this, contractors (suppliers) and their staff (also suppliers) must fully understand customers' needs and meet these needs by doing things right first time. Customers will compare the quality of service they have in mind with that provided by suppliers and their colleagues while they are doing whatever is needed to satisfy the contract. In this way, the customers' greatest or worst expectations may be realised.

> Whether or not a provider becomes a winner will depend upon how internal and external customers perceive the quality of service afforded them by suppliers.

Customer charters

Some training providers have now prepared 'user charters' for their customers. The charters set out mutual responsibilities and describe standards of service that customers may expect to receive and also what the user agrees to do in return. The idea is an extension of negotiated learning provision that has formed the basis of learning contracts for many years.

Customer satisfaction

Satisfaction implies the fulfilment of a desire or need. Satisfying the bare needs of the end-user of a service is thought by some to be all that is required to discharge fully the responsibilities of the supplier. This may be true when outcomes are compared with specification and contract, but some customers may expect more and it is that little extra attention to detail or effort to please that goes a long way to building good customer relations.

It has already been suggested that whether we like it or not customers compare the quality of service they get from different suppliers. They compare and assess staff and resources, staff attitudes toward them, whether the supplier listens courteously to them, language usage, speed of response to their requests and how complaints are handled.

> Managing customer care and taking responsibility for achieving customer satisfaction lies with the training provider. However, the ultimate judge of whether or not needs and expectations have been met lies with the end-user.

Customer services and liaison

The role of **customer services** is becoming increasingly important in backing up a customer-centred quality education and training service. Since quality may be defined in terms of customer expectations, the concept of a quality service can be related to training provision in much the same way as to that provided by a five star hotel. Customer service in a college is provided by the student services unit, the aim being to treat learners decently, ensure that they gain access without a lot of hassle, make them feel at home and provide ongoing support.

Access and initial assessment

Matching individual needs and expectations with related education and training provision is the key to success in the attainment of competence in an occupation or subject. Gaining access to suitable learning opportunities has, in the past, not always been easy. In some cases it has been at best a compromise between what the customer was seeking and whatever course or training programme was already available. Today, there is a demand for more flexibility and a wider range of training provision. A bespoke rather than off-the-peg service is required. This is needed to fulfil the expectations of individuals and employers seeking to supply quality products and services provided by a well-trained and competent workforce.

In order to meet the challenge, providers may need to set up or improve access and initial assessment. A more responsive vocational education and training service is called for. For example, a central admissions unit located within the student services unit could help to improve matters.

The role of student services

Student services deals with matters affecting the learner as a customer. In some cases this work is undertaken by a **student counsellor** working alone but with access to all provider departments, support services and external referral agencies. Not all providers operate these services, although it is now becoming a necessity rather than a luxury as competition for customers increases.

With the introduction of NVQs (National Vocational Qualifications), higher priority is being given to providing the kind of facilities that are needed to back up assessment and accreditation of prior learning and experience. Customers seeking information on accreditation and curriculum entitlement (their share of the education and training cake) now expect a better deal than that on offer in the eighties and previously.

Customers need to gain access to the right person to help them without first being needlessly directed from one place to another. They deserve to be interviewed in a quiet, comfortable and private room. They require to be treated in a sensitive way by supportive and honest people who know what they are talking about. They are, after all, customers without whom the business would fail.

Induction and initial assessment role
Another key role of student services would be to facilitate access to learning and to make it easy for customers to get out of the system what they need rather than what happens to be on offer. A model that might suit colleges, but which is transferrable to other training providers and employers, is shown in Figure 4.2.

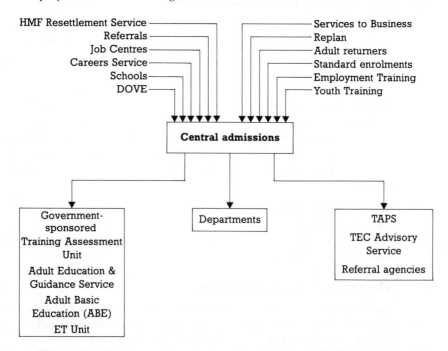

Figure 4.2 Role of customer support services – access and initial assessment

Working on a systems approach, customers would be directed to the central admissions unit which would act as a filter. Competent staff would offer a user-friendly counselling and guidance service to those looking for learning opportunities.

For many customers, mainstream education and training provision would be geared to satisfying their needs. Such people would be directed to the department where adequately-trained academic staff would be able to give detailed information on subjects and routes to progression. Customers would be set on the right track – that leading to the achievement of their goals.

Customers with learning difficulties or problems that cannot readily be resolved and those needing help with career choice would be referred to qualified staff based in support units.

Complaints and their resolution

Complaints and their resolution can take up a lot of time and resources, and if perceived as being a nuisance will probably result in scant attention being paid to the complainer. To treat a customer in a condescending, slighting or inadequate manner would not in the long run be very sensible. Resentment would surely result. Ill will and grumbles are quickly spread around a group and the wider network of friends and other contacts inside and outside the organisation. The end result could be loss of business to other providers of similar training who happen to be better at handling customer relations.

An attempt should be made to calm angry customers who are upset about something. The person dealing with the complaint should then try to look at the problem from the customer's point of view and maintain a positive attitude. Entrenched positions and emotional outbursts should be avoided. If there is the likelihood of personality clashes occurring, perhaps counsellors, student union representatives or their equivalents could be brought in to serve as mediators.

> Someone will have to co-operate with complainers, deal with them skilfully and hopefully turn them into satisfied customers.
>
> Opportunities should be sought for staff to develop the assertiveness that will result in positive reactions by customers and suppress or restrain conflict.

Customer loyalty is important. If they are to keep coming back, time must be found to deal with legitimate complaints. How customers see you and what they think of you and the organisation you represent will be influenced by the image you portray.

The risk of alienating customers should be reduced by treating complaints as opportunities to check provision and to locate and correct sources of non-compliance that have led to the complaints.

Internal conflict and the way in which a complaint concerning a member of staff is handled may cause ripples throughout the entire organisation. Scapegoating is not unknown in educational circles. Trainees know just how to wind up trainers and set one against another. Some misfits holding high offices, when acting upon complaints from people, are inclined to make ill-informed judgements without carefully checking the source, causes and validity of the grievance. The complaint may or may not be due to staff shortcomings. A better way is to consult with all implicated and listen to all shades of opinion before taking a decision. The origin of a complaint may derive from failures in organisational systems and not from individuals.

Maintaining a quality service depends to a considerable degree on job satisfaction. Unhappy staff are unlikely to continue to meet the challenge of putting the customer first. Having the will to provide an excellent service is essential to everyone working in the business.

Governors and board members

The **governing body** is the controlling body of a college and it may comprise about 20 members drawn from a diverse population. A **board of directors** is a group of people who officially administer a company. In each case its role is to monitor, direct and control the actions, affairs, policies and functions of the organisation. The way it performs its functions will have implications for the customer.

There should be considerable involvement by everyone in customer-care activities. A strong commitment to operating total quality policies and procedures should be demonstrated by those responsible for managing the organisation. But attempts to impose 'top–down' enforcement of such policies will probably be unsuccessful. In the eyes of the customer it is the person at the point of contact that is the provider, so the success of quality assurance in action will depend on 'bottom–up' commitment and ownership of quality policies and procedures.

The people who count most are the people at the sharp end, in the area of provision where there may be most difficulty or competition. It is these people who reward the customer with the kind of service that they require or in some cases demand.

First impressions count

Customers are the providers' greatest assets. Holding an inventory of high-class resources will not alone ensure a successful business. Pursuing a sound customer relations policy is important to the survival of the provider, as is recognising that individual needs are important to customers. Customer care is focused on understanding and acknowledging that customers will, from time to time, be seeking help and advice. They will be interested in what the provider can genuinely do for them and not in any kind of sales pitch or unrealistic hype.

No attempt should be made to fob off customers.

The customers' first impressions will colour the way in which the organisation is viewed. An indifferent attitude can be very obvious to a potential customer. It is how customers perceive the service that will encourage them to buy or register with the provider and come back for more, or alternatively to join the band of customers who did not come back.

How successfully the first contact is managed can be critical to the development of a business relationship. Poor telephone techniques can very quickly upset potential customers. A quick acknowledgement when the phone rings while you are busy or an offer to ring back soon is better than subjecting the caller to the 'music box' ordeal. When internal lines are engaged it is cheaper and easier for the customer to hang-up and ring another provider who maintains sufficient lines.

Automatons mindlessly mouthing the now compulsory and increasingly-lengthy telephone greeting without a trace of sincerity can be off-putting to callers. All that is needed is a telephone technique that conveys to the customer a sincere, warm and friendly attitude toward them and an interest in what they are saying. Sending a 'We're here to help' message is more profitable than issuing a 'Get off the line, you're interrupting me' signal to the caller.

It is likely to be receptionists or other support staff that will be the first people the customer will meet face-to-face. Initial needs will be revealed to reception staff and customer satisfaction will depend on how well they meet expectations. Training staff will need to be aware of this fact and understand the implications of liaising and working together.

It is a well-documented truth that the customer is the most important person that anyone in business is likely to come into contact with. They should not be treated as an interruption to our work, but as the purpose of it. It is also readily acknowledged that the customer is not often dependent upon the provider supplying them, but the provider is always dependent upon sufficient customers buying their product or service.

There is now widespread agreement that a lot of customers do not come back after a bad experience with provider's staff or as an outcome of the services offered not meeting contracted requirements. Exit reviews and early leaver surveys will show where customers' perceptions of the course programme or service offered reveal shortcomings or nonconformances. Time spent listening to customer suggestions is not wasted. What they have to say can prevent further failures. Whenever feasible and corrective action is proposed, there should be a rapid response and evidence of positive developments aimed at putting matters right.

Eliminating faults and improving unsatisfactory elements of provision should be given high priority and schedules for surveying arrangements and for correcting deficiences should be devised. The following guide for assessment has been suggested.

> 'Deficiences are corrected fairly rapidly; action plans are formulated and implemented, and highly efficient methods exist to direct management attention to quality concerns.'[3]

Notes

1   Dorset Training and Enterprise Council's *Training Provider Quality Survey Manual,* p. 24, Bournemouth, May 1991. (The Dorset TEC's Manual was itself modelled on the Coventry and Warwickshire TEC publication *The Training Provider Quality Survey Manual,* published in 1990.)

2   Ibid. p. 25. (Author's interpretation.)

3   Ibid. p. 21.

CHAPTER FIVE

TQM and BS 5750 in Education and Training

Chapter coverage

Aim of BS 5750
  Why bother?
TQM in education
  Targets
  Customer needs
  Continuous improvement
  Audits
The link between TQM and BS 5750
  Strengths of BS 5750
BS 5750 in education and training
  How BS 5750 might work in practice
  Planning and documentation
  Contracting
  Key steps in contract review
Launching initiatives
  Educational aspects
  Recruiting clients
  Induction
  Administration
  The Health and Safety at Work Act
  Training plans and programmes
  Learning opportunities and methods
  Curriculum entitlement
Operation and management of an organisation
  Staff
  Correlation – mission v. reality
  Quality system elements

The aim of BS 5750

The aim of the BS 5750/ISO 9000 series of standards is to prevent faults and errors in the activities of the organisation which affect the quality of the product or service the customer receives. It does so by requiring that management systems and procedures are established, documented and maintained. Achievement of the BS 5750 standard demonstrates to your customers that you provide products or services to the required quality.[1]

Why bother?

Many customers now insist on dealing only with organisations with BS 5750 certification. Now, the Training and Enterprise Councils (TECs) require all training providers with whom they contract business to achieve quality standards prescribed by the TEC concerned. Manufacturing organisations seek out suppliers who operate within a framework of quality assurance principles defined in systems such as BS 5750. It is therefore not surprising to find that those awarding contracts will likewise seek out training contractors who meet appropriate quality standards. Furthermore, to survive in business there will be a need for contractors to demonstrate commitment to a process of continuous quality improvement in all aspects of their operations.

When awarding contracts, TECs and other sponsors of education and training may give preference to those who 'establish and maintain a valid coherent quality management system'[2] or providers with BS 5750 certification, assuming that the contracted level of quality can be delivered. Benefits to the provider of effectively evaluating where they are with respect to given quality standards are that they will become more effective and therefore more profitable, with a greater probability of survival.

Providers should be able to capitalise on an enhanced reputation brought about by achieving **approved training organisation status** and BS 5750 criteria. Greater influence and a wider customer base will result from achieving a high quality development rating as an outcome of quality audits.

TQM in education

In a total quality environment there is a need to first find out what the customer requires and then to set about effectively and efficiently meeting those needs. Involvement of the whole workforce in building quality into the service delivered and a commitment to doing the right things correctly is emphasised. This demands a quality-assured, well-managed and adequately-resourced provision, backed by a team of staff who are committed to a company-wide total quality approach to their work. Without staff support it is not possible to implement a total quality policy.

Targets

Achieving total quality is a target at which much effort will be directed, but unlike a penalty kick for goal it may take some time getting the desired result. Sudden and dramatic 'once and for all' attainment of quality objectives is not a realistic proposition. A commitment to quality improvement lasts for ever.

For a training provider a useful time to introduce a total quality policy is when establishing training requirements with clients. Supply-led programmes continue to generate interest and income, but demand-led products are more likely to sustain the business, provided that the supplier is able to give customers what they want. It is therefore essential to maintain a dialogue with TECs and the public at large, and involve them in the development of learning opportunities.

Once contact is made it is necessary to demonstrate commitment to delivering a quality product and to improve continuously the service to customers. This will be evidenced by the quality of training perceived, the range and scope of provision offered and the general effectiveness of working.

Good communication is an essential requirement of any people-based business. Having the ability to anticipate the needs of industry and to communicate the relevance of your training provision, plus the capabilities of your systems and staff in meeting those needs, is a benefit of TQM.

Defining the needs and wants of community client groups and negotiating how they may be serviced is a feature of teamworking within a total quality framework. This focusing of attention on the customers' requirements is a component of the total quality concept that operates at team and individual level. Ownership is reflected in the quality performance criteria and targets self-imposed by staff for all organisational activities.

> The systematic application of procedures for assuring quality demands the co-ordination of effort and continuous monitoring of all activities.

Customer needs

Good customer relations is an important feature of a total quality operation. When customers initiate enquiries that cannot be dealt with over the phone it may be useful to make an appointment to see them. When they arrive let them enjoy a pleasant, welcoming atmosphere communicated by the staff involved and the premises, and when the interview is over avoid communicating the 'Well, that's that, now let's get rid of them' attitude.

When customers call it will often be necessary to identify their training needs and expectations. This is the time to build their confidence, to ask and answer questions, to seek information and above all, to listen to what they are saying. There should be plenty of opportunities for them to clarify points and to get a complete picture of what is agreed. They will need sufficient information about what is involved and the extent of suggested programmes. But avoid jargon and never go over the top with detail.

Customers will appreciate the personal touch that leads to a feeling that they are being taken care of by an understanding person. Providers' staff will be trained to treat customers as they would friends, to watch for distress signals and to volunteer help without always waiting for customers to ask for it.

Having established customers' needs and wants it will be time to motivate them by identifying benefits and indicating rewards. But let customers decide what they will do. Avoid persuasion, pressure and intellectual coercion. Where possible, link the proposed programme with progression to long-term objectives and concentrate on helping customers get what they really need.

Responsiveness is the ability to react quickly or favourably to a training need. Customers will expect providers to respond rapidly to reasonable requests and to somehow adjust provisions to meet their special needs. In a total quality maintained environment the provider will find the right solution to their problems and bring to their attention the service that is available. In some cases, introductory courses may be the answer.

Potential customers will be attempting to assess the credibility and competence of the supplier during the early stages of negotiation. This is when having a sincere belief in what you are doing and establishing your commitment will help the customer form a positive view of the provision. Sometimes giving a few personal details about tutors who will be involved can pay dividends.

TQM ensures that a reliable and consistent service is operated. This entails action planning with the customers and suppliers, and delivering what you promise, plus a bit more if possible. It demands that the supplier gets the quality right by meeting all contracted customer requirements.

Giving value for money is considered by some to be an essential feature of a quality service. If this is to be achieved there must be an ongoing drive to seek to improve the service and to react promptly to feedback obtained. There is also a need to determine, or at least estimate, the degree of customer satisfaction achieved and to maintain a sharp lookout for gaps and weaknesses that break the quality chain.

Continuous improvement

Tender loving care does not stop at the contracting stage. Total quality features subtly and gradually spread throughout the organisation although progress can be speeded-up by regularly monitoring activities and trying to measure improvements in services provided.

It is unlikely that any form of assessment of the operational effectiveness of TQM will be devised although failures in the supplier–customer chain will be detected. Essential features to be satisfied include: the involvement and commitment of all staff in TQM; the need to ensure that the service is being operated at the right time, place and quality level; and generally according to the agreed contract or customer requirements and expectations.

Audits

Total quality levels can be enhanced through the use of surveys and audits designed to keep policies and targets under constant review. Apart from the audit of formal, documented policies, procedures, work instructions and associated documentation and records contained within the quality manual, there are less formal aspects of operation to be monitored. They include the degree to which individual personal interests have been served and the amount of enjoyment and satisfaction derived from participating in programmes. Other important indicators of quality of service provided include:

- gains in knowledge, qualifications, intellectual satisfaction and work skills;
- improvement in customer job and career prospects;
- pleasure derived from meeting other people, usefully occupying spare time and the social aspects of utilising leisure time in an educational or training environment.

Providers may wish to measure progress along the total quality road using performance indicators of their own choosing.

The link between TQM and BS 5750

BS 5750 is accepted as an established quality system, but TQM is dependent upon the existence of an underlying quality system, such as BS 5750. The standard could be thought of as a launching pad for total quality. However, the total quality concept also guides management thinking when planning the implementation of BS 5750. Both appear to be mutually dependent on one another and when linked draw on the implicit strengths of each concept.

The total quality concept has already been considered[3] and it can be argued that TQM is a total management strategy comprising many interdependent features of resource provision and programme delivery. This makes it difficult to attempt a comprehensive audit of total quality since its very being relies on an indeterminate number of individual ideas, beliefs, values and actions. It is staff attitudes and shared bases of behaviour that together make up the organisational culture, with some groups leading or lagging behind others.

> Total quality policies extend to all departments and to be successfully implemented emphasis must be placed on total commitment and involvement of all staff. Total quality is a philosophy rather than a system with standards that ensure conformance, as in BS 5750.

Strengths of BS 5750

In order to meet the demands of objectives set out in a quality policy it is necessary to develop a quality management system. BS 5750 is not a bureaucratic entity. It is a quality system that relates mainly to the product and/or service provided. Such a system will be based upon a logical approach to quality management that is founded upon standards. These quality assurance standards will contain criteria demanding that things are done right according to a documented procedure.

Outcomes in the form of products or services must actually match specifications given in the documented standard. However, the standards are not imposed upon the providers and they are not set in concrete. Providers will relate the BS 5750 standard to the approved processes and practices already operating in-house. Where an internal quality audit suggests that things are not right providers will need to redefine their own quality policy and standards. Quality cannot be effectively controlled without proper standards.

> The writing of standards should reflect a systematic approach to meeting customers' requirements.
>
> Those who control work have the responsibility for quality and key management objectives will include the need to be able to pass the initial and final assessments, the subsequent audits and then to continue to meet standards.
>
> Within a structured quality management system, staff will be encouraged to reduce complaints and to improve continuously the processes or products by regularly monitoring the service and taking corrective action as required.

BS 5750 in education and training

BS 5750 is a quality standard. It provides a framework of structured quality elements that may be adapted to the needs of training providers. By implementing a quality system based on BS 5750, learning opportunities for all users may be improved. Training inputs and processes may be quality assured, thereby forming a basis for providing the service in line with total quality philosophy.

Earlier attempts to assure a quality service were related to the award of Approved Training Organisation (ATO) status. ATO status was given as a reward to training providers who met certain Training Agency (now Department of Employment Group – Training Enterprise and Education Directorate (TEED)) quality requirements. The experience gained during preparation for such awards can now help organisations who are preparing to meet BS 5750 standards within government-sponsored training provision.

Today, the Training Enterprise Councils (TECs), having set themselves quality goals, support the notion of quality-assured training contractors. TECs must ensure the quality of their training providers by having in place an agreed and effective quality assurance system embracing all vocational training providers. As sponsors and customers of training providers they will expect value for money in return for contracts awarded. Renewals or further contracts will depend on how effective the provider's quality assurance systems are seen to be. Providers must demonstrate a commitment to an adequately-managed quality assurance initiative. This will encourage movement toward continual improvement that will be monitored using quality probes, surveys and audits.

Self-assessments, carried out during internal quality audits, will normally be backed up with the external seal of approval given by authorised independent or third-party assessors. From 1992, there will be links with ISO 9000 and EN 29000.

TECs are developing strategies which will ensure that training contractors review and audit what they are offering customers. In this way, quality is systematically appraised and procedures implemented to ensure that actual provision meets the TEC quality requirements.

BS 5750 is transferable from service and manufacturing industries to education and training. Self-regulation and meeting the requirements set out in BS 5750 standards will probably be a prerequisite to contract award and access to funding mechanisms.

How BS 5750 might work in practice

An examination of the fundamental terms and definitions relating to quality given in BS 4778 *Quality vocabulary*[4] promotes insight and understanding about quality concepts. Once the concepts have been analysed, attempts may be made to implement and apply a system such as BS 5750.

Measures of service quality will include the degree of conformity to standards (the fulfilment of a specified requirement) and service reliability (consistently performing a specified function).

Training providers will handle a mix of products and services that will involve tangible products, such as bread baked by trainees during a practical programme, and intangibles, such as a process-based service, for example operating a reception facility. Quality may be related to the design of the service, programme or product, or to implementation of the curriculum. In each of these instances, the quality requirements and needs can be identified and specified by writing performance criteria. Quality control activities are aimed at eliminating poor performance and non-conformances, and promoting an effective service.

> The quality manager will plan and implement quality policy but it is the assessors, moderators and auditors who will monitor, evaluate and assure all aspects of the provision. They will either verify that the needs and requirements of the customer or end user have been adequately met or they will recommend corrective action.

Mistakes are evidence that people are trying to do things for themselves. Managers need staff who are able to think for themselves and use their initiative – without this creativity the organisation would soon decline. On the other hand, no business can survive by relying on a team of incompetent people.

When preparing to implement BS 5750, delivery of effective training programmes to internal and external customers (provider's staff, workplace trainers, careers staff, trainees, employers, sub-contractors and other stakeholders) is just as much an essential requirement within education and training as elsewhere.

> The lead time between application for BS 5750 and final award may be upwards of 18 months.

Planning and documentation

Effective management of TQM and quality assurance programmes requires that a carefully-documented quality plan and supporting documentation are maintained. The plan will specify the systems needed to ensure the effective deployment of resources and contracted product and service quality.

Documentation should be kept simple and restricted to that necessary to support the service, and work instructions should be provided that clearly describe features to be carried out. Records should be maintained to provide evidence that provision conforms to specified quality.

The secrets of success are maintaining constancy of purpose and working to a documented plan.

> This is where a comprehensive quality manual, containing quality policy and procedures, backed by written work instructions and supported by suitable training, can help guide people towards meeting the requirements of BS 5750 and total quality.

Contracting

A **contract** is an agreement entered into by a person or company to deliver goods or services, or to carry out some function on mutually agreed and binding terms.

When introducing TQM, existing contracts should be reviewed in order to ensure that needs, requirements, standards and other relevant criteria are recorded and clearly understood by all parties. The content of contracts should be feasible and attainable. There will be a need to accommodate any special or non-standard processes or products. New or additional assessment specifications, training techniques and resources should also be identified. Any additional information required to facilitate the tender or contract should be obtained before training or hire of resources begins.

> In a training context the provider would need to agree with the purchaser what is to be supplied as a result of individual enrolment to a course or programme, or in the case of contracted, fully-costed training what will comprise the training package.

The key steps in negotiating contracts suggested in BS 5750[5] are given in Figure 5.1 overleaf. Each step should be defined in a procedure and as they are performed records should be made and kept.

Key steps to be taken should include:

- Ensuring that the requirements are clearly understood and agreed by both parties, and that they are then properly recorded and kept.
- Discussions by both parties of any difference or non-conformity to the specified requirements and the recording as part of the contract documentation of the conclusions reached, together with how the differences are to be resolved.
- Both parties going through a defined process to ensure that they have the necessary resources, organisation and facilities to conform to all the requirements in the contract.

Source: BS 5750: Part 4 (1990), para 4.3.

Figure 5.1 Key steps in contract review

Launching initiatives

Educational aspects

How can we show our customers that we mean business when it comes to putting their interests first? How do we communicate this urgent need to our staff and how do we know when we are meeting customer requirements? A possible approach might be to get top managers to throw their weight behind a drive to provide a quality customer service and to secure the help and commitment of the entire workforce in meeting the challenge.

Starting with a knowledge of customer needs, and backed by a properly resourced operation, the provider will set quality targets defined in a policy, contract or specification. Written procedures and work instructions contained within the quality manual must be supported with records and documentation. This will enable a systematic approach to be adopted whereby everyone concerned will have a clear picture of what is required of them. Staff operating within a total quality context will follow procedures when delivering the service, ensuring that targets, goals and standards are achieved. They will also respond to changes in customer requirements as they occur. By continuously monitoring the quality of service, potential problems and sources of complaints can be eliminated. This leads to increased efficiency.

Perhaps total quality can best be implemented by making sure that everyone is aware of the need to maintain an unbroken chain of supplier–customer quality, from start to finish, when seeking to meet customer requirements.

The text that follows is devoted to considering possible approaches to preparing for, and introducing, total quality when recruiting and inducting customers.

Recruiting clients

Before launching programmes and enrolling clients it is important to take account of requirements expressed by stakeholders concerning vocational education and training, and academic provision. Competition and the freedom of prospective clients to exercise choice demands that programmes are developed to satisfy particular client groups and their specific needs.

There is a need to offer good value for money these days and to take account of as many shades of opinion as possible when planning provision. The Careers Service and Adult Guidance Service maintain close liaison with training providers and each offer comprehensive advice and guidance for providers and potential clients.

When setting up a recruitment process it is useful to gather and analyse enrolment data and enquiries for education and training provision, and use the results to establish trends and enrolment patterns.

Target groups

The category and numbers of learners comprising each target group to be recruited will be stated in the provider's operational plan. There will be a need to facilitate easy access to provision and to take account of equal opportunities policies, other legislation and quality-related factors. Enrolment procedures and practice must take account of customer requirements and contract specifications.

Target groups will probably include: 16–19 year old, full-time students; trainees seeking vocational awards leading to NVQs; those with special educational needs; international and European Community students; part-time, employed students (day release); customers using the Government Training Credits Scheme; together with employers and others using 'services-to-business', income-generating resources.

Induction

To **induct** trainees is to install them formally in a company or training scheme or to initiate knowledge of a particular **organisational area** or **workplace**. **Induction** is the act of introducing new starters to the provider's organisation soon after their enrolment. The process allows a **training agreement** to be negotiated. The effectiveness and completeness of induction planning and delivery will be reflected in what the newcomers learn, understand and agree, and the attitudes they form toward the provider. Subsequent performance may depend to a considerable degree on the kind of deal they get during induction.

The provider's organisation

The primary induction presentation should include a description of the provider's organisation and an explanation of its **mission**. Organisations vary considerably but all must operate within a **legal framework**. Reference should be made to the training provider's structure, but too much detail is likely to confuse trainees.

Trainees will need to get a clear picture of how each part of their organisation fits with other parts and in particular how the work of their section or department fits into the whole scheme of things. Whether the provider is large or small, motivation and commitment to high-quality performance will be enhanced if trainees can see how their personal occupational skills will be utilised.

> The auditor will check that the provider, together with trainees, has examined the purpose and operation of the organisation and that the trainees have a clear picture of its structure. Checks will be made to confirm that the provider has explained to trainees how their job skills and occupational area role is matched with opportunities within the training organisation and that they understand what they have been told.

Induction programme for new starters

First impressions are important. How we feel about someone when meeting them for the first time will influence our attitude towards them on subsequent meetings. The same goes for trainees joining a training programme. They will appreciate a proper induction. A better attitude will result if a little time is taken to welcome newcomers, make them feel at home and settle them into their new surroundings. The likelihood of their leaving due to anxiety or confusion will be reduced if they are properly integrated into the programme and with the people they meet there.

Induction is the time to give information about the organisation that will affect the new starters and to introduce them to their supervisors, the job and the training opportunities available to them.

A typical outline induction programme listing some factors that will be of benefit to new trainees is given in Figure 5.2. As can be seen in this figure, the programmes cover some of the aspects of policy and procedures that are important to new starters and to the success of the business.

The organisation
- mission
- history and development
- structure and management
- training provision and services.

Personnel matters
- reception process
- policies, rules and procedures
- education and training
- disciplinary and grievance procedures
- services to learners
- health, safety, first aid and hygiene, housekeeping and protective clothing
- race relations and equal opportunities
- welfare and trainee benefits.

Facilities
- washrooms and toilets
- first aid room, cloakroom, lockers, common room and refectory
- parking
- telephones.

Study centre and workplace
- tour of premises
- money matters
- learning arrangements
- standards and quality assurance (BS 5750)
- resources, equipment and methods
- assessments and performance appraisals.

Staff
- supervision
- trainers
- support staff and other workers.

Monitoring
- help available
- follow-up meetings
- guidance and counselling
- exit surveys.

Figure 5.2 The induction programme

The content of the induction will vary according to the needs of individuals concerned and those of the provider. The duration and phasing of the induction will depend upon induction policy. In some cases, a general induction covering the programme suggested in Figure 5.2 may be delivered, followed by mini-inductions spread over a defined period.

Care should be taken to provide a good reception and make the newcomer feel welcome on the first day. Key information should be shared first. Information overload should be avoided.

A typical **workplace induction** programme is given in Figure 5.3. Trainees will already have received a general induction and the building craft skills induction programme would be delivered on joining the construction department. All newcomers to practical work need an induction. This is especially true in labour-intensive occupations and where power tools, lifting, scaffolding and heavy plant are involved.

Due to the nature of construction work and the people working in craft and related occupations too much passive listening and paper-based activity may not be welcomed. As it is necessary to make an impact when delivering the induction, a good deal of hands-on activity could usefully be provided. This is allowed for in the programme of suggested activity that emphasises site safety and safe working practices. The induction timetable prepares trainees for dealing with hazards that may be encountered when working on-site. It may be the only time that trainees will gain prior insight into potentially dangerous aspects of construction work.

Day	9	10	11	12	1	2	3	4	5
Mon 9/7	Assemble, welcome by head and tour of department Meet staff		Outline of scheme and induction programme			Health and Safety at Work Act (1974) First aid films Accidents and fire precautions Electricity at Work Regs. (1989) COSHH			
Tues 10/7	Training log-books Recording procedures Administration		Banking and finance matters			Site safety Introduction to working platforms			
Wed 11/7	Union representative UCATT		Scaffolding			Erecting scaffolding			
Thurs 12/7	Portable power tools		Hand tools			Lifting and transporting, and stacking materials			
Fri 13/7	Starting, stopping and maintaining mixers and compressors					Mixing concrete and mortars			

Figure 5.3 The induction programme – building craft skills

Programme content enables trainees to experience a systematic, concentrated induction into the use of tools and equipment connected with their future work role. This, hopefully, will promote safe working practices and reduce the risk of injury while at work.

Policies

Policies are plans of action adopted by a company and **procedures** define courses of action to be followed in order to achieve the desired policy outcomes. The trainees will need to become fully conversant with the provider's policies and procedures.

Trainer responsibilities

A **trainer** is a person employed to plan and arrange practice and instruction that will provide opportunities for trainees to reach an agreed standard of proficiency or to enable them to meet performance **criteria** specified in a given training programme or unit of competence.

Resources that will be used throughout the training and learning programme must be selected and evaluated so that trainees derive maximum benefit from the learning experience in terms of time, money and energy invested.

Training plans covering content, resources to be employed, timing and mode of delivery must be prepared during the planning stage prior to delivery. Any plans produced must be reviewed and updated in the light of experience gained during their use.

Auditors will probably check with trainees that providers have explained their responsibilities as trainers and facilitators of learning. Auditors will need to be reassured that trainees have understood the documented procedures.

The auditor will check that the provider can justify the use of the methods and resources used throughout the induction programme. Validity against procedures specified will be tested.

Plans covering the induction programme will be checked to ensure that training methods applied are as specified.

Trainees rights and responsibilities

A **right** is that which is due to a person. Rights include legitimate curriculum entitlement and specified privileges or allowances resulting from training with a particular provider.

Auditors will check the training provider's explanation of the trainees' rights and responsibilities against requirements. They will satisfy themselves that the trainees have understood these in respect of the training to be undertaken and support that may be expected.

Administration

The process of managing the training programme is called **administration**. There are certain administrative procedures that trainees must be familiar with. During induction sessions, trainees are normally provided with sufficient information on administration and other procedures that they will come across during their training within the provider's area or at work placements. A checklist of administrative documentation is useful as an aid when delivering the induction (see Figure 5.4).

- Offer of employment.
- Training agreement.
- Training programmes.
- Training plans.
- Performance criteria and units of competence.
- Assessments and reviews.
- Individual action plans.
- Planned work experience.
- Work-based training paperwork.
- Off-the-job training.
- Diaries and log-books.
- Skills test paperwork.
- Records of achievement.
- Identification and initial assessment/preparation.
- Guidance and counselling provision.
- Health and safety policy.
- Travel claims.
- Sickness and absence reporting.
- Equal opportunities policy.

Figure 5.4 Checklist – administration documentation

During induction, routine policies and procedures will need to be explained, related documentation issued and samples completed. Trainees will need to understand training agreement factors, such as those shown in Figure 5.5, before signing their training agreement declaration (see Figure 5.6). Where possible, trainees must learn to handle procedures and documentation by **carrying out** activities as and when they naturally occur rather than as exercises.

Form of agreement	
Expectations	
Trainer	**Trainee**
Trainee will:	**To receive:**
• participate willingly	• induction and initial assessment
• attend training sessions	• action plan
• read and follow all workplace and college rules and conditions	• training plan
	• planned work experience
• comply with the law (Health and Safety at Work Act 1974, Electricity at Work Regulations 1989, etc.)	• off-the-job training
	• liaison support
	• guidance and review
• maintain contact with trainers and supervisors	• assessments
	• record of achievements
• report absences, hazards and accidents	• insurance cover
• keep a diary and log-book.	• safe working environment
	• protective clothing.
Other factors	
Outcomes	**Administration**
• identification of:	• equal opportunities
strengths	• status of trainee
interests	• attendance pattern
aptitudes	• hours of work
abilities	• holiday entitlement
• training potential	• sickness reporting
• work skills and competence	• grievance procedures
• experience	• disciplinary procedures
• suitable employment	• safety and hygiene
• NVQs or other awards.	• first aid and accidents
	• counselling
	• company rules and regulations.

Figure 5.5 Training agreement factors

Training Agreement

Trainee's name . . . .

Address . . . .

. . . .

. . . .

I have read and I understand the agreement that we have negotiated and declare that I will follow the rules and regulations set out in the Agreement.

Signed . . . . Trainee

Signed . . . . Employer

Date . . . .

Figure 5.6 Training agreement declaration

Auditors will confirm whether or not the provider has successfully communicated accurate information on administrative and other workplace or training provider procedures. Examples of forms correctly completed by the trainees and submitted to the scheme manager or employer may be called for to support the documented procedures in this area.

Health and Safety at Work Act

Consideration of the implications for providers and trainees of the Health and Safety at Work Act 1974 is given in Chapter 1. It is however essential that providers can demonstrate that, during induction, they have explained the employer's and the trainees' responsibilities under the Act.

The auditor will check that providers monitor the safety of their working environments and that they publish and implement fire, accident and emergency procedures, and maintain appropriate records.

Training plans and programmes

Documents detailing personal training programmes will need to be produced jointly by providers and trainees. Plans must detail methods, resources and opportunities by which **negotiated objectives** or **performance criteria** may be achieved. Targeted review interview dates must be agreed, together with estimated dates for completion of training.

The documents serve as evidence that a programme of formative reviews and assessments has taken place. Review sheets and records of achievement can be filed in the trainees' portfolios of records and used to support claims of competence in a given area.

Personal programmes will be examined by auditors to ensure that proposed training is based on units and elements of training relating to the trainees' occupational area. Trainees may be asked to confirm that their training programmes were negotiated and agreed by them in co-operation with the provider.

Learning opportunities and methods

Trainees should be given time to discuss with the provider what **learning opportunities and methods** will be made available to them during their training programmes. The way people prefer to learn and the pace of learning varies from one person to another and there is no set pattern that suits everyone. For these reasons it is essential that method and content is negotiated and agreed as far as is possible during the induction period. Work methods available should be chosen to suit the trainees' occupational areas and personal needs.

The auditor will require to see evidence that providers have allowed trainees to agree or disagree with their training plans and methods of learning and, as far as possible, to have modified methods and plans to suit individual needs, capabilities, aspirations and motivations.

Providers have an obligation to check that trainees understand instructions and to give them sufficient opportunities and encouragement to ask questions and challenge training provision.

During discussions with trainees it will become obvious to the auditor either that trainees have been given opportunities to ask questions about their training programmes and to give opinions on their proposed training; or that their programmes have been imposed without adequate negotiation.

Curriculum entitlement

Curriculum provision, implementation and audit process[6] is discussed in some depth in Chapter 11 but it is important to incorporate certain key features in any TQM plan. Important features would include:

- access
- appropriateness
- quality
- entitlement
- integration
- progression
- balance of theory/practical
- assessment
- monitoring and evaluation.

A thorough understanding of the concept of customer entitlement will be embedded in each of the provider's departments. Account must be taken of this factor when planning the training provision. In particular, there will be a need to provide a flexible and accessible competence-based system offering what the customer requires and, where possible, training that leads to certification, NVQs and other recognised awards.

Operation and management of an organisation

In some cases, the introduction of TQM calls for a complete review of the organisation's structure and the need to change and strengthen processes and procedures, as necessary. Total quality will need to be phased in over a period as it is unlikely that considerable change[7] will be implemented in the short term.

There may be problems when implementing a formal total quality policy due to the fact that there will be staff who consider that they already have too much on their plate. If staff believe that they are already overworked they will not welcome the added burden of taking on board the latest 'flavour of the month'. It may not be easy to convince them that TQM does not necessarily entail vast amounts of additional work. It may be more rewarding for staff to discover for themselves that it is in their interests as much as the customers' to integrate TQM into their daily work. Hopefully, some will find that when procedures are working well and total quality philosophy is accepted by all, they are better able to utilise their time and energies, so reducing frustration.

> **More effective formal and informal links with employers and target groups, and better communications in-house, may be needed to help suppliers deliver the right quality consistently.**

Staff

Human resources are the most valuable asset in any service business. No business can flourish without a skilled and dedicated workforce that is able continuously to meet customers' needs effectively and profitably.

Workshop sessions involving every member of staff are an essential prerequisite when launching a comprehensive quality programme. Awareness-raising sessions must be aimed at giving everyone a clear view of the needs of customers and the importance of helping to achieve improvement in performance of all operations.

When initiating change, such as the introduction of TQM or BS 5750 systems, it is important to consult with those who will be involved in the process. Conflict can easily result when people do not understand what is involved when changing routines. Even worse is the situation where unqualified people are asked to implement changes or where people lack those competences needed to undertake the work reasonably well. Adequate staff development training will be an essential prerequisite when linking TQM to present systems or implementing a total quality concept across the provision.

Systematic evaluation of training needs

Each member of staff will be entitled to a staff development review conducted by a designated person at least once a year. Reviews may cover the individual's performance throughout the past year and anticipate likely training needs in the future. The reviews serve to provide opportunities for managers and staff to exchange ideas about future commitment to the development of competence necessary to perform effectively at work.

Where training is required an action plan will be agreed and training records will be maintained.

Staff development

There should be systems for staff induction, training and development. Staff must be adequately qualified and competent to carry out their duties. Effective performance of their role will depend on there being in place opportunities and procedures for staff to reach the standards needed to operate at the specified quality level.

A set of questions to audit the quality of staff training is shown in Figure 5.7.

- Do all new staff participate in an induction programme?
- Is a staff appraisal system operating?
- Does the appraisal system include all staff?
- Are staff development and training needs identified and is updating facilitated?
- Is there a system for recording training?
- Has a staff audit been conducted and competences recorded?
- Are staff competent to carry out their role and undertake their responsibilities?

Figure 5.7 Quality audit – training

Correlation – mission v. reality

Some mission statements express high ideals and sincere intentions that may or may not be achievable. An example is shown in Figure 5.8. Training provider managements have been known to make a good deal of fuss about the precise wording of the mission statement. It is put on the agenda of an endless series of meetings and eventually a form of words that seems appropriate is agreed and a statement is published. The academic board rubber stamps it and then the board of governors is asked to approve the statement which is then widely promoted. Fine so far. But what happens next? Sometimes, not a lot!

This organisation aims to contribute to the prosperity, well-being and quality of life of the maximum number of people, businesses and other organisations within the catchment area by effectively providing high-quality education and training.

Figure 5.8 Mission statement

A total quality approach would call for the use of probe questions, audits or reviews designed to provide evidence of quality of performance. Reviews could include a comparison of what the reality is against the mission statement. Consideration could be given as to how achievement of the aims could be met in practice and then some form of measurement applied to estimate how far the organisation is in meeting them.

The mission could be intended to promote and adopt a philosophy of commitment to quality, and continuous improvement and fulfilment of long-term service to clients. Alternatively, a hidden agenda might be to stay in business at any cost and to maintain short-term profitability.

Audits of service design, delivery and results, and the monitoring and evaluation of service provision would go some way to providing evidence of the extent that the reality actually reflects mission aims.

Quality system elements

Guidance on quality system elements is given in BS 5750:Part 4 (1990) and a cross-reference of elements referred to in the text is given in Figure 5.9. The primary aim is to assist those managing a business to achieve the requirements of BS 5750:Parts 1, 2 and 3 by explaining what has to be done.

Quality elements may be related to the design, implementation and delivery of quality training since many of the BS 5750 elements are readily transferable to training provision and other occupational areas.

Training **inputs and processes** may be seen as being those resources and systems applied when designing and delivering the curriculum while **product or service** is defined as output that an organisation supplies to a user. In this case, it is learning, experience, achievement, performance and the demonstration of competence.

Notes

1   Alison Foster, 'Explaining Quality Systems', in *Training Tomorrow*, September 1990 Issue, p. 38, MCB University Press Ltd, 1990.

2   *The Training Provider Quality Survey Manual*, Coventry and Warwickshire TEC, 1990.

3   See Chapters 3 and 4 of this book.

4   BS 4778:Part 1 (1987), *Quality Vocabulary*.

5   BS 5750:Part 4 (1990), p. 5, para 4.3.

6   See Figure 11.1 Audit – recruitment and induction process on page 248.

7   See Chapter 2 – Introducing change.

8   BS 5750:Part 4 (1990), Appendix A *Cross-reference of quality system elements (BS 5750 Part 4 and BS 5750 Parts 1, 2 and 3)*, p. 12.

Appendix A. Cross-reference of quality system elements in this Part of BS 5750 and BS 5750 : Parts 1, 2 and 3

Table 1 provides a cross-reference of quality system elements in this Part of BS 5750 and BS 5750 : Parts 1, 2 and 3.

Table 1. Cross-reference of quality system elements in this Part of BS 5750 and BS 5750 : Parts 1, 2 and 3

Subclause numbers in this Part of BS 5750	Title	Corresponding subclause numbers		
		BS 5750 : Part 1 (ISO 9001/EN 29001[1])	BS 5750 : Part 2 (ISO 9002/EN 29002)	BS 5750 : Part 3 (ISO 9003/EN 29003)
4.1	Management responsibility	4.1[2]	4.1[3]	4.1[4]
4.2	Quality system	4.2[2]	4.2[2]	4.2[3]
4.3	Contract review	4.3[2]	4.3[2]	[5]
4.4	Design control	4.4[2]	[5]	[5]
4.5	Document control	4.5[2]	4.4[2]	4.3[3]
4.6	Purchasing	4.6[2]	4.5[2]	[5]
4.7	Purchaser supplied product	4.7[2]	4.6[2]	[5]
4.8	Product identification and traceability	4.8[2]	4.7[2]	4.4[3]
4.9	Process control	4.9[2]	4.8[2]	[5]
4.10	Inspection and testing	4.10[2]	4.9[2]	4.5[3]
4.11	Inspection, measuring and test equipment	4.11[2]	4.10[2]	4.6[3]
4.12	Inspection and test status	4.12[2]	4.11[2]	4.7[3]
4.13	Control of nonconforming product	4.13[2]	4.12[2]	4.8[3]
4.14	Corrective action	4.14[2]	4.13[2]	[5]
4.15	Handling, storage, packaging and delivery	4.15[2]	4.14[2]	4.9[3]
4.16	Quality records	4.16[2]	4.15[2]	4.10[3]
4.17	Internal quality audits	4.17	4.16[2]	[5]
4.18	Training	4.18[2]	4.17[3]	4.11[4]
4.19	Servicing	4.19[2]	[5]	[5]
4.20	Statistical techniques	4.20[2]	4.18[2]	4.12[3]

[1] EN = European Standard.

[2] Full requirement.

[3] Less stringent than BS 5750 : Part 1.

[4] Less stringent than BS 5750 : Part 2.

[5] Element not present.

Figure 5.9 Cross-reference of quality system elements[8]

CHAPTER SIX

Service Design

Chapter coverage

Developing a learner service model
    Service design
    Why customers seek education and training opportunities
    Customer entitlement
    Curriculum planning
    Curriculum development
    Contracts and action plans
    Providing equal opportunities
Access
    Initial assessment
    The role of central admissions
    Training and development needs analysis
    Meeting training needs
    Skills audit
    Making initial assessments
Establishing an assessment centre
    Resource implications
    Centre staff
    Assessment centre manager
    Assessors
    Administrative support
    Co-ordinators
    Staff training and development
    Staff accreditation
    Accommodation
    Hardware and consumable materials
    Recording assessment

Disseminating information
Claiming competence
Learning resources
Marketing
Marketing the service

Developing a learner service model

Service design

The commercial success of a business depends upon providing the customer with the proper mix of professionalism, technical expertise, value for money and quality of service. Considerable value derives from involving employees in service design. A business can only respond properly to customers' needs if the workforce is clear about what is to be provided, backed by adequate information flows. In a competitive market, the ability to maintain a close relationship with customers puts the provider in a strong position to retain their business and to offer complementary services.

Good design will help training providers to adopt a strategic approach to achieving the quality of service that will influence educational and commercial success and meet customer requirements. Used effectively, planning and design can help reduce costs, improve all aspects of the provision and lead to better competitiveness and greater market share.

Quality probe – service design

- Is the design process an integral part of strategic and operational planning and defined in the quality policy?
- Does the design system extend to all aspects of the service provision?
- Is the design system producing an effective product or service that may be supplied efficiently?
- Do the design team understand the needs of your customers and take account of feedback from end users and knowledge of other providers' services?

Why customers seek education and training opportunities

Some clients apply for courses in order to satisfy a need to learn that may be linked with accomplishment, recognition, ambition and prestige or self-respect. Others enjoy relaxation, entertainment and the social interaction that some programmes promote. Added to the list is the important need to survive and this is a key reason why many people seek training opportunities in order to gain marketable skills. Competence derived from training will open doors to work where new skills can be applied and higher remuneration received.

Included in the latter category would be gaining knowledge, skills or work experience that would enhance career prospects, promotion or employment prospects, should a planned change of occupation be sought. Where the need to update or to improve academic and work-related qualifications prompts a person to train, it is likely that further learning opportunities will relate to a need to build on existing strengths. People also join courses to learn theory and gain experience, and later obtain accreditation and validation of competences. Such motivators provide a potent drive to satisfy the need to achieve, to satisfy a challenge or the desire to master something new. This need is felt by the individual concerned and others may be quite unable to detect that person's real reasons for wishing to join a course.

The training provider needs to be prepared for anything when it comes to a customer's personal needs and reasons for seeking help. Unfortunately, many will have aspirations and needs that neither they nor the provider can hope to fulfil. Careful initial assessment may, in some cases, be necessary in order to avoid later disillusionment and feelings of failure.

> **It will not always be possible to negotiate entirely individual learning programmes especially where only limited budgets and staffing are available. Alternative methods of study, such as open learning, may need to be recommended to meet the customers' needs.**

Customer entitlement

Curriculum entitlement gives learners the right to participate in certain learning experiences and to work towards recognised outcomes, such as NVQs and other vocational qualifications. Providers of the service that customers will use have an obligation to deliver quality training and to satisfy contracts made.

Attention should be focused on the curriculum to be offered, the processes that will facilitate learning and the environment in which learning will take place. Eligible learners should have access to suitable learning opportunities and learning methods that suit them.

Programme **content** will often necessarily relate to the customers' needs to achieve performance criteria that lead to demonstration of competence, as defined by lead industry bodies, and to NVQs. In the schools sector, attainment targets form part of the National Curriculum.

> The minimum entitlement should comprise negotiated content, negotiated and pre-specified outcomes, individual progression opportunities and learning experiences which are the same for everyone.[1]

Curriculum planning

The curriculum may be defined as the planned experiences offered to customers by the provider through their participation in a training programme and associated learning opportunities. The diagram shown in Figure 6.1 shows the curriculum development process.

Each component is interrelated with the others. The process of curriculum development should be ongoing with continuous adjustments being made as a result of feedback from the monitoring and evaluation elements.

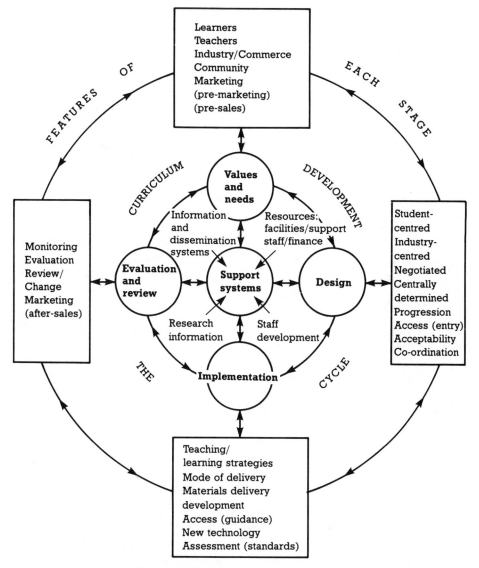

Figure 6.1 Process of curriculum development[2]

Quality probe – curriculum development

- Is there a curriculum development plan?
- Is there a documented procedure for:
    identifying and analysing client training and development needs?
    defining key occupational purpose, roles, units and elements of
      competence and performance criteria?
    devising curriculum strategy and plans?
    resource planning?
    structuring the teaching and learning programme, and selecting
      programme content, resources and support?
    designing teaching and learning strategies?
    monitoring and evaluating responsiveness, quality, efficiency and
      effectiveness of outcomes?

Further Education Unit (FEU) suggests that 'Curriculum planning must take account of three "levers" for change: curriculum development, staff development and institutional development, and that to be successful all three must be roughly in phase and supported.'[3]

Contracts and action plans

As in the procedure for contract review set out in BS 5750[4], the provider and the customer (end-user) should ensure that requirements of the service to be rendered are clearly understood and agreed by both parties and then properly recorded and kept. Resources and facilities should be available to ensure conformance with the contract made.

This procedure might best be carried out in the assessment centre where all that is on offer could be outlined. As curriculum entitlement is about what learners should have access to and receive, it would be useful at this point to compare what is offered with that suggested in the FEU statement:

> The minimum entitlement should comprise negotiated content, negotiated and pre-specified outcomes, individual progression opportunities and learning experiences which are the same for everyone.[5]

A decision might then be made about the course or learning opportunity to be undertaken. A contract, agenda for action or action plan could then be negotiated and signed by the assessor and the customer. This document may later be used as an instrument for recording outcomes of subsequent reviews and assessments, and ultimately to evaluate conformity to specified requirements. If this procedure is systematised the results can be used to review, evaluate and develop the quality of the curriculum on offer across the organisation.

Providing equal opportunities

An important duty of training providers is to operate a policy that provides for equal opportunities and to supply a service that takes account of the customers' rights to receive quality training regardless of social and religious background, ethnic or national origin, marital status, age, intellectual or physical capacity, and gender. The system for promoting equal opportunities may be documented in both the quality policy statement and in the quality manual.

In certain instances sponsors may insist upon seeing for themselves that a provider actually operates an equal opportunities policy backed by documented procedures. With this in mind, the flow chart (in Figure 6.2 overleaf) and quality probes in this section may be of use when auditing the existing provision and reviewing procedures relating to equal opportunities policy.

Quality probe – equal opportunities policy

- Does your policy take account of the customers' rights to receive quality training regardless of social and religious background, ethnic or national origin, marital status, intellectual or physical capacity, age and gender?
- Are some groups under-represented? Are you targeting the right market? Is the publicity and advertising material appropriate and is the marketing operation effective?
- Do you promote multicultural activities? Are there opportunities for consultation and participation by customers from minority groups in the planning of provision?
- Are relevant opportunities available to all who seek to use your service? Have you outlined provisions fairly and honestly? Are entry requirements and selection methods fair and effective? Are employers involved in planning provisions?
- Is your equal opportunities system adequately resourced?
- Do you provide unbiased counselling, guidance and advice?
- Do you operate an effective induction programme and are there procedures for helping newcomers settle in?
- Are teaching and learning styles appropriate? Can programmes be adapted to suit individual requirements? Is adequate tutorial, peer group, non-contact and off-site support available?
- Do your staff take positive action to publicise and implement equal opportunities policy, and is good practice operating at all levels of the provision?
- Are assessment procedures fair, valid and appropriate to the user group?
- Are equal opportunities processes monitored and evaluated during internal quality audits? Does your provision comply with current legislation?

Quality probes may be designed for any aspect of equal opportunities provision. In the Coombe Lodge Report, *Women in Further and Higher Education Management,*[6] Steve Crabbe gives a Checklist for Equal Opportunities (Gender), and explains that the draft checklist has been written 'in order to focus attention on the steps needed to be taken to

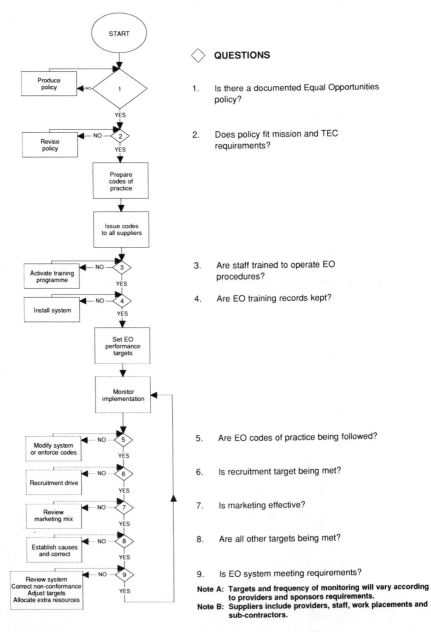

QUESTIONS

1.   Is there a documented Equal Opportunities policy?

2.   Does policy fit mission and TEC requirements?

3.   Are staff trained to operate EO procedures?

4.   Are EO training records kept?

5.   Are EO codes of practice being followed?

6.   Is recruitment target being met?

7.   Is marketing effective?

8.   Are all other targets being met?

9.   Is EO system meeting requirements?

Note A: **Targets and frequency of monitoring will vary according to providers and sponsors requirements.**
Note B: **Suppliers include providers, staff, work placements and sub-contractors.**

Figure 6.2 Implementing equal opportunities

ensure that educational establishments are providing equal opportunities with respect to issues of gender and sex discrimination.' The checklist contains a section which may be used in a quality probe relating to customer access.

Quality probe – equal opportunities (gender)

- Have steps been taken to ensure that both sexes are treated fairly in terms of selection and recruitment for courses and subject options? Have staff been alerted to possible unconscious prejudice and stereotyping in selection techniques, interviewing and publicity for courses?
- Are careers teachers and advisers aware of possible sex-stereotyping when giving guidance to learners on employment and training?
- Are amenities and facilities for learners in all buildings and departments equally available to both sexes?
- As far as you are concerned are you providing equal opportunities to those with whom you are involved?
- Are you free of bias when counselling, giving guidance or enrolling?
- Are you happy with the facilities provided for both sexes?

Survey equal opportunity arrangements within your organisation. List improvements in provision of equal opportunities that you feel would be helpful and plan their implementation.

Access

Initial assessment

It is important to assess all people seeking access to vocational education and training opportunities, the purpose being to help in the planning of training and to promote occupational competence.

The object of **initial assessment** is to help trainers and learners sort out what it is that they wish to achieve. Action plans can be produced and relevant training arranged to meet needs as far as is possible, bearing in mind available resources and the ability of individuals to attain their occupational aims. Some of the purposes of initial assessment and review are set out in Figure 6.3 overleaf.

Individual training programmes may be based on outcomes of the analysis of training needs.

Matching individual needs and expectations with related education and training provision is the key to success in the attainment of competence in an occupation or subject.

- To help clients clarify training and development needs and create an action plan.
- To invite clients to get existing skills accredited and to plan the learning of new skills that can help them develop or enhance career opportunities.
- To prioritise the importance of action plan content and to derive a sequence of learning, bearing in mind costs and benefits of the decisions made.
- To monitor and record progress against earlier action plans. To clarify confusion or lack of understanding. Then adjust the current action plan accordingly.
- To write aims and objectives designed to enable the sought-after skills to be defined and understood.
- To identify tasks and workplace activities that will enable new skills to be learned and practised, and existing skills to be accredited.
- To agree the settings and context in which the achievement of competence may be demonstrated and accredited.
- To analyse and reflect upon the relevance of the clients' experiences to the achievement of competence.
- To review supporting evidence of competence and to allow for guidance, counselling and monitoring of the learning process and outcomes of assessment.
- To carry out accreditation processes for prior learning and to discuss how best to integrate new competences when learned into daily workplace activities.

Figure 6.3 Purpose of initial assessment and review

Access to suitable learning opportunities has, in the past, not always been easy and at best a compromise between what the client was seeking and whatever course or training was ready-made. Today, the demand for a wider range of training provision is clear. This range is needed to fulfil the expectations of employers seeking to provide quality products and services backed by a well-trained and competent workforce. A responsive vocational education and training service is called for.

In order to meet this challenge, providers will need to set up a central admissions unit or otherwise improve access and initial assessment.

The role of central admissions

Reception or central admissions staff will probably be the first to deal with the client. In some cases this work is undertaken by a **counsellor** working alone but with access to all provider departments and support services or external referral agencies. Not all providers operate these services, although it is now becoming a necessity rather than a luxury as competition for business increases. With the introduction of NVQs, higher priority is being given to providing quality facilities needed to back up assessment and accreditation of prior learning. Clients seeking information on accreditation and curriculum entitlement (their share of the education and training cake) now expect a better deal than before.

Clients need to gain access to the right person to help them without first being needlessly directed from one place to another. They deserve to be interviewed in a quiet, comfortable and private room. They require to be treated in a sensitive way by supportive people who know what they are talking about. They are, after all, customers without whom the business would fail.

The induction and initial assessment role

A key role would be to facilitate access to learning and to make it easy for clients to get out of the system what they need rather than what happens to be on offer. Working on a **systems approach**, clients would be directed to the **central admissions unit** which would act as a filter. Competent staff would offer a user-friendly counselling and guidance service to those seeking learning opportunities.

For many clients, mainstream education and training provision would be geared to satisfying their needs. Such people would be directed to the department where adequately-trained staff would be able to give detailed information on subjects and routes to progression. Clients with learning difficulties or problems that cannot readily be resolved, and those needing help with career choice, would be referred to qualified staff based in support units.

Assessors experienced in initial assessment procedures and the accreditation of prior learning would link with subject specialists able to offer in-depth study guidance to clients. At peak periods, key staff would be seconded to the central admissions unit in order to cope with heavy demand. At other times, close liaison would be maintained. Terminals provided would enable clients to access national and local databases.

Training and development needs analysis

It is likely that anyone who is working or preparing to work will have some learning need. The way in which our working environment is changing today calls for rapid responses from the workforce. The rate at which technology is changing, how we need do things and what we need to do at work, together with more demanding customer expectations, mean that we have to do something about keeping up-to-date. We need constantly to adjust to the demands made of us and learn new things that will help us to move on. We need to be competent whether our status is that of trainee, skilled worker, supervisor, trainer or assessor.

A **needs analysis** is client-centred and may include training needs relating to an individual, group, industrial or commercial enterprise, institution or other external agency. Such needs are often classified as being **demand-led**.

Needs may also be anticipated by a supplier of training or education by referring to lead body documentation, a syllabus, new legislation, market trends or otherwise predicting the likely demand for a particular learning service. Such provision is described as **supply-led**.

Whether demand-led or supply-led the design and implementation of the curriculum should satisfy expectations of the clients and fulfil their needs.

Meeting training needs

Once needs have been identified, information on the availability of education and training opportunities should be readily available to all clients wishing to gain access to the provision. This is where suitable databases can be helpful to providers seeking to meet individual training needs. Qualifications and training opportunities on offer would be accessed using the database. User terminals would input and access data needed to maintain the service at the right standard and an input/output model would serve to match, as far as possible, supply and demand.

A database, such as the one shown in Figure 6.4, could be operated by central admissions. It would provide details of what is on offer to clients who arrive seeking information and guidance as to how their needs might

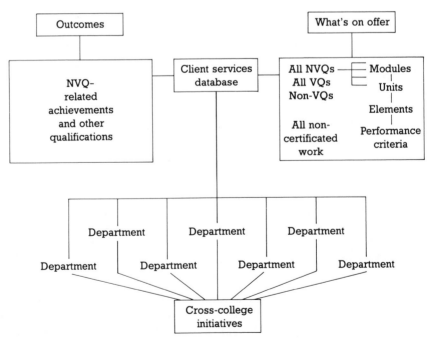

Figure 6.4 Central admissions database

be met. Once again, qualified staff would be on hand to supplement the details provided by the database. Outcomes of training in the form of NVQ-related achievement and other qualifications may be fed back into the database and this data is useful when monitoring and evaluating the training provision.

Training manager's requirements and trainee choices could be input to the database, together with initial assessment needs-based data, selection test results and action plan content. A best match could be obtained and this, together with data relating to NVQs[7] and other qualifications, would formulate performance criteria to be used as a basis for negotiating the training programme. Trainee achievement would also be input to generate performance indicators as a measure of outcomes of training, qualifications gained and other scheme-specific statistics.

Skills audit

Whether an assessment and review of learning needs is carried out with an experienced trainer/counsellor or alone by **self-analysis** may not be too important. What is important is for people to be able to identify what skills they already have.

Those involved in the analysis should be encouraged to talk about their needs during initial assessment or when the training group first assembles. Some will be surprised to find themselves in a situation where their personal views are sought. For many this will be the first time.

If people are asked to write a list of things they need to know, without any kind of help, prompting or support, they may become confused. They may feel that they are not yet in a position to tell someone else what it is that they wish to learn.

Taking into account their background knowledge, standard of basic education, special learning difficulties and what they hope to achieve during subsequent training, it may be possible at this stage to agree realistic expectations and outcomes that will go some way to balance individual and organisational needs.

Alternatively, a comparison could be made of what they can do against a **checklist of competences** relating to their occupational area. The resulting skills audit can then be compared with a list of competences that will be needed to work at the right standard. Personal development needs that do not directly relate to work skills may also be identified during the process.

> The difference between what they are competent to do now and what they will need to be able to do in future is known as the training gap. Once this gap has been agreed the next stage will be to establish a priority for learning.

Quality probe – identification of training needs

- Is the objective of carrying out the identification of training needs during initial assessment to help trainers and trainees clarify learning needs and to create an achievable action plan?
- Is there evidence that a documented procedure for ongoing analysis of training needs is being implemented in the workplace?
- Are systems for recording, categorising and prioritising individual and organisational needs operating?
- Is positive action being taken to ensure that both sexes are treated fairly in terms of equal opportunity and avoidance of sex discrimination?
- Is the action plan content and sequence of learning prioritised so as to give the best match between trainees' and employers' needs?
- Are clients asked for their ideas about training programme content and method, and to identify tasks and workplace activities that will enable them to learn effectively?
- Are the employers' needs and expectations as far as trainees are concerned taken into consideration when matching training with identified learner needs?

Subsequent assessments

Formal assessments can be made throughout the training programme. Informal assessments may also be made and these involve negotiating with trainees or carrying out **trainee-centred reviewing**.

Criterion-referenced testing, in which a trainee is assessed relative to certain pre-determined standards, specified in performance criteria, may be used in preference to **norm-referenced testing**. The latter compares the trainee's performance with other trainees or to an average for a group of trainees. With criterion-referenced tests the trainee will pass if performance against standards meets the standard. This system of assessment depends to some extent upon the trainer adopting a modular approach to training where successful completion of one learning step leads on to the next.

Making initial assessments

The methods used for making assessments will normally be chosen to suit the person to be assessed. If self-assessment is not possible then assessment may be made with the trainer and trainee working together using methods such as:

- checklist or series of structured questions;
- guided individual discussion;
- group discussion;
- setting trainees tasks or problems;

- observing trainees in the workplace during the course of their normal work;
- observing trainees undertaking set tasks specified by the lead body, award body, employer, workplace trainer, assessor or other agent.

The Employment Department Group – Training Enterprise and Education Directorate (TEED) state that 'The highest priorities should be given to things that matter most in the job'[8] and suggest that 'A set of structured questions can uncover a lot of information about the person's skills and attitudes; combined with an informal invitation to carry out a number of simple tasks, giving quite an accurate initial assessment.'[9]

Quality probe – initial assessment staff

Are initial assessment staff able to:

- Explain the purpose of initial assessment and process of negotiation and specify their own role in the process?
- Explain criteria on which performance standards are set?
- Identify an appropriate range of assessment methods?
- Use suitable assessments to measure trainees' performances or help them to carry out self-appraisals against performance criteria?
- Operate a recording and reviewing system founded on the use of initial and ongoing formative assessment?

Establishing an assessment centre

Resource implications

During the early stage of planning it will be necessary to research and inform management of resources needed to establish an assessment centre, to provide assessment on demand and to implement fully NVQ assessment, accreditation and certification policies and procedures.

Typical enabling objectives concerning the resourcing and setting up of assessment centres are:

- To investigate resource implications of the design and implementation of a documented system for admissions, accreditation of prior learning and achievement (APLA) and other NVQ assessment processes.
- To develop an assessment system compatible with the quality policy statement.
- To promote the status and use of record of achievement (RoA) as a pre-entry instrument to continuing education and training, and as a means of focusing on the needs and achievements of the individual.

- To initiate developments which extend RoA and individual, action-planning processes into learning opportunities and experience.
- To investigate the implications for the provider of competence-based skills testing including the provision of assessment on demand, in line with NVQ requirements.
- To co-operate closely with pre-16 institutions in order to provide a smooth transition on entry to continuing education and training or employment.
- To support and co-ordinate development with that of other assessment centres and make recommendations for future innovation.

Centre staff

An interdisciplinary team could be established which would work towards the creation of a coherent policy of assessment, accreditation and candidate-centred learning support. This would map onto the training provider's operational plan and departmental plans with the aim of endorsing learner entitlement.

Assessment centre manager

Ideally, the centre manager would be a person with a wide experience of the world of work, business, continuing education and training. Major functions of the manager would be maintaining open-access, supervising centre staff, providing educational guidance and negotiating action plans with candidates. Co-operation and communication links would be sought with central admissions, especially when counselling prospective candidates and preparing initial portfolios.

Assessors

Qualified assessors would be needed to review portfolios of achievement or other supplementary evidence and where necessary to set up demonstrations of competence and assessments.

Administrative support

Support for the centre would include an administrative facility that would handle assessment procedures, accreditation, certification and recording. This facility would liaise with Training and Enterprise Councils (TECs), NCVQ, lead bodies and awarding bodies. It would also maintain close links with the Careers Service, the organisation's central admissions unit, employers and other interested parties.

Co-ordinators

A typical role for a co-ordinator concerned with assessment process would be:

- To work with co-ordinators from other departments or assessment centres and to monitor the effectiveness of organisational policy and practice.
- To facilitate departmental developments by becoming familiar with issues and identifying appropriate procedures to be employed.
- To have oversight of departmental assessment centres and modularisation projects, and to share developments and good practice with other co-ordinators.
- To act as a focal point for information and to publicise good practice within the department.

Staff training and development

There will probably be a need to raise staff awareness of national developments in:

- assessment and accreditation of competence and prior learning and achievement;[10]
- supporting the delivery of learner entitlement and the need for continuity of learning and progression;
- investigating and supporting strategies for embedding NVQs in the training provision.

Quality probe – staff development

- Is there a documented staff development policy for teaching and support staff?
- Is there a staff development plan?
- Is a staff appraisal and identification of training needs system working effectively?
- Are staff training features regularly monitored?
- Are the outcomes of training evaluated against the plan?

Staff accreditation

The Training & Development Lead Body's (TDLB) standards-setting work is playing a major role in elevating the status of training and development. In setting standards for education and training providers and their staff, the foundations for competent performance in training and development have been laid. TDLB's work will reinforce and add to the framework for accrediting qualifications already in place and it is anticipated that NVQs for professional trainers will soon become a requirement for all those involved in training and staff development.

> 'The training both by specific training to perform assigned tasks and general training to heighten quality awareness and to mould attitudes of all personnel in an organization is central to the achievement of quality.'[11]

Accommodation

The assessment centre and interview rooms should be of suitable size to accommodate effectively the number of clients using the service. Planned provision would ensure a safe, healthy and welcoming environment fit for the purpose to which it will be put.

> Accommodation and resources should be adequate, regularly audited, well maintained and suitable for purpose and use in the context of supporting training and development.

Hardware and consumable materials

Materials and resources will have to be procured to support activities relating to the assessment service. Sub-contractors and suppliers should have the capability of delivering products or services of the required quality. Internal suppliers of reprographics and facilities to produce assessment documentation, records of achievement and logbooks should consistently meet the requirements of users, whether they be candidates for assessment or centre staff.

> Quality of materials and equipment needed to operate the centre, whether for inclusion in product or service, must conform to specified quality standards.

Recording assessment

Current practices

When defining quality procedures and systems for evaluating achievement it will be necessary to carry out research designed to identify current practices and proposed methods of assessing and recording outcomes.

Typical enabling objectives concerning the identification of current practices would include the need to:

- Identify accreditation of prior learning and achievement (APLA) and NVQ-approved systems of assessment which could be implemented in the assessment centre.

- Carry out research to identify current recording and assessment practices operating within the organisation and by competitors. This can be done through visits, attendance at meetings, conferences and seminars and from written information.
- Compare other accepted and approved NVQ recording and assessment practices with one's own. Discuss their suitability and validity for implementation as NVQs and other competence-based qualifications become available.

Disseminating information

Embedding good practice

Having established examples of good practice it will be necessary to disseminate information on approved good practice, via departmental assessment teams, for further discussion by course teams and subsequent embedding within the total training provision.

Typical enabling objectives concerning embedding good practice would be to:

- Specify systems of assessment which would be implemented in the assessment centre.
- Provide examples of approved good practice when assessing, guiding and counselling in order to assist staff training and development.
- Identify counselling, assessment and mapping procedures and systems to be adopted for each learner.
- Devise a strategy for embedding procedures and developing good practice across the organisation.

Claiming competence

Client portfolios

Portfolios of evidence, contents of National Records of Vocational Achievements (NROVAs) and other evidence of prior learning and achievement (APLA) in training and education, presented by candidates for assessment, may be likened to **purchaser supplied products** or 'free issue' provided by the customer to the manufacturer or supplier of a service or end product.

In each case, the onus for validity and conformity to specified requirements rests with the customer. In the first instance, responsibility for correctly assembling relevant, current and reliable supporting evidence lies with the candidate seeking accreditation. In the second instance, verification of conformance to specification, freedom from defect and properly protected products (training purchaser's software, resource kits, assignments, coursework, homework and project work) lies with the provider's customer.

Another interpretation of the purchaser supplied product would be the referral agent's services supplied to the provider's customer, including counselling, guidance, remedial tuition or other products or services that serve to support the main training programme supplied by the provider.

To provide for assessment on demand and to implement assessment and accreditation policies and procedures it will be necessary to provide an opportunity for persons without formal qualification to claim competence as a result of their experience and prior achievement.

Typical enabling objectives concerning provision of assessment on demand and accreditation of prior learning and achievement would include the need to:

- Investigate the means of establishing provision for assessment on demand of:
  practical skills;
  related theory (supplementary or underpinning knowledge).
- Provide an assessment framework to accredit previous achievement and experience.
- Identify counselling, guidance, assessment and mapping procedures and systems available to each user.
- Offer advice on further study required to attain NVQs or other qualifications at appropriate levels.
- Review existing assessment methods and recording systems and formalise data collection using a computer-based system for recording achievement and competence.
- Monitor utilisation of assessment centres and carry out user-satisfaction surveys.

Learning resources

Learner-centred resources
In order to provide user support it will be necessary to undertake a review of learner-centred resources that would be required for use in the assessment centre.

Typical enabling objectives would include the need to:

- Catalogue current, learner-centred learning materials and assessment documents, and identify priority areas for resource development.
- Research and evaluate externally-generated learning material packages, including standard assessment materials from examining and awarding bodies.
- Create a resource bank and carry out licensing and copyright transactions in connection with open-learning materials and other bought-in resources.

- Modularise programmes, revise schemes of work, assignments and learning opportunities to conform with new and amended units, elements and competence statements provided by lead bodies.
- Liaise with other assessment centres in order to identify strengths, opportunities, successes, common problems and weaknesses.

Marketing

Marketing the service

In order to enhance utilisation of the assessment centre and its staff it may be necessary to market the service to employers and the general public. Well-targeted marketing can be used to make potential customers aware of the provider's name and service.

Market research enables the provider to focus resources on those programmes and services that are most likely to create or meet public demand and generate, where appropriate, a profit. Research can limit the risk of wasting resources on projects that come to nothing.

Quality probe – market research

- Is there a documented system for collecting and interpreting data that will help get products and services to the end user?
- Is data gathered from internal workforce and archives as well as from external sources?
- Is there a research plan and if so does it define information to be gathered, research methods and researchers? Does the operational plan specify objectives and describe implementations?

The marketing plan would normally cover the four Ps:
- Product;
- Place;
- Price; and
- Promotion;
with additional features, such as monitoring user's, employer's and sponsor's perceptions of the service, quality of communications and feedback.

Action planning is to identify market forces operating within the provider's area of activity, to devise objectives describing how target group needs may be serviced and to develop a strategy and operational plan for meeting those needs.

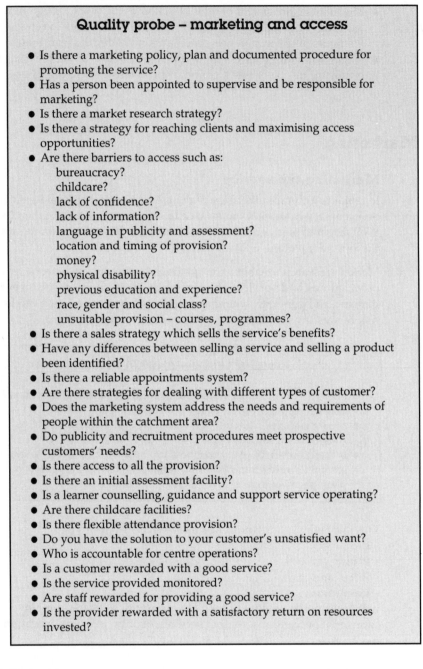

Quality probe – marketing and access

- Is there a marketing policy, plan and documented procedure for promoting the service?
- Has a person been appointed to supervise and be responsible for marketing?
- Is there a market research strategy?
- Is there a strategy for reaching clients and maximising access opportunities?
- Are there barriers to access such as:
    bureaucracy?
    childcare?
    lack of confidence?
    lack of information?
    language in publicity and assessment?
    location and timing of provision?
    money?
    physical disability?
    previous education and experience?
    race, gender and social class?
    unsuitable provision – courses, programmes?
- Is there a sales strategy which sells the service's benefits?
- Have any differences between selling a service and selling a product been identified?
- Is there a reliable appointments system?
- Are there strategies for dealing with different types of customer?
- Does the marketing system address the needs and requirements of people within the catchment area?
- Do publicity and recruitment procedures meet prospective customers' needs?
- Is there access to all the provision?
- Is there an initial assessment facility?
- Is a learner counselling, guidance and support service operating?
- Are there childcare facilities?
- Is there flexible attendance provision?
- Do you have the solution to your customer's unsatisfied want?
- Who is accountable for centre operations?
- Is a customer rewarded with a good service?
- Is the service provided monitored?
- Are staff rewarded for providing a good service?
- Is the provider rewarded with a satisfactory return on resources invested?

Notes

1 *Towards a Framework for Curriculum Entitlement,* p. 16, FEU, London, 1989.

2 *Strategy and Processes,* FEU, London, 1986.

3 *Towards a Framework for Curriculum Entitlement*, p. 4, FEU, London 1989.

4 BS 5750: Part 4 (1990), p. 5, para 4.3.

5 See note 1, p. 4.

6 A. Spencer, N. Finlayson and S. Crabbe, Coombe Lodge Report, Vol. 20, No. 3, 'Women in Further and Higher Education Management', pp. 173–4, The Further Education Staff College, Coombe Lodge, Blagdon, Bristol, 1987.

7 NCVQ database information is accessed by: classification (industry, occupation, training category and subject); level; awarding body; and title. Full information on each qualification is available, including a description of the qualification, who it is for, the level of qualification, its structure, its component parts, and what is required in order to obtain it.
   Welcome to the NCVQ Database, National Council for Vocational Qualifications, London, 1990.

8 *Literacy and Numeracy – a guide to practice*, Training Agency (Now the Employment Department Group – Training Enterprise and Education Directorate [TEED]), Sheffield, June 1989.

9 Ibid.

10 L. Walklin, *The Assessment of Performance and Competence*, Stanley Thornes (Publishers) Ltd, Cheltenham, May 1991.

11 BS 5750: Part 4 (1990), p. 10, para. 4.18.

CHAPTER SEVEN

Service Delivery

Chapter coverage

Process control
  Process inputs
Manpower
  Labour
  Attitudes
  Trainers and support staff
  Trainer competence
  Health and safety
  The training cycle
  Human resources
  Timetabling
Machines
  Capital equipment
  Teaching and learning hardware
  Plant and equipment
  Reliability
  Availability
  Maintainability
Materials
  Educational technology
  Producing software
  Audio-visual aids
  Open-learning packages
  Reviewing learning materials
  Checking out systems and facilities
Methods
  Implementing an equal opportunities strategy
  Communication skills

Feedback
Teaching and learning modes
Using computers and data-processing aids
The trainer as systems analyst
Introducing new resources
Measurement
Reviewing learner progress
Inspection and testing
Systematic monitoring and evaluation
Milieu
The learning environment
Financial resources
Physical resources
Resource centres
Purpose and aims
Work placements

Process control

The importance of finding out what the customer wants and providing it at the right quality cannot be underestimated. In order to get it right first time, every time, there is a need to change the emphasis from evaluating results or outcomes to designing systems and planning and controlling inputs. Effort should be directed, in the first place, to ensuring that those involved in manufacturing, providing a service or delivering education and training operate within a quality-assured environment.

The quality of process inputs should be controlled rather than relying solely upon feedback from results achieved. The object is to prevent snags and failures occurring in the first instance. Inspection will not solve the problem if results do not meet standards. It is too late to shut the door after the horse has bolted. The process should be systematically controlled from raw material to finished product and end user, and from access and design of training to evaluation of service provided.

The target should be zero defects achieved by teachers, trainers and support staff working correctly all the time. This in turn, means working within documented quality systems, keeping to recommended or specified procedures and seeking out and eradicating sources of non-conformance and problems. A policy of no failures should prevail. The degree of customer satisfaction will be indicated by feedback from audits of trainee and employer perceptions of learning provision and outcomes.

Customer complaints result in actual costs in terms of staff time spent trying to put things right or at least reaching acceptable compromises. Opportunity costs will also be incurred from not being able to do something more productive and there will be loss of goodwill.

Nowadays, more than ever before, customer service is probably the most vital part of a training provider's business. Customers are the most important people to be found in reception, the training department or workplace.

Process inputs

The 6Ms approach to quality control covers six types of variable input that may be involved in a process:

- Manpower   (*all* trainers and support staff with their experience, knowledge, skills and attitudes).
- Machines   (capital equipment, teaching and learning hardware).
- Materials   (software and expendable resources).
- Methods   (delivery modes – teaching and learning methods).
- Measurement   (reviewing, testing, examining, assessing, monitoring and evaluating).
- Milieu   (learning environment, work placement, laboratory, classroom or workshop).

The above list shows that inputs may comprise a mix of human, physical and financial resources, and are therefore subject to breakdown, loss of efficiency and effectiveness, or in the case of labour and finances – withdrawal. Each variable will therefore need to be carefully controlled if the process is to conform to customer expectations and yield satisfactory results.

Manpower

Labour

Many service organisations are very labour-intensive and people who have appropriate know-how and skills predominate. People are the major resource employed by training providers and business reputation is built on the perception customers gain during their interaction with them. A business can only be as good as the people who work there, but people alone cannot ensure success. Another ingredient is needed – money, to fund material resources and to service loans. Without adequate funding to provide better facilities a better service may not be possible given that existing human and physical resources are being employed effectively doing the right things right, first time.

Attitudes

When learners are asked why they choose to use a particular training provider a range of different reasons is given. However, one response is forthcoming time and time again – 'Because I get good service there. They make people feel welcome. They look after me and I get what I need from them.'

The attitude of providers' staff towards learners can, in the long term, make or break the business. Problems can arise as soon as people arrive at the reception desk. First impressions count. Customers do not expect to be kept hanging about by stressful staff who appear to be otherwise occupied, to be absorbed in paper shuffling and routine administration or a seemingly never-ending telephone conversation.

> **Remember that you are not doing enquirers a favour by attending to them – it is their right. It is your responsibility to treat them as the most important people in the place. Avoid the risk of adding to the list of customers who never came back.**

When delegates reach the training area, smartly-dressed, helpful professionals should be there ready to create the right caring image.

When customers appear to be having difficulty in finding their way or needing help, do we ignore them and leave them to sort it out for themselves or do we offer help? Instead of being always on the lookout for people who may need help, all too often staff look the other way. Offering help only when people corner you is not good enough. Telephone enquiries likewise warrant a well-mannered response and the same polite treatment as during a face-to-face encounter. Delays can be very frustrating and are difficult to tolerate.

> **Customers are not an interruption to our daily routine. They are the reason we are in business. Without them we would not have the job.**

As in other businesses, when it comes to product knowledge it is important to demonstrate a sufficient understanding of all aspects of the training provision offered. Delegates' enquiries require answers that give accurate information. They will expect providers to know about all features of the training on offer.

> **It should be remembered that customers may not be dependent upon you, but that you are dependent upon them. They have a choice of where to shop for training and positive attitudes to customer care can help them make that choice – your provision or a competitor's.**

Trainers and support staff

Customers will expect trainers and support staff to be experienced, knowledgeable and skilled, and to have supportive attitudes. When delivering training they should be capable of managing the learning process, choosing appropriate resources, using language consistent with the learners' needs and expectations, and maximising learning outcomes.

Trainer competence

Trainers will need to be able to demonstrate awareness of the uses of computers and other data processing aids in the teaching of their subjects. This is an area that has regularly been designated by the Department of Education and Science (DES) as a National Priority Area for staff development training. There is a need to focus attention on the growing importance of information technology and microelectronics in modern training practice.

> Trainers working in a quality-assured environment will be able to demonstrate competence in setting up and using microcomputers and associated hardware units; selecting and using program packages; maintaining storage and retrieval systems; and ensuring that environmental conditions are non-hazardous.

Health and safety

Learners will expect their trainer to be fully conversant with ergonomic considerations and all aspects of the Health and Safety at Work Act 1974 relating to the training programme and, in particular, to equipment that will be used while learning.

For example, it is possible that working with visual display units (VDUs) may, under certain conditions, cause or contribute to health problems relating to posture and vision. Operators have complained of eyestrain, headaches, migraine, nausea, backache, muscular and visual fatigue, eye irritations, rashes and other symptoms associated with their employment.

> The trainer must be aware of these and other hazards that may exist while people are at work. Information technology trainers should be vigilant when trainees are working with computers or in electronic offices particularly where VDUs are in constant use.

The training cycle

In mainstream education the process known either as 'staff appraisal' or as 'systematic evaluation of in-service training need' is now widespread. Staff are entitled to (or are required to participate in) regular reviews or appraisals in order to make known their recent achievements, and also to identify updating and training needs.

Systematic reviews of training needs should be conducted and satisfactory arrangements for the training of staff to bridge training gaps identified should be negotiated. A similar system of validating sub-contractors in terms of their personal competence or by audit of their quality system should be operated by training providers who buy in the services of consultants and training delivery agents.

Qualifications, such as the City & Guilds trainer and assessor awards and others validated by the Training and Development Lead Body, have been adopted by many training providers wishing to assure the competence and credibility of their trainers and satisfy the TECs' and other training contractors' quality requirements.

New standards-based NVQs in training and development are being developed by the National Council for Vocational Qualifications (NCVQ) to fit into their overall national structure of NVQs. The qualifications are designed to cover the whole of the training cycle (see Figure 7.1)[1] and to fit into providers' strategies of **human resource development (HRD)**.

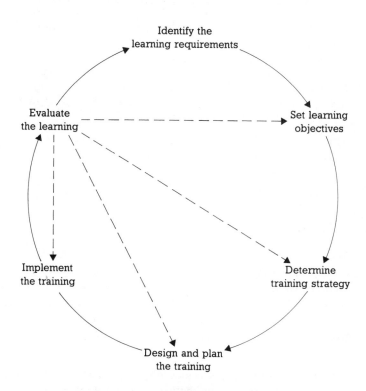

Source: J. Kenney and M. Reid, Training Interventions. Reproduced by permission of the publishers, The Institute of Personnel Management, IPM House, 35 Camp Road, London SW19 4UX.

Figure 7.1 The training cycle – planned training

When assessing staff achievement in connection with workplace trainer and assessor awards, staff achievement and underpinning knowledge should be assessed on the job against suitably-defined performance criteria. Training records should be maintained.[2]

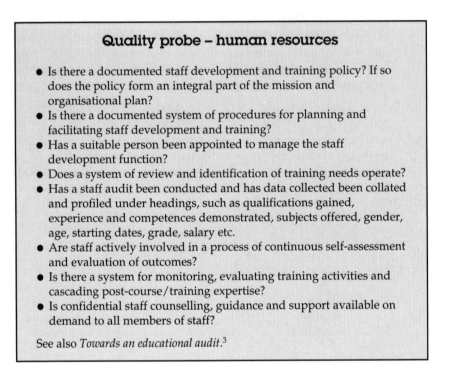

Quality probe – human resources

- Is there a documented staff development and training policy? If so does the policy form an integral part of the mission and organisational plan?
- Is there a documented system of procedures for planning and facilitating staff development and training?
- Has a suitable person been appointed to manage the staff development function?
- Does a system of review and identification of training needs operate?
- Has a staff audit been conducted and has data collected been collated and profiled under headings, such as qualifications gained, experience and competences demonstrated, subjects offered, gender, age, starting dates, grade, salary etc.
- Are staff actively involved in a process of continuous self-assessment and evaluation of outcomes?
- Is there a system for monitoring, evaluating training activities and cascading post-course/training expertise?
- Is confidential staff counselling, guidance and support available on demand to all members of staff?

See also *Towards an educational audit*.[3]

Timetabling

Efficient timetabling of courses, staff and rooms is a necessary prerequisite to effective delivery of training. A good deal of time can be spent struggling to equate staff, accommodation and resource availability with demand for assessment, training provision, tutorial periods, counselling sessions and guidance slots. This is where computer-assisted timetabling can help to match resources with demand.

Use of computer-assisted timetabling can enhance human and physical resource utilisation, facilitate record keeping and provide feedback to the management information system in terms of performance indicators.

Machines

Capital equipment

Colleges are centres of communal investment in plant, equipment, learning materials and (most of all) professional expertise. Within them resides wide experience of vocational education, including professional skills of design, delivery and assessment.

College plant and equipment exist for education, not primarily for production. As publicly-funded, but responsive, institutions they must have the long-term interests of communities in mind as well as short-term demands for occupational competences.[4]

> Trainers are expected to be competent in the use of a range of training resources in different contexts. They will need to be able to evaluate the strengths and limitations of each resource employed and select appropriate machines, materials or aids, taking into account learning outcomes and, where possible, individual learning styles.

Teaching and learning hardware

Managers now operate in a climate of reduced funding support from external agencies. They have to make teaching and learning resources go further so that survival and growth depend on their ability to remain effective while suffering from cutbacks and intense competition. They have to become more accountable to stakeholders who are looking for a value for money service and to justify expenditure against operational objectives and out-turns.

An obvious way of staying in business is to maintain the quality of training outcomes while reducing the unit costs of providing the service. This may be easier said than done. Unlike machines in industry, it is not normally possible to turn up the wick and get the educational hardware working faster. Similarly, the drive to get people working more effectively rather than harder can be relatively slow to take off.

> The answer may lie in the need for the provider to improve resource utilisation, to seek out and cut back on waste and to operate a planned approach to resource acquisition rather than resorting to the year-end spend-up.

Quality probe – plant and equipment

- Is there an inventory of training resources?
- Is there a documented system for checking that all plant and equipment is sufficiently utilised and efficiently and effectively deployed?
- Is there a named person with overall responsibility for all aspects of testing, servicing and operating the provider's plant and equipment?
- Are resources tested, inspected, serviced and maintained according to manufacturers' schedules and in accordance with legislation?
- Are users trained and competent in the use of resources and are associated health and safety regulations consistently applied?
- Is usage monitored and recorded and are the resources cost-effective?
- Are there any resources that are obsolete or giving poor performance and are these adversely affecting provision? Can important areas for improvement of service delivery be identified?
- Does the range of resources available meet contractual requirements and the needs of learners, employers, sponsors and staff employed in using the plant and equipment?

Reliability

Reliability is a term that will be familiar to educationalists. It has long been used in relation to the quality of testing and assessment, but its application to training resources in the form of hardware and machines may not be so well understood.

Reliability, in a general sense, is defined in BS 4778: Part 2 (1979) as 'The ability of an item to perform a required function under stated conditions for a stated period of time.' This concept can be useful in the training business where machines and resources used in support of programmes offered must be available for use when required. The overhead projector must work when switched on, the video emit good sound and vision quality, and computer systems must not malfunction. The reliability of resources purchased by the training provider will be reflected in failure rates, serviceability and maintenance costs which in turn will affect cost-effectiveness calculations and customer perceptions of the service provided.

Availability

Resources should be accessible and capable of being used to perform their intended purposes. Procedures for obtaining resources when needed and if necessary at short notice should be operating. The storeperson philosophy of yesteryear, where all stocks should be kept safely under lock and key and should preferably never be withdrawn from the store, may not be valid today.

Maintainability

The **useful life** of a resource should be estimated so that a renewal programme may be costed and implemented thereby reducing the probability of an unacceptable failure rate while in service or unrepairable failure. Too much downtime and corrective maintenance performed after breakdown is a sure sign that items are being misused, servicing is ineffective or that there is an absence of planned maintenance.

Inspection, test and maintenance schedules must be designed and servicing schedules prepared so that the efficiency and effectiveness of resources may be prolonged and the effects of wear-and-tear offset by preventive maintenance. Servicing records should be kept.

It may be necessary to reproduce, circulate and control copies of manufacturer's instruction manuals and maintenance logs. Staff will need to be trained to maintain the resources unless leasing or maintenance contracts are arranged. The economic quality level should be determined for each type of resource.

Materials

Materials are the items needed to carry out a particular activity whereas **materiel** is the name given to the materials and equipment of an organisation. Materiel therefore includes all that comprises part of the contract, supplies, systems for delivering specific training programmes and presentation materials. Material specifications may be drawn up that list the supplies needed to resource particular training programmes.

Documented procedures for control of related paperwork, such as lead body regulations, awarding body circulars and performance criteria, reference materials, assessment specifications and records of achievement, should be in operation. Any document changes should be controlled.

Educational technology

Educational technology embraces all that is involved in the design and implementation of systems of teaching and learning, and all that is involved in supporting these systems. Resources in the form of hardware and software are important elements of the educational and training system and given that training providers fund the human resource and hardware necessary to support the training provision, software production will normally be devolved to individual trainers or to groups of trainers.

Producing software

Software is a term used to describe the instructions a computer follows when carrying out tasks. Special programming languages are used to communicate these instructions to the computer. A set of instructions is called a program.

The term 'software' is also used in educational technology and in this case it relates to the provision of visual aids, handouts and other paper or recorded resources rather than hardware in the form of machines or other equipment used to produce or display the material.

> Preparation of high-quality training sessions depends upon the availability of good-quality support materials. Designing and producing effective software are demanding aspects of a trainer's role.

Audio-visual aids

Using audio-visual aids introduces materials in a way which increases the impact of information being shared with the learners. Today, a great deal of effort is being devoted to devising ways and means of improving the presentation of information. The role of audio-visual aids and computers as supplements to boardwork, textbook and trainer talk is growing in importance. As with any information to be communicated, planning is essential to success.

> Planning should include both design and the reasons for using the resource.

> The effect of aids on learning outcomes should be critically evaluated. Where necessary modify the aids before using them again.

Open-learning packages

Many open-learning schemes require the use of self-instructional resources and these often include **learning packages**. The packages contain materials that will support the learner when studying. Printed materials, audio-visual media, computer-assisted learning programmes and practical work may be available for use. Packages may support the study of whole units or separate elements that comprise the unit, or they may cover modules requiring study periods varying from a few hours to several days. Complete courses may take weeks or even months to work through.

Provider's of open-learning services will need to have in place adequately resourced open-learning centres with tutorial help and support staff on call. A system for booking physical resources and obtaining help from adequately qualified tutors, counsellors and guidance staff will need to be documented and facilitated.

Reviewing learning materials

In order to test the applicability of learning materials in relation to stated learning objectives it is necessary to carry out a review and evaluation of lesson outcomes. The materials to be evaluated may take any form, including completed assignments or skills tests, and learner achievement records or review sessions would provide feedback for analysis.

In the case of audio-visual aids that have been used in the teaching process, learners should be asked to judge the effectiveness and value of the contribution that aids have made to their learning outcome.

Provider's staff will need to be able to demonstrate awareness of the uses of learning resources, computers and other data processing aids in the teaching of their subjects.

Checking out systems and facilities

An audit of existing training and learning strategies can lead to improvements in delivery systems. The quality and effectiveness of learning in the provision can be enhanced by checking things out.

Quality probe – checking staff back-up

Check out security arrangements. Arrange for staff to get help in the evening. While in a quality-assured system things do not normally go wrong it makes sense to produce a contingency plan to cope with such things as blown fuses, lamp failure, wiring problems, running out of resources, and the intriguing task of locating a technician.

Methods

All training activities including curriculum planning, delivery and evaluation together with processing of associated paperwork must be carried out under controlled conditions. In a manufacturing situation, processes are controlled in order to provide an assurance of their capability to work to specification. This control should also apply to methods used in education and training.

Process capability may be thought of as being the limits of inherent variability within which the teaching and learning service operates. It gives an indication of the ability of the staff and systems to carry out consistently and correctly training requirements and meet customer contracts. Where variations exist, attempts will be made to control the degree of variance in service provision and to influence the capability to improve and develop methods.

Important features of the process to be controlled include:

- learning programme structure and related performance criteria;
- documented work instructions and session plans;
- teaching and learning environment;
- methods, resources and process records.

Providers will need to operate a range of training methods and be able to identify the strengths and limitations of each. Trainers employed will need to be able to select and apply strategies that will achieve specified outcomes while taking account of learners' needs and preferred learning styles. Learners may be categorised as having one of three commonly demonstrated styles: dependent, collaborative or independent.

Dependent learners prefer to be told and shown, to be encouraged and motivated by the trainer or others. In order to get the best out of them, trainers will need to give a lot of support and reward them by praising achievement.

Collaborative learners relate well to the trainer and seek to support, 'dance with' and match their behaviour with that of their mentor. They do not need to be driven or persuaded to attend to what is being said or done.

Independent learners look upon the trainer as a facilitator of learning who primarily manages resources but is on hand should help be needed. They are well-motivated. They set and monitor their own learning agenda and progress.

> A quality-assured provision will operate a delivery service that takes account of the degree of learner dependence involved.

Implementing an equal opportunities strategy

It has been reported in FEU publications that in terms of culture there is considerable evidence of insensitivity and misconception relating to the background experience and aspirations of the different ethnic minority groups. Providers must be aware of this possibility and ensure that negative attitudes to minority groups and racism in the classroom or work placement do not develop.

Choice of methods, resources and usage of language should be consistent with equal opportunity legislation. Learning opportunities should be managed so that learning is maximised for all clients regardless of sex, ethnic origin, religious persuasion, age or marital status.

Communication skills

Trainers will need to be able to deploy a range of communication skills appropriate to content and context of training sessions. The better the match between trainer style and preferred learning style the more effective will be the training experience and the learning outcome. Regrettably, it is unlikely that teaching and learning styles will be compatible in every case, but this should not deter the trainer from seeking to find a method that will promote co-operation and useful learning.

A trainer would be expected to demonstrate competence in effective communication when explaining a learning task, its purpose, processes involved and the product or service to be delivered.

Feedback

In industrial terms, the **feedback** concept applies to linking a system's outputs to its inputs, thereby monitoring what is going on and keeping the system under control. In a training context, feedback provided by various methods of review and assessment gives information about the learner's progress.

Being able to give and receive feedback is an important skill for trainees, trainers and assessors.

Receiving **positive feedback** about learning outcomes and achievements is good for learners but **negative feedback**, given skilfully, can also aid learning.

In a quality-assured environment the trainee, trainer and assessor will need to be able to share their perceptions of the good and not so good aspects of the training provision.

Giving and receiving feedback

Feedback may be obtained during performance reviews where learners are able to find out just how well they have done. They are able to compare and verify with the training provider their outcomes against performance criteria. Where there is a need to do better, they can discuss how they could go about reaching the standard required.

> The provider will need to comment on learning outcomes and offer advice as and when required.

Even when the assessment confirms that criteria have been met, feedback can be valuable in that constructive criticism and review encourage the development of a healthy rapport and learner confidence. The value to learners of self-referenced feedback is recognised as being of great value. It is what the learners say, think and do about their achievements or failures that really counts.

> When operating within a quality system it is necessary to provide reinforcement in the form of feedback and to discuss with learners how criteria have or have not been achieved.

Feedback given in a thoughtless manner is unhelpful. Learners will know when they have not done well, there will be no need to tell them. Providers should 'own their feedback'. They should accept responsibility for what they say to learners. They should ensure that their comments are understood by learners and that what is said is valid.

> If, when giving feedback, the provider can start by recounting some of the good aspects of the learner's outcomes they will be more ready to listen to what follows. There will be a greater probability that subsequent supportive criticism will be well received and will be acted upon.

Teaching and learning modes

The service may be provided using a variety of training methods that are developed around key functions, such as specifying performance criteria, selecting session content, organising resources and activities, and interacting with the learners. The methods used may be chosen from a well-established list ranging from learner-centred discovery learning to very formal prescriptive teaching. The list will include structured interactive teaching that involves the teacher and learner in working at learning activities in close relationship, with each influencing the content and quality of learning outcomes. Unstructured methods, self-directed, tutor-supported study and guided discussion and review may also be favoured. In some cases, learning outcomes may depend largely upon learner activity and degree of self-motivation.

The range of resources that could be used include a stick of chalk, audio-visual aids, computer-assisted learning facilities, work experience and many others. However, the importance of effective use of learning resource centres cannot be overstated. In today's harsh financial climate there is a real need to evaluate currently-used teaching methods and explore the possibility of adopting ways of maximising learner progress in terms of self-development and achievement of prescribed performance criteria. Ways of better utilising staff must be found and teachers will need to keep an open mind about concepts, such as the use of team teaching, resource-based learning, open learning and facilitating the requirements of larger groups of learners.

Open learning

Open learning provides a relatively new opportunity for people to learn. Open learning schemes enable people to make choices of what they will learn and within reason when, where and how they will achieve their goal. Many schemes have no formal entry requirements and no rigidly-fixed assessment methods. Participants are encouraged to go at their own pace, negotiate tutorial help as and when required and use whatever learning resources they feel best suited to their preferred learning style.

The system

The system should take account of the needs of four key types of customer: the learners, the sponsors, the resource designers and the delivery agents. Here, the concept of internal suppliers and customers works to promote a better quality service for the end user – the learner or sponsor.

> A prospective learner will depend upon the system to deliver what they have decided to learn in a form that meets their requirements.

Sponsors such as the TECs, employers and civil service departments will be seeking value for money since they will be paying some or all of the costs involved in supporting trainees or employees.

Designers of self-instruction materials and open-learning support systems will be suppliers of resources to customers in the form of learners and the delivery agents. The notion of suppliers of quality-assured products and services will therefore apply.

> Delivery agents will be expected to carry out an identification of training needs and negotiate with the learner how best to match provision with requirements. This may involve recommending and providing the open-learning materials required to support learning effectively.

Using computers and data-processing aids

The role of the trainer is to some extent changing to that of a facilitator and manager of learning, and the increased use of computers in learning will accelerate the change in role brought about by the introduction of computer technology. Computers have already had a dramatic effect on teaching and learning methodology, and their application seems limitless.

There is no doubt that computers can and do influence the efficiency of learning. They allow students, freed from the time constraints that were previously imposed by laborious calculation, graph drawing, typing corrections and reworking, more time to devote to learning new principles.

Computer-assisted instruction and related learning methods make possible the provision of flexible learning opportunities, with the computer replacing the trainer for some of the time. Without the computer, many flexi-study and open-learning programmes would be unsustainable, and the special needs of underachievers would not be as well catered for as they are with computer-aided teaching programmes.

Trainers and learners can achieve educational outcomes of a higher quality and wider scope than might otherwise be achieved by utilising the computer's ability to:

- store information;
- make decisions about data with which it is fed;
- carry out tasks at high speed;
- communicate a mass of information in an easily understood format.

Administrative duties, record keeping, timetabling, statistical returns and much of the work concerned with 'managing colleges efficiently', 'resource management', 'strategic and operational planning' and many other non-teaching tasks that may now form part of the trainer's role encourages the use of computers in education.

The trainer as systems analyst

Before involving the use of computers when delivering training it will be necessary to review the existing teaching and learning system and carry out a feasibility study, in order to decide whether it would be in the best interests of the learners to change things.

It may well be that the learners will be better off if things are left as they are, but if the intention is to introduce computers, any feasibility study should include a survey of available resources and the additional cost involved in making the change.

Quality probe – introducing new resources

- Is there a real need to introduce change or is there another way of achieving similar outcomes without the need to buy in additional resources?
- How would the proposed change benefit internal suppliers and customers and the end users?
- How will proposed change enhance efficiency and effectiveness of the provision?
- Would new equipment supplement or replace existing resources?
- Is a new resource compatible with existing systems and would the change, if implemented, be cost-effective?
- Will the processes affected by the proposed change and the end product meet customer requirements?

Measurement

Providers will need to have in place a system for reviewing processes and outcome, monitoring progress and evaluating the extent to which performance targets are being met. The scope of monitoring activities will embrace the achievement of individual learner's performance criteria, group goals and contracted targets agreed with the TECs and other sponsors. The system will also facilitate measurement of the extent to which learning outcomes match contract specifications and customer expectations.

Where mismatches between expectations and outcomes are perceived, systems designed to identify, remedy and control the source of non-conformance to contract should be activated. Details of the deviation from specification should be documented and action taken to eliminate the possibility of a recurrence.

The person responsible for maintaining control of the delivery system should adjust documentation and record changes. Training programmes, schemes of work and session plans should be updated accordingly.

Reviewing learner progress

A system for reviewing learner progress provides an example of how the concept of monitoring activities against performance criteria or personal training programmes may be facilitated.

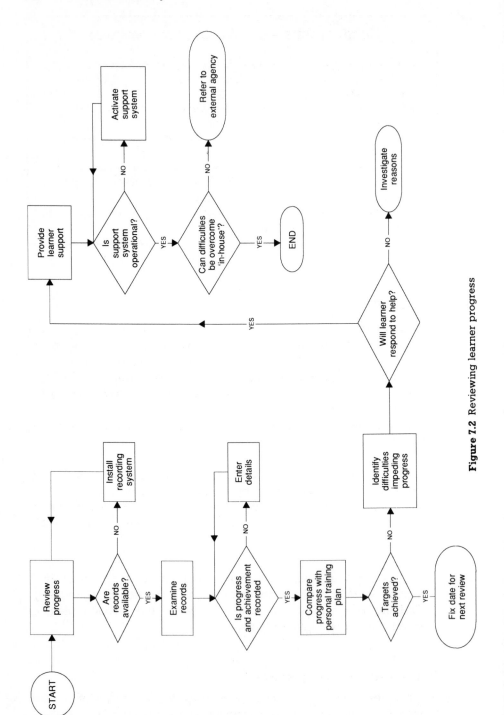

Figure 7.2 Reviewing learner progress

The flow chart given in Figure 7.2 shows the importance of reviewing progress and keeping records of achievement. Where difficulties that impede progress are identified there is a system for providing learner support that addresses a number of possible needs and outcomes.

Charts may be produced where systems and documented procedures for the measurement of other parameters are required.

Inspection and testing

BS 5750 requires that the quality system should incorporate planned and documented procedures for inspection and testing prior to the release of a product or service.[5] The standard describes three phases where inspection, verification or testing may take place. The phases which also apply to training and education provision are:

- An initial inspection when receiving purchases, sub-contracted items or service. (In the case of a training provider this means assessing incoming trainees, learners, part-time teachers' services and capital equipment or consumable resources.)
- In-process checks during service delivery. (In the case of a training provider this means: continuous assessment and reviews of progress against action plans; checking training provided and progress against training programmes and contracts; learner profiling; records of achievement; making log book entries; and recording competences gained.)
- Checks of performance against plan or contract prior to final release to a customer. (In the case of a training provider this applies to final reviews, skills testing, formal examinations, summative assessments, assessments in the workplace against specified performance criteria, and recording and accrediting learner achievements.)

Systematic monitoring and evaluation

Providers are required to carry out systematic monitoring and evaluation of educational and training processes. This, together with the need to maintain quality in an efficient and effective organisational environment, is now fast becoming a universal requirement.

Monitoring is the process of observing activities and gathering information about them. This enables under-performance and poor service to be detected before it is too late to do anything to put matters right. Control of training systems can be maintained by continuously reporting on method, content and outcomes, and taking corrective action where necessary. Changes can be made in response to feedback coming from the monitoring process and this helps to prevent making the same mistakes the next time round.

Evaluation is a process of establishing the efficiency and effectiveness of the learning process when measured against some standard, or assessing its worth in terms of client learning and achievement of competence. Monitoring and evaluation is discussed in greater depth in Chapter 9.

> Monitoring and evaluation is one of the keys to validating policies, plans and procedures operating within the organisation. Feedback will be obtained about whether or not training provision adequately meets clients' requirements.

Milieu

The learning environment

Customers entering the provider's reception area should perceive a warm, welcoming atmosphere and get friendly and helpful service from staff. However, the age of some buildings and the condition of the fabric can be off-putting to people. While buildings cannot be demolished and replaced overnight an attempt can be made to provide reasonable comfort and quality of accommodation.

Repair, maintenance and security of facilities will reflect the size and targeting of budget allocation and the importance management attaches to promoting a good image and sending positive messages about themselves to prospective clients. In order to obtain or maintain an edge over competitors, organisational culture and objectives should encompass the requirement that all staff use the facilities to best advantage and strive at all times to meet customer expectations.

> Quality systems should reflect the need to provide an environment that will enhance the effectiveness of learning with built-in flexibility to cope with change.

Quality probe – learning environment

- Is there a list of accommodation with details of features, such as location, seating capacity, furniture and fitments, electrical power specification, audio-visual aids, boards, flip chart stands etc.?
- Is there a flexible and reliable booking system?
- Can unused capacity be rented or otherwise utilised?
- Have ergonomic factors been reviewed and is the accommodation fit for intended purpose?
- Is the accommodation safe, hygienic, adequately equipped with fire fighting and other essential protective equipment, free of hazard and up to legal standards.

Financial resources

It is said that money does not grow on trees. This is certainly true in the training world today where miracles are expected from shrinking resources. In this climate, it is necessary to become more effective in order to survive and the need to conserve resources and eliminate waste requires managers to make some unpleasant decisions.

There is now a need to give a value-for-money service and this means improving efficiency – getting a quart out of a pint pot and using the profits from the second pint to fund improvements and further development.

Physical resources

Physical resources comprise machines, buildings, classrooms, laboratories, workshops, materials, stock, products and services. These, together with other equipment, represent the business assets. Where resources are up-to-date, the marketing plan can be implemented without problems, but an audit of the age, condition, and currency of assets should be carried out to ensure that new contracts won can in fact be met at the right standard.

Availability of appropriate resources will affect growth and reliability of service, and freedom from breakdowns will go some way to helping the provider to retain or increase market share.

Resources centres

A learning resources centre (LRC) is a collection of learning resources together with some equipment for their manufacture and use by learners and provider staff. A **library resources centre** will contain book collections and will also operate information storage and retrieval systems.

An important role of LRCs is that of providing information and materials that will help staff keep up to date with developments in their subject specialisms. Learners and the public at large can use LRCs to help them pursue their studies or occupy leisure time. By increasing control of their own learning through flexible open-access to learning resources available in centres, new patterns of learning behaviour become possible.

Purpose and aims

A learning resource service exists to serve clients, whether they be part-time or full-time trainers or learners. Such a service should implement the policy of using resources efficiently to support learning. It should offer facilities that draw upon all available methods, resources and media, and integrate these with established teaching and learning techniques in the most effective way, so as to achieve educational and training aims.

In assisting with this type of innovation in learning and teaching methods provision should be designed to:

- Encourage the effective use of all appropriate media and materials in the support of learning programmes.
- Make readily available to staff, materials and equipment that will enable them to develop and capitalise on their delivery skills.
- Create the environment, facilities and materials for learning through which individual learner differences in abilities, learning skills and speeds may be catered for.

Microfiche catalogues give details of books, slides, records and laser discs, cassettes, videos, microcomputer programs and other resources held. There is normally a reference section that holds encyclopedias, dictionaries, subject bibliographies, abstracts, indexes, expensive reference works, trade catalogues, industrial directories and very comprehensive sources of information of all kinds. British Standards, study and information packs and archive materials, including old newspapers, are normally also held. Updated computerised data may be available from electronic information services such as *Prestel, Ceefax, Oracle, Reuters* and on-line searching.

Equipment should be installed so that users may watch videos or listen to audio-cassettes and enable copies for private study to be taken in accordance with current copyright law.

Microcomputers, word-processors and software should be available for the preparation of assignment work.

Work placements

Trainees who will soon be starting work at their placement or employing organisation will need to be adequately briefed about attendance arrangements.

Recruitment or monitoring officers will need to operate a documented procedure for recording negotiated arrangements agreed with work providers or employers.

A carefully-planned induction to the placement and related training environment should be arranged. Visits should be made in order to check the quality of training and validity against the training programme.

Although employers and employees will be aware of their responsibilities under the Health and Safety at Work Act there will always remain an element of danger in any location where work is taking place. For this reason practical training at the placement will need to be monitored.

Action should be taken, in line with current legislation, should nonconformance be detected. Similar action would be taken when discrimination in any form or breaches of equal opportunities are reported.

Notes

1 J. Kenney and M. Reid, *Training Interventions,* Institute of Personnel Management, London, 1986.
'Planned training can be defined as the processes involved in:
- deciding whether training can help to resolve or prevent a problem, and if so determining whether training is the most cost-effective approach;
- identifying what learning is needed and setting learning objectives;
- deciding which training strategy or strategies to adopt and planning appropriate training programmes and arrangements to meet this need;
- implementing the training and ensuring that employees are assisted to acquire the skills, knowledge and attitudes they require;
- evaluating the effectiveness of the learning at appropriate times during and after the training; and
- satisfying any residual learning requirements.'

2 L. Walklin, *The Assessment of Performance and Competence,* Stanley Thornes (Publishers) Ltd, Cheltenham, 1991.

3 *Towards an educational audit,* (RP304), FEU, London, 1989.

4 *The College Does It Better,* p. 7, FEU, 1987.

5 BS 5750:Part 4 (1990), para. 4.10, p. 8.

CHAPTER EIGHT

Service Results

Chapter coverage

Reviews
Assessment of learner progress
   Achievement criteria
   Quality indicators
   Final assessment and testing
   Quality assurance in accreditation
   Validity and reliability
   Assessment and test records
   NVQ assessment model
   Assessment and test status
   Statistical techniques
Nonconformance
   Nonconformity
   Corrective action
Effectiveness of teaching and learning
   Planning and delivering training
   Assessing
   Performance indicators
   Customer perception of the provision
   Employer perception of the provision
Service audit reports
   Evidence
   Report and summary
Implementing the recommendations

Reviews

An impartial examination of outcomes is carried out in order to assess how well customer requirements are being met and to identify system deficiencies.

Internal audits should be used to review constructively service results and associated functions, procedures and responsibilities, rather than to confirm that uneconomic detection methods are actually disclosing system shortcomings. Audits will reveal whether or not the supplier is providing services and products of suitable quality at lowest cost; and whether or not the users are receiving satisfactory service at a reasonable cost to themselves. Preventive measures designed to avoid nonconformances will also be checked.

In-house questionnaire completion, employer surveys, work-placement monitoring, minutes of programme review team meetings, course team reports, records of achievement and associated documentation can all be used to confirm that customer requirements are being met or alternatively to generate evidence supporting proposals for corrective action. TEC quality surveys may also indicate that there is a need to take action to correct nonconformance.

An ongoing total quality development plan is a dynamic process and audit outcomes will be used to generate changes leading to updating and continuous improvement of provision.

Assessment of learner progress

One of the main purposes of the service review is to establish the degree to which learner entitlement and requirement has been satisfied. In order to do this, the progress of learners must be clearly and readily recognisable from induction until they leave. An effective system must be in place that will enable individuals or trainee groups to be identified and progress confirmed throughout the entire course or training programme. This process could be likened to aspects of manufacturing inspection and test status, from design to delivery. Adequate procedures must be available and designed to recognise whether or not learners are making satisfactory progress in meeting requirements.

Achievement criteria

Criteria must be provided that will enable assessors and auditors to monitor provision and trainee achievement. Where trainer or teacher-controlled monitoring is in operation, particular care must be taken to ensure that programme performance criteria are clear and unambiguous.

In some instances, sampling procedures will be in place as a means of verifying conformance to quality specifications. While BS 5750: Part 1 does not require that statistical sampling be implemented, it may in some cases be helpful to use curriculum plans and procedures that enhance confidence in quality level.

> Monitoring and assessment records must be kept and must identify the person responsible for verifying conformance to training programme specification.

Quality indicators

Quality indicators point out or recommend features of good practice that might be addressed when assessing the quality of inputs or processes. Indicators may be listed and weighted according to some scale so that they may be used to estimate the extent to which the quality element criteria, subjected to audit, have been met.

Performance indicators

Performance indicators are used to monitor, evaluate and control performance against pre-set targets, and are calculated using data collected from current activity or events that have already happened. They provide inputs to management information systems and tend to relate rather more to planning and control of resources and outcomes than directly to operational quality matters. Interpretation of indicators and remedial action can however lead to improvements in quality.

Final assessment and testing

Qualifications are being developed to standards and levels acceptable to the National Council for Vocational Qualifications (NCVQ). These qualifications identify competences to be achieved and demonstrated to the required standard by the learner. This approach suggests new responsibilities for both learner and trainer if competence is to be developed, practised and assessed through relevant learner-centred activities. The assessment of competence is a key activity, both to identify achievement and as the basis for accreditation.[1]

> The range of activities within which assessment will take place requires those involved with the assessment of learner achievement to be adequately trained and capable of undertaking assessment and testing.
>
> Before seeking accreditation and certification of NVQ competences the responsible person must ensure that all performance criteria have been demonstrated, assessed and recorded.

Assessing competence

A systematic approach similar to that shown in Figure 8.1 will be needed for assessing achievement. The process normally adopted involves the person seeking confirmation of achievement (described as the candidate), the teacher or trainer providing the training, and the assessor or observer carrying out the assessment. A countersigning officer will validate the maintenance of standards.

Assessment procedures would, in some cases, take account of the outcomes of formative assessments already carried out, together with records of achievement and supporting documentation.

Assessment procedures must be set out in the quality plan and records kept of all assessments carried out.

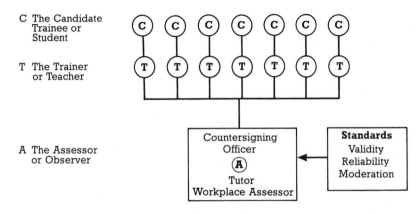

Figure 8.1 Assessing competence

Mode of assessment

The method used will be matched to the particular need for monitoring, assessment, test or examination. The instruments, processes and performance criteria involved in evaluating achievement or performance of the training programme will need to be specified and documented. The process could be likened to the final inspection and testing of a product or service used in business to ensure conformance to requirements.

Performance-related assessment methods include: live observations; reviewing video recordings; and guided discussion with candidates and work providers backed by the examination of records, procedures, systems, documentation, assignments and resources.

Formal assessment may include invigilated examinations and skills testing.

Quality assurance in accreditation

In order to ensure continuing credibility of NVQ awards and consistency of evaluation it is necessary to employ assessment methods that will limit variance in quality of accreditation. Each and every element of competence must be assessed to standards indicated by the performance criteria and examinations must be marked and evaluated to nationally recognised standards.

NCVQ are concerned with making sure that the assessment method adopted captures valid evidence of competence, although it does not specify particular types of assessment to be used.

An invalid assessment was reported concerning a trainee who was taking a practical skills test involving standards specified in an awarding body log book. The trainer, acting as an assessor, unwittingly treated the carpentry and joinery skills test as a coaching session. Throughout the assessment he gave instructions, explained what was to be done next, passed tools and even told the trainee the angles at which to saw timber and the nail size to be used to fix the members. When told by a passing supervisor that the skills test would have to be repeated under specified test conditions the trainer blinked disbelievingly.

A quick check on the assessment process revealed a serious non-conformance. There were no documented procedures. The test was invalid. The trainer was doing what he thought best, but it happened to be incorrect. Had the supervisor not intervened, the trainer would have signed-off the trainee as being competent on that NVQ element. Imagine what could happen later on-site if the trainee, now fully accredited as a competent person, had to perform the work unaided, or perhaps more complex skills that had earlier been similarly 'demonstrated under skills-test conditions'.

> Assessments must be carried out according to procedures specified by the awarding body for the particular NVQ.

This requirement is not new. For many years, BTEC moderators and City & Guilds assessors and other awarding body validators have been monitoring standards across the country. Proposals for offering programmes and provision for implementation and accreditation to required standards must be validated by the awarding body, before the go ahead is given to centres. Verification of implementation by the centre to agreed standards required during delivery of the programme is part of normal monitoring processes, as is a review of outcomes.

> Validation of assessor competence in terms of ownership of occupational area knowledge and skills, plus the ability to review, assess and accredit candidates to agreed standards, is essential

to the maintenance of quality of assessment. Assessor competence is the key requirement for valid and reliable assessment of learner achievement.

All assessment specifications, instruments, test papers, resources and skills tests must be controlled and validity maintained. Consistency and reliability must be assured.

Validity and reliability

When planning training and assessment we must ensure that the content and process is **valid**. The assessment method must fit what is to be assessed. This means that the accreditation of competence covers what is required to be achieved in terms of performance criteria.

In order to be properly validated, competence must be demonstrated and assessed under conditions as close as possible to those under which it would normally be practised.

It is of the utmost importance to ensure that candidates will be able to perform competently in their occupational roles, anywhere, to standards specified in award documentation.

Assessments must be **reliable**. The extent to which an assessment of competence is consistently dependable and reliable when carried out by different assessors, by a single assessor with different candidates, or at different times of day and in different places, is a measure of the **reliability** of the accreditation.

Performance criteria usually provide a description of conditions and standards against which competence will be judged. Competence is then confirmed by completing all the criteria for success on a 'can-do' basis. This limits, to a considerable extent, subjectivity and variation in assessors' opinions.

General factors that may affect reliability include the form and content of the assessment and the environment in which it takes place. Assessor-related factors include the spoken or written language used for instructions, cultural bias and supervision style. Candidate-related factors include an individual's mental, physical and emotional state, their degree of motivation and their relationship with the assessor.

Providers must develop quality systems for monitoring training and assessment procedures. All assessment specifications, instruments, test papers, software, resources and skills tests must be controlled and validity maintained. **This is necessary in order to ensure that national and local standards are maintained**.

Consistency and reliability of assessment in recording achievement must be maintained. Qualifications awarded should reflect their worth, regardless of the location in which training and assessment takes place.

Assessment and test records

In a quality-assured system it is helpful to maintain an assessment record of training outcomes and achievements. Data stored would include a combination of performance evidence and supplementary evidence, in-line with the NVQ assessment model (see Figure 8.2).

Records of submissions to awarding bodies, HMI, validator and moderator reports and other documentary evidence of verification and inspection of service provision must be kept.

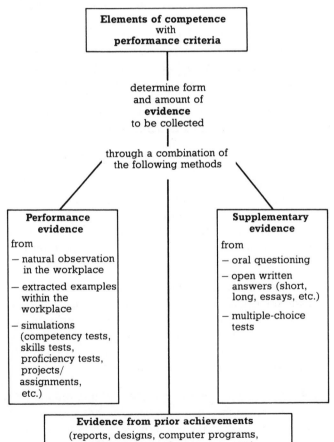

Figure 8.2 NVQ assessment model

Assessment and test status

The status of assessment resources and processes could be classified as 'awaiting validation', 'suitable for intended purpose' or 'unsuitable for intended purpose'.

> Ongoing evaluation of materials and administration must be carried out and only those facilities that meet assessment specifications or requirements should be used. A system for recording the status of the provider's assessment and test service must be maintained.

Statistical techniques

Statistical techniques may be used to gather quantitative data on any aspect of service provision and related outcomes. An analysis of the data would yield essential information about the effectiveness, efficiency and quality of operations, and knowledge of the provider's capability in meeting demands made of the service.

The capability of a service can be investigated by making regular visits and selecting and measuring a number of current or very recent programme outcomes. The data collected will provide evidence of the kind of variability to be expected. Typical indicators include: qualifications gained; retention rates; customer destinations; progression to continuing education, training or employment; and customer satisfaction.

> Data gathered would be used in the analysis of performance indicators. These inform the management information system and aid planning.

The data-gathering activity may be compared with those techniques used in industry for verifying the acceptability of process capability. In a training context, every instructor, every physical resource and every procedure will have inherent variability. Training is a people-intensive business, and people are individuals, so it would be unreasonable to expect that they will behave like precision machinery with high repeatability levels.

Machine capability can be enhanced with maintenance or replacements, but people have off-days and may often vary in their performance levels, from class to class, on the same day. Even so, in the end, the training must be accomplished satisfactorily and customer requirements must be consistently met. The introduction of quality circles involving all concerned in providing the service is seen as a way of motivating staff, improving quality and satisfying customers. But there is also the requirement to provide adequate resources and training, backed by precise work instructions and a reward of some kind.

In order to meet contractual requirements it may be that staff will need to bring themselves up to standard by seeking staff development training, counselling or support.

Nonconformance

Nonconformity

Nonconformity is 'the nonfulfilment of specified requirements'.[2] Procedures must be established to ensure that nonconformance of any aspect of training provision or contract is readily identified and rectified under supervision of the responsible person. All instances of nonconformance must be reported to the quality manager.

The main sources of nonconformance in education and training are:

- programme design and delivery;
- physical and material resources;
- teaching and training staff;
- support staff; and
- the learners themselves.

A nonconforming training product or process must be effectively prevented from being offered until documented procedures for going ahead have been negotiated, concessions made or corrective action taken. Such action should include prevention of recurrence. Documentation relating to any complaint or incident must be stored and be available for subsequent retrieval in the event of further review or audit purposes.

Where frequent absence, lack of progress, poor co-operation or other learner conformance occurs, the source could be behavioural. In this case, counselling, guidance and negotiation may resolve the problem and restore control. Alternatively, and as a last resort, sanctions may have to be applied.

In a manufacturing context, defective items would be identified, segregated and disposed of. Control procedures would be brought into play and defectives would be marked, removed from production lines and placed in quarantine stores or other holding areas. We cannot very well do this with learners, although on occasion the idea of following the commercial procedures may seem to be appropriate or even appealing.

If a learner consistently fails to meet performance criteria or assessment standards then remedial classes, retraining and retest, or transfer to another programme may be the answer.

Nonconformity reviews should be carried out by sifting through data gathered from many sources including:

- assessment records, records of achievement, NROVA content, port-folios, log-books, assignments and attendance registers;

- quality records and in-house documentation;
- customer (learner/sponsor) complaints;
- sponsor's reports;
- reports of shortcomings in learning materials, teaching and learning resources, and delivery processes.

Where audits reveal instances of nonconformity, details should be recorded on a nonconformance note similar to that given in Figure 8.3.

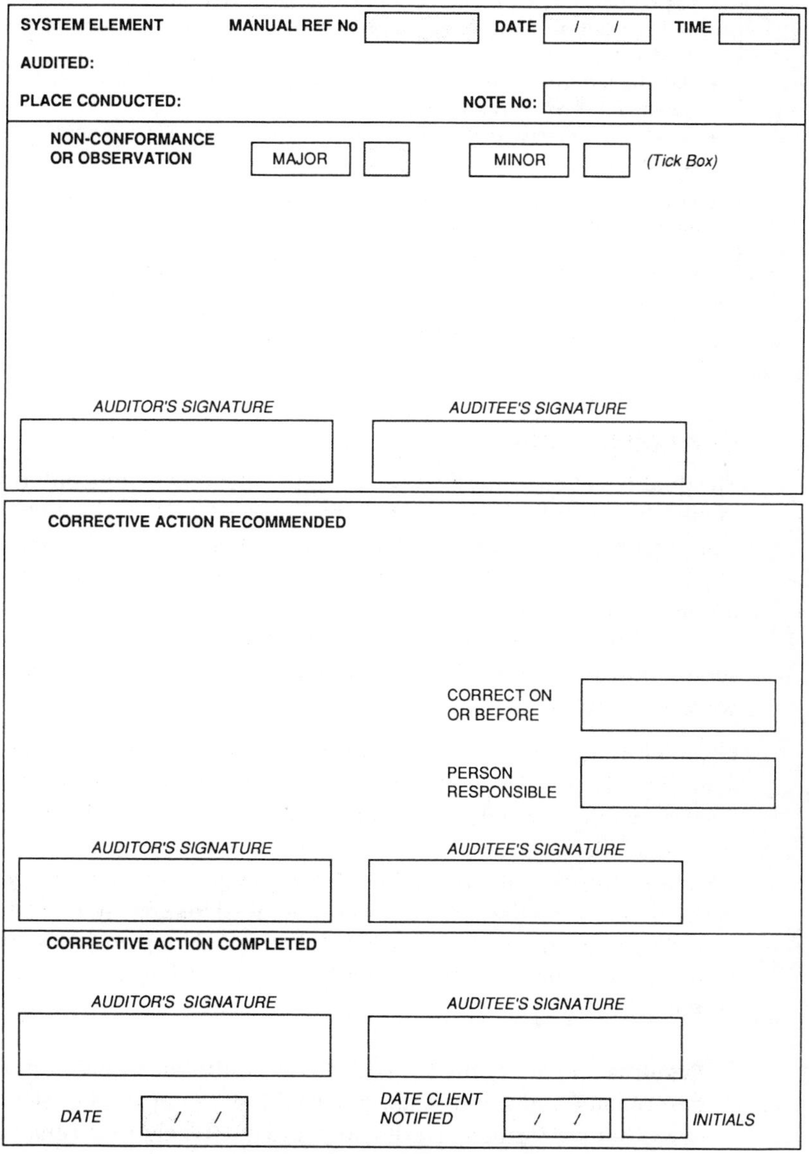

SYSTEM ELEMENT AUDITED: MANUAL REF No [ ] DATE [/ /] TIME [ ]

PLACE CONDUCTED: NOTE No: [ ]

NON-CONFORMANCE OR OBSERVATION [MAJOR] [ ] [MINOR] [ ] *(Tick Box)*

AUDITOR'S SIGNATURE *AUDITEE'S SIGNATURE*

CORRECTIVE ACTION RECOMMENDED

CORRECT ON OR BEFORE [ ]

PERSON RESPONSIBLE [ ]

AUDITOR'S SIGNATURE *AUDITEE'S SIGNATURE*

CORRECTIVE ACTION COMPLETED

AUDITOR'S SIGNATURE *AUDITEE'S SIGNATURE*

DATE [/ /] *DATE CLIENT NOTIFIED* [/ /] [ ] *INITIALS*

Figure 8.3 Nonconformance note

When documenting nonconformance the provider may wish to record information, such as that listed in Figure 8.4.

Records should include the following:

- course or programme identification;
- stage or scheme of work week number;
- number of learners involved;
- nature and extent of nonconformance;
- assessment of the problem and how this was resolved;
- action taken to correct the cause of the problem at its source and prevent recurrence;
- distribution list for copies of documentation specifying corrective action to be taken and records to be kept;
- details of persons responsible for authorising and implementing corrective action.

Information relating to the nonconformance and corrective action taken must be communicated to all concerned.

(Author's interpretation of information given in BS 5750: Part 4 (1990), para 4.13.)

Figure 8.4 Recording nonconformance

Corrective action

The quality system must facilitate prompt detection of nonconformity and identification and correction of assignable causes. Well-documented and maintained procedures for identifying trends toward nonconformance must be in place. Where audits or performance indicators signal an unsatisfactory trend, corrective action must be taken before nonconformance occurs. Recurrence of nonconformity of training product or service must be prevented by implementing effective monitoring and corrective action.

Changes in training process, resources employed or procedures resulting from corrective action must be carefully monitored and evaluated, to ensure that they are effective in the long term. Details of changes must be recorded. Manuals (and where applicable codes of practice) must be updated. However, the procedure does not end here. Staff must be made aware of the corrective action process and need for vigilance. The provider and staff concerned must learn from the incident and aim to search continuously and relentlessly for ways of further improving quality systems.

Systems must address purchaser (student/trainee/sponsor) complaints and comments, must take account of success rates and other performance indicators and must include the analysis of processes in order to prevent potential nonconformance.[3]

Effectiveness of teaching and learning

Formal periodic and systematic reviews are carried out to ensure continuing effectiveness of the service provided. Reviews of the design and outcomes of training programmes will embrace the need to establish that these are designed to meet customers' needs. This is true whether customers are trainees or employers. Audit checks will be made to ensure that outcomes are monitored and evaluated against criteria, such as those contained in personal training programmes, and that achievements are recorded.

Planning and delivering training

Structure

A review of performance will focus on key elements of service structure, such as identification of learners' needs, induction, goal setting and action planning, programme planning, teaching and learning strategies employed, assessment specification and implementation, and a general evaluation of programme planning and delivery.

Providers must ensure that training programmes are designed to match the need of individual customers and that training is compatible with the needs of employer and trainee. Providers must arrange a schedule for internal audits to be regularly conducted. The audit procedure should be documented and persons responsible nominated. Service audits will seek to establish that the programme delivered complies with the written contract or training agreement.

A selection of individual training programmes will probably be selected at random and checks made to confirm that the customers are getting what the provider contracted to supply. Guided discussion with the delivery agents and subjects named in the personal training programmes, and employers, may be undertaken as a way of assessing programme delivery, outcomes and degree of satisfaction.

NVQs

Now, more than ever before, there is a need to design training programmes that will result in learners achieving approved qualifications recognised within the NVQ framework. Sponsors of vocational training, such as the TECs, will require providers to deliver NVQs that are relevant to the employer's or trainee's occupational area. Failure to do so may result in the sponsor withholding approval and funding for proposed contracts.

Assessing

Procedures and methods used must be suitable for the intended purpose and adequate for assessing the effectiveness of the learner's achievement.

Where possible, learners should be involved in the design of appraisal schemes, in evaluating their progress and monitoring the effectiveness of their teaching and learning programmes.

The documented initial assessment procedure must result in the generation of a negotiated programme and timescaled action plan containing a description of units, elements and performance criteria to be achieved. Checks will be made to confirm that the programme agreed is relevant to occupational requirements and identified needs. Prior learning, experience and achievement must be taken into account and, if necessary, assessment instruments will be administered to confirm claims made by candidates.

When designing the training programme, assessment plans will be approved by course teams, informal assessment will be encouraged and formative and summative assessment procedures employed. Methods of assessment specified will be related to the appropriate learning objectives, performance criteria or competency statements.

Integrated assignments and work-based training will include some form of assessment and there will be internal moderation procedures for validating assessment criteria against training programme units, elements and performance criteria.

Trainee reviews will be conducted using a documented procedure that will allow progress against individually negotiated targets. System audits will involve the need to check that:

- reviewers have been adequately trained and are competent to conduct reviews;
- trainees fully understand the purpose of reviews and the process involved;
- reviews take place as per the documented schedule;
- actual performance against individual training programme confirms that training and learning opportunities are valid;
- feedback is helpful, constructive and aids motivation;
- corrective or remedial action is taken as required;
- review outcomes are documented, agreed and signed by trainee and reviewer immediately the review is concluded.

Outcomes will need to be reliably established and learner achievement must be free of variance brought about by the inconsistency of reviewers, assignment markers and assessors.

Knowledge of results and feedback of learner performance will be constructively presented and entered on the candidate's record of achievement. Records will be kept of accreditation and certification of learner achievement and there needs to be a documented procedure for processing results.

Performance indicators

Programme criteria will be used as measures of fulfilment of programme aims and objectives. Poor curriculum design and the reluctance of individual members of staff to adopt work instructions agreed by course teams will cause problems and lead to system 'failures'. This will give rise to the need to take remedial action.

Remedial action plans must be produced and implemented to correct procedures where requirements have not been, or are not being, met. The responsible person will ensure that shortcomings in resources and methods are rectified at the earliest possible opportunity. Remedial action taken must be recorded.

Input and output statistics may be compiled using suitable parameters as yardsticks against which to estimate the effectiveness of the service provided. Where possible, operational procedures should be simplified and the risk of errors decreased.

Customer perception of the provision

Key criteria for judging the effectiveness of provision will be the degree of compliance with the contract, individual training programme and action plan. The customers' declared perceptions of the quality of service provided will however depend on how positive they feel about the processes experienced and the value to them of the products they come away with during and after training.

When reviewing service results it can be useful to collect information about learner perceptions of the training programme and of the service generally. There will be differences in the features of the service that will be selected for audit. The needs of individual learners and of particular occupational areas will vary, but for many it will be important to determine whether or not there is sufficient learner participation and active involvement in the learning process. Another key feature to be sampled might be the degree to which transferable skills are incorporated in the programme of workplace activities and across programme design elements.

The effectiveness of the accreditation of prior learning and experience will be assessed, as will opportunities for clients to negotiate individual learning programmes. Learners' comments on course provision and delivery will be sought and an evaluation made.

The integration of theory and practical work, and the relevance of training to the learner's chosen occupational area will be evaluated against individual training programmes or contracts. This will entail the need for providers to operate adequate reviews and systems for reporting progress.

Where reviews indicate deficiencies in the provider's ability to meet customer requirements there must be procedures for making necessary alterations to meet expectations. The image gained of the organisation will depend largely on drop-out rates and the extent to which programme aims and objectives have been fulfilled.

Early leavers

A system for leaver analysis may be operated and evidence of remedial or necessary corrective action being taken, as a result of the review and evaluation of learner achievement, will be assessed by internal auditors. Analysis of data held in management information systems may be helpful when following up achievement and checking on customer destinations.

Destinations

Monitoring learner destinations will reveal the causes of system 'failure' evidenced by drop-out or non-completions (other than losses due to employment, progression and the like). Cause and effect diagrams may be useful when attempting to find the root cause of nonconformance or failure to meet contract, and when making changes leading to improvements.

Employer perception of the provision

It is important to recall that the provider's staff may serve many internal and external customers and that while the learner is the central player, sponsors and employers are also very involved in the process. Without sponsors the number of customers in training would be considerably reduced. Therefore, it follows that receiving value for money, as perceived by those who are paying for the service delivered, is important to survival.

Responding positively to customer needs and meeting customer quality requirements is the individual responsibility of each and every person working for the provider. Service reviews will require that information is collected about employer perceptions of the provider's training programme and chain of service supplied in general. Each link in the chain will be a person supplying services to a particular standard and receiving services from others. The quality chain must be unbroken and this is where carrying out routine self-audits against written procedures and work instructions can go a long way towards assuring conformance.

Quality will be assessed bearing in mind the need for the provider to meet customer requirements continually and consistently. Auditors will be looking for evidence that sponsors and employers have been encouraged to become involved in setting realistic and achievable standards, and in programme design and implementation. The active involvement of clients in the many aspects of delivery, assessment of competence at the workplace, accreditation and certification will probably be monitored also.

It is the user or the customer who will pass judgement on the quality of service provided. The opinions of others may not count for much.

Service audit reports

Each provider will have a master quality manual that describes all elements, processes, procedures and records in use. Copies of a survey manual containing elements, such as those listed in Figure 8.5, will be used to aid internal service audits. The survey manual will probably be more widely available than the comprehensive official reference quality manual. Due to the need to maintain accuracy and authenticity the number of copies in circulation will be restricted to perhaps the quality manager and chief executive.

Quality elements:

- quality policy
- roles, responsibilites and accountabilities
- quality planning
- quality procedures
- implementation of quality procedures
- health and safety
- equal opportunities
- marketing and promoting programmes
- premises and equipment
- design of training programmes incorporating NVQs
- design of training programmes meeting needs of customers
- staff selection, training and responsibilities
- audit and review
- selection and control of training sub-contractors
- selection of work placement sub-contractors
- review and evaluation of work placements
- initial assessment and action planning
- trainee reviews
- trainee success evaluation
- capacity to correct unsatisfactory elements.

Figure 8.5 Provider quality survey manual elements

Fully documented procedures with outline flowcharts and detailed work instructions will be contained in the provider's quality manual and used by auditors as the source from which to develop an audit trail. Examples of documentation are given in Figures 8.6, 8.7, 8.8, 8.9a and 8.9b.

DORSET SKILLS TRAINING	
Quality System Procedure	No: AA-001
Title TRAINEE REVIEW PROCEDURE	Page 1 of 3

Scope

This procedure relates to all trainee reviews instituted by authorised staff concerning trainees involved in the following aspects of their training programme under the contract for Dorset Skills Training.

　i)　Work experience with a work placement accepted under the quality criteria relating to the procurement of such a work placement.

　ii)　Directed training with a sub-contractor approved under the relevant quality criteria but not listed under i).

This procedure relates to:

　i)　Youth Training.
　ii)　Employment Training.
　iii) Foundation Training.

Responsibility

It is the responsibility of the training co-ordinator to ensure that this trainee review procedure is maintained.

It is the overall responsibility of the quality manager to ensure that corrective action regarding nonconformance is taken in accordance with the procedures.

It is the overall responsibility of the quality manager to ensure that the corrective timescales are adhered to.

Originator	Quality manager	
Approved	Head of training programmes	
Date of Issue	July 1992	Issue Number 1

Figure 8.6 Trainee review – scope and responsibility

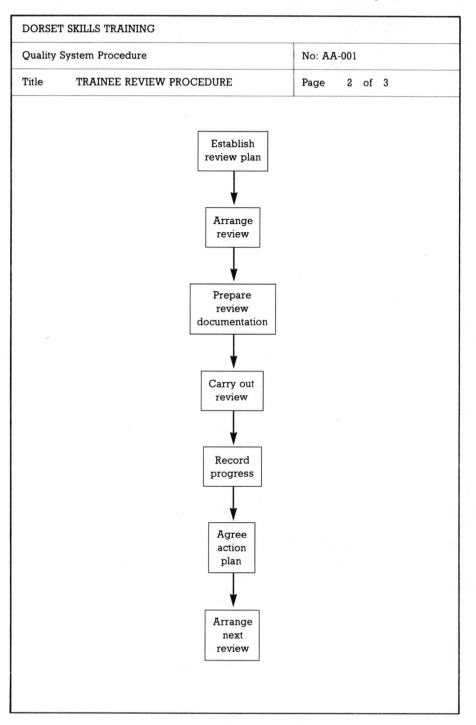

DORSET SKILLS TRAINING

Quality System Procedure | No: AA-001

Title   TRAINEE REVIEW PROCEDURE | Page   2   of   3

Establish
review plan

Arrange
review

Prepare
review
documentation

Carry out
review

Record
progress

Agree
action
plan

Arrange
next
review

Figure 8.7 Trainee review flowchart

DORSET SKILLS TRAINING	
Quality System Procedure	No: AA-001
Title TRAINEE REVIEW	Page 3 of 3

Procedure	Documentation ref:
1.1 Establish for each trainee at induction, a review plan specifying minimum of four negotiable target dates per year pro rata	
1.2 Transfer trainee review plans to master review programme forward planner.	10/A
2.1 Arrange the review and ensure that the employer's representative, supervisor/trainer and trainee are notified of the arrangements.	
2.2 Update master review programme forward planner.	
3.1 Compile a set of review documents.	9/1/A, 9/2/A 10/B, 10/C 10/D, 10/E
4.1 Ensure that the review group comprises: the training co-ordinator, trainee and other interested persons, e.g. careers officers, employers, work-based supervisor, TEC etc.	
4.2 Carry out the review and evaluate progress to date and outcomes of action agreed during previous review.	
5.1 Agree and record progress in each category specified in the review sheet.	
6.1 Identify trainee requirements and agree action to be taken and target dates for completion.	
6.2 Negotiate date of next review.	
6.3 Ensure that the reviewer, trainee and interested persons sign and date the review sheet, where appropriate.	
6.4 Issue trainee with original review sheet.	
6.5 File review sheet copy in trainee file.	
6.6 Update trainee review plan and master review programme forward planner.	
7.1 Store the records securely in the training co-ordinator's office.	

Document key

10/A	Master review programme forward planner.	Originator	Quality manager
9/1/A	Personal training plan (YT)	Approved	Head of training programmes
9/2/A	Personal training plan (ET)		
10/B	YT review sheet	Date of Issue	July 1992
10/C	Occupational training review sheet (ET)	Issue Number	1
10/D/E	Attendance record sheet NROVA		

Figure 8.8 Trainee review procedure

DORSET SKILLS TRAINING	
Quality System Procedure	No: AA-001
Title **TRAINEE REVIEW PROCEDURE**	Page 1 of 2

WORK INSTRUCTION

The training co-ordinator will:

1.1   Complete trainee review plan.

1.2   Arrange trainee review.

1.3   Carry out the review.

1.4   Complete trainee review sheet.

1.5   Issue trainee with completed review sheet.

1.6   Arrange next review date.

1.7   Return trainee file to training co-ordinator's office.

Figure 8.9a Trainee review work instructions

DORSET SKILLS TRAINING	
Quality System Procedure	No: AA-001
Title TRAINEE REVIEW PROCEDURE	Page 2 of 2

WORK INSTRUCTION

The Dorset Skills Training secretary will:

1.1   Maintain master review planner.

1.2   Compile a set of review documents including –

YT personal training plan	9/1/A
ET personal training plan	9/2/A
YT review sheet	10/B
ET occupational review sheet	10/C
Attendance records	10/D/E.

1.3   Photocopy completed trainee review sheet and place in trainee file.

1.4   Update master review planner.

1.5   Store trainee file in the training co-ordinator's office.

Figure 8.9b Trainee review work instructions

An *aide-mémoire* or checklist of specific and open-ended questions to be asked about execution of responsibilities and implementation of procedures will be prepared by the auditor. The list should be comprehensive enough to guide discussion and enquiry, and enable sufficient evidence to be collected that will reliably verify procedures. Examination should also reveal nonconformance. The object of the audit is to find out whether or not the quality system is meeting customer requirements.

Evidence

The scope of a review will be defined according to the needs of the organisation concerned. There can be no single descriptor that will meet every requirement, but certain features are found to be common to many types of review. One of the most important features is the need to select and gather evidence. During audits of provider's systems, information about the effectiveness of the training services against contracts and specified performance criteria is gathered. Opportunities for learners to acquire skills and experience in the workplace are noted. Feedback from learners about their activities on the provider's premises and the benefits and disadvantages of working in particular placements is collected.

Reliable data is needed for use when assessing evidence, drawing conclusions and making recommendations. Data-free reviews and subjective opinion will not normally be reliable. The value of data gathered will be limited as there is a need to support judgement with hard evidence.

Sources of reliable (if not recent) evidence may be derived from a study of annual reports, minutes of course team meetings and leaver surveys. Current information, such as regularly-updated performance indicators, can normally be obtained from the provider's management information system.

Analysis of review material and its interpretation will be quantified and summarised in a report of the review findings.

Report and summary

Findings, including a list of major and minor deficiencies and non-conformances discovered during audits or reviews, will be included in a report of service results. This will be presented, together with a summary of data gathered. An interpretation of the quality of service provided will be reported, together with conclusions and recommendations. Comments will be justified and recommendations clearly defined. Operational constraints should be recognised and care taken to ensure that recommendations are realistic and possible to implement.

The draft may incorporate details of changes recommended, together with suggested means of implementation. A final report will normally be circulated.

Implementing the recommendations

The implementation phase of any plan to introduce change must be carefully handled (see Chapter 2). The organisational climate, as perceived by employees, will be shaped by the effectiveness of supervisors in managing organisational behaviour, interpersonal relations and their own leadership styles.

The role of steering groups, using a form of critical path to implementation, based on a timescale agreed with the staff, is another important feature of planning for change. The group will initiate action on report recommendations and disseminate information regarding the project. It will monitor and evaluate progress and ensuing change in the area of implementation, and the effects of implementation (anticipated and unexpected) on other parts of the organisation.

A constructive approach is needed. This should be aimed at creating the right conditions before introducing changes and be backed by reasonable and adequate consultation with the staff affected by proposed changes.

Once the climate is judged to be satisfactory, staff will be given responsibility for planning and implementing changes. Before doing so, it is essential to obtain the commitment of those concerned in doing what needs to be done and setting targets for completions, reviews and progress reports. People will work more effectively and efficiently when reasonable deadlines have been agreed.

Some managers fail to understand that initially not everyone in the organisation will necessarily benefit from change in the same way that the business as a whole or the management team itself might. It is important to ask 'What's in it for the other players?' Simply trying to sell the proposals will not do. Bottom-up processes can and often do work, provided that genuine openness is practised and there is adequate consultation, listening and empowerment of the staff. Staff will need to own the process of change for they are unlikely to welcome its imposition.

Quality probe – service results

- Do outcomes consistently conform to contracts negotiated with purchasers?
- Does the product or service meet the requirements and expectations of the clients or users?
- Are assessments valid and reliable?
- Are results correctly recorded?
- Are nonconformances controlled?
- Is necessary corrective action taken?
- Is statistical data analysed in terms of performance indicators?
- Is our service reliable and do we deliver value for money?

Notes

1 L. Walklin, *The Assessment of Performance and Competence,* Stanley Thornes (Publishers) Ltd, Cheltenham, June 1991. (A practical guide that clearly describes the sequence of planning, teaching and assessing activities necessary to ensure that learner competence can be developed and levels of achievement monitored.)

2 BS 4778:Part 1 (1987), *Quality vocabulary,* p. 9, para. 3.20.

3 *Guidance notes for the application of BS 5750/ISO 9000/EN 29000 to education and training,* p. 10, para. 4.14, BSI Quality Assurance, Milton Keynes, Sixth draft, January 1991.

CHAPTER NINE

Monitoring and Evaluating the Service Provision

Chapter coverage

Systematic monitoring and evaluation
    Quality assurance aspects
    The purpose of M&E
    Gathering data
    Analysis of strengths and weaknesses
    Considerations
    Operational features
Suggestions for successful implementation

Systematic monitoring and evaluation

A matter that now concerns all teachers, trainers and providers is the systematic monitoring and evaluation (M&E) of educational and training processes. This, together with the need to maintain quality in an efficient and effective organisational environment, is now fast becoming a universal requirement.

Monitoring is the process of gathering useful information and 'keeping the train on the rails'. In other words, by continuously observing and reporting on method, content and outcomes, control of the educational experiences can be maintained. This monitoring process enables under-performance and poor service to be detected before it is too late to do anything to put

178

matters right. Where necessary, changes can be made in response to feedback coming from the monitoring process and this helps to prevent making the same mistakes the next time round.

Nonconformances and problems detected by the monitoring process should be corrected at once.

Quality probe – monitoring

Is there a system and documented procedure for monitoring service processes and gathering relevant information?

Does the system cover:

- the design of training provision?
- the direct observation of the training or support process in action?
- interviewing the target group?
- data collection?
- analysing the effectiveness of the training provision?
- post-training support?

Evaluation is a process of establishing precisely what has happened during an educational or training experience and the effect it had on the learner. The efficiency and effectiveness of the learning process may either be measured against some standard or an attempt may be made to judge or assess its worth in terms of client learning and achievement of competence.

Assessing the extent to which both the organisation's and the client's objectives have been met is an essential part of any evaluation process. Feedback from monitoring and evaluation of performance-related activities is one of the keys to validating policies, plans and procedures operating within the organisation.

From the provider's point of view, feedback will be obtained whether or not course planning and provision actually meet clients' needs and more detailed criteria, such as:

- meeting organisational objectives for the course and client group;
- providing learning opportunities and experiences that usefully and effectively enable clients to achieve specified performance criteria and attain their personal training-related goals;
- organising instruction and providing continuity, sequence and integration of learning experiences;
- enabling a process of monitoring and evaluation to take place.

Evaluation of feedback shows how the provision is succeeding in achieving its objectives and meeting users' requirements.

Quality probe – evaluation

- Is there a system and documented procedures for evaluating the training provision?
- Does the system include procedures for:
    gathering information and evidence?
    analysing and assessing data gathered?
    comparing actual outcomes with intended outcomes?
    disseminating results, conclusions and recommendations for change?
    continuous improvement?
    resourcing the cost of changes?

Quality assurance aspects

Quality conscious organisations in the education and training business will be aware of the need systematically to monitor and evaluate their inputs and outputs. Policies and procedures relating to provision, total quality management and BS 5750 will require that monitoring and evaluation becomes an integral part of management philosophy. Organisations do not have to get involved in quality assurance processes but, as Deming suggests, 'Survival is not compulsory.' It is therefore reasonable to assume that organisations need to do something about embedding monitoring and evaluation into everyday activities and, in particular, to sample clients' perceptions of the service provided.

The purpose of M&E

The key purpose of a M&E system is to collect and use information which will improve awareness of providers' courses and facilities available to potential learners and employers. The quality of the overall package (learning opportunities, resources, course material, instruction, assessment, environment and other features) offered to clients will be made public. The validity of provision to current and predicted industrial, commercial, education and training needs will be confirmed.

General aim

The aim of introducing a system is to review, refine and implement techniques for monitoring and evaluation in order to enhance the quality of education and training provision, and promote client satisfaction.

Specific objectives

Typical objectives of providers' M&E systems are to:

- review and refine the work already undertaken in departmental course evaluation and to form an overview of monitoring and evaluation across the organisation.
- develop a system of monitoring and evaluation of provision at course level, integrating qualitative and quantitative strategies.
- exploit the potential of management information systems for monitoring and evaluation purposes.
- develop and implement procedures for course evaluation within the context of strategic management.
- apply and evaluate the systems developed and monitor and adapt as appropriate.
- produce interim reports and, where necessary, identify future strategies, participants and course teams.
- provide staff development opportunities and management support for all M&E activities.
- disseminate information about the system and implement M&E strategies throughout the organisation.
- develop and enhance the quality of provision to clients.
- share information and outcomes with clients, partners, other providers and services.

Gathering data

Information is selected and gathered to suit the needs of individual departments while providing essential data needed to inform the management information system. The provider's managers should be able to assess processed data in terms of:

- its usefulness in achieving the aims and objectives of the provider's mission and operational plan;
- the ease with which the information can be collated, assessed and effectively used, in order to achieve the specified objectives from the points of view of:
    the provider's management;
    course provision and departmental management;
    course teams and curriculum development;
    client's perceptions of the provision and outcomes.

Systematic monitoring and evaluation is not only worthwhile but essential to effective management and planning at all levels. The process should be refined and simplified as far as possible so that it becomes an integral operational element of the provision.

Quality probe – gathering information

When planning the evaluation process:

- who will design the evaluation system?
- what key questions will be asked?
- how will information be gathered?
- how will the data gathered be collated, analysed and summarised?
- who will process the data and identify strengths and weaknesses?
- what will be done as a result?
- how will recommended action be prioritised and implemented?
- how will modifications to processes be resourced?
- who will monitor the implementation of changes?
- who will be responsible for the process?

When gathering information:

- who should be asked for information? (Will staff, users, employers, sponsors and third-party observers be consulted?)
- how will data be captured? (Will interview, questionnaire, checklists and training programme records be used?)

Analysis of strengths and weaknesses

Strengths

- Practical information for managing the provision will become available including:
  recruitment pattern;
  analysis of client group data;
  profile of entry;
  marketing.
- Information for improving the provision relating to:
  initial assessment;
  induction;
  interviewing;
  planning and preparing the programme content;
  planning and delivery processes;
  balance of the provision.

Weaknesses

- Too much information may be gathered about the environment, facilities, accommodation etc., rather than highlighting main problems.
- Course monitoring is better analysed separately.
- The evaluation programme may become too complex and will fall into disuse.

The process of collection and analysis of information must not become too time consuming.

Considerations

The process of sampling client groups and evaluating existing M&E strategies within a department can give rise to a number of features for consideration:

- raising more questions than answers;
- staff development needs;
- the need for customisation of documentation;
- the M&E teams' requirement for time and other resource support in order to operate;
- ideas for rationalisation of policies and procedures;
- the need for additional instruments relating to areas of special interest;
- the validity of information collected and the subsequent analysis, synthesis and evaluation of the processed data.

Other important issues that may be identified are:

- a need for the design or refinement of operational systems;
- a review of curriculum entitlement for clients and associated provision design considerations.

Operational features

The size of groups sampled may affect the reliability of information gathered. Conclusions drawn from relatively small and possibly unrepresentative samples may be invalid and open to misinterpretation. However, contributors to the process, such as students, employers, sponsors and provider's staff are generally supportive and helpful.

Positive and constructive views of the environment, course style and content will impact on action planning and lobbying of departmental and provider's management. Confirmation of clients' high regard for staff professionalism and provision is gratifying when forthcoming, but some comments heard may be very controversial and of considerable concern if staff are adversely criticised. When comments are critical of a particular lecturer or trainer it is difficult to know how best to handle this information.

The mode of completion of a course M&E questionnaire (the instrument) may affect the responses, depending on whether or not clients are supervised while form-filling. The issue of confidentiality in respect of data gathered from clients must also be considered.

In order to facilitate meaningful returns from clients, some instruments used may need rethinking with regard to language, presentation and in some cases purpose. Time and labour to customise the instruments will then be needed. Teams sometimes change instrument content or layout to suit their particular needs and subject areas, and these adaptations often prove helpful.

Some questionnaires tend to invite negative and unhelpful comments from clients. If this is the case, changes will be needed so as to encourage constructive criticism. Groups surveyed should include a representative sample from each main vocational area.

Participants may question the validity of collecting and analysing data and information if nothing appears to happen after questionnaires have been completed. They should perceive that action has been taken and that results are being achieved in response to their comments. This applies equally to the implementation of action called for within departments or across the whole organisation.

Course team meetings are very useful in terms of interchanging views, ideas and progress. Teams see the benefits of process and outcomes, but the question of funding for research must be resolved early in the process. Pressure on staff time tends to raise questions from them on just what can be done without additional time allowance.

Teams develop into very cohesive, mutually supportive and competent units. This developing expertise proves invaluable when embedding M&E systems throughout organisations.

Pressure on departments to perform, in terms of staff/client ratios or unit costs, raises questions about the quality of course provision. When clients raise complaints about courses or other aspects of provision there is a tendency for them to expect immediate positive changes. When these changes are not forthcoming there is often a sense of disappointment and frustration.

Once clients have completed questionnaires their interest is aroused and they understandably wish to discuss the findings. This takes time and if the M&E process becomes operational, staff will have to take on-board work involved in operating the system. It is therefore necessary to stress the need for adequate resourcing if the type of activity undertaken by M&E teams is to be extended to the entire provision.

Excessively long questionnaires may be off-putting to clients sampled and M&E teams may be concerned about the considerable volume of data generated. Probably the most time-consuming element of the process will be extracting information from questionnaires for analysis. A team may well take an hour to extract information from a sample of 25 forms.

The workload generated by responses from a small sample, when scaled up on a pro rata basis to departmental or organisation-wide implementation, requires structured guidance and training in large-volume data handling and processing for the team. Labour and technology to handle the data generated would also be needed. Presentation of this information in a numerical and (where useful) graphical format could be carried out using a computer and spreadsheet program.

The administration of questionnaires, collation of responses and handling of related documentation is a huge task. If it is to be done properly and the outcomes are to be acted upon it needs managing. It is suggested that one person be given a sufficient time allocation and responsibility for managing the M&E process across their department. Otherwise a team of several staff could be employed in monitoring and evaluating the operations and clients' opinions of the provision.

Providers need to undertake this activity if they are to be responsive to the needs of clients and employers, to continue to attract learners and to deliver education and training in accordance with departmental plans.

Embedding any development, such as M&E, requires a certain ownership by M&E team members and clients. As stakeholders in the outcomes they must be convinced of the relevance of the process and resulting benefits, and not feel trapped within a paper-bound context. Sensitive negotiations will be required to assure staff that the process is not a thinly-disguised appraisal exercise. It would be naive however to hide the fact that issues of appraisal are explicitly raised by client and employer perceptions of the course or training programme, and of the provider.

M&E is an implicit part of the culture of curriculum development, delivery and the evolving of effective provision. We all monitor and evaluate experiences to a larger or lesser degree, but a formal M&E process does consume a good deal of time.

With the TECs and other sponsors demanding formal M&E as an explicit part of the curriculum the following issues will need to be addressed by staff and providers' managers:

- staff development needs;
- administrative staff costs and needs;
- the course team structure and timetable for meetings;
- M&E policy, procedures, processes and products.
- ongoing customisation to suit various course teams and subject groups;
- the individuals who will undertake quality assurance aspects of M&E.

With regard to actions and outcomes deriving from the processes of M&E analysis, it is necessary to give careful consideration to the allowance for an appropriate lead-time to implementation of improvements. If staff and clients are to have confidence in the system, specific observable outcomes in terms of client achievement and course development will need to become apparent reasonably quickly.

An analysis of M&E factors could well give statistical force to the need for additional funding for organising and taking practical action in terms of enhancing facilities. Needs relating to the environment, customer care and the client services department, for example, could well be highlighted, together with other non-teaching support requirements involving additional financing.

Information gleaned about marketing education suggests that clients may first learn of the provision either from promotional material, open nights and friends or by contacting the organisation directly. The careers person is a key figure in terms of clients finding out about continuing education provision. Regrettably, providers' publicity material is often not widely available in schools or in other locations where it might profitably be displayed or distributed. Further education enrolment is, in some cases, difficult and time-consuming. Procedures for gaining access are frequently neither clear nor user-friendly.

Informal discussions with teachers and others indicates that, as in many cases where change or innovation is in progress, there can be feelings of uncertainty and temporary loss of direction. While academic staff, backed by support staff, are willing to give of their best to make things work and take on board new concepts, they need support and guidance at all stages of implementation.

M&E team members have to work very hard to gain greater insight and experience while undertaking M&E trials and developmental work. In some instances, team members need positive direction so that all members will reach the intended location rather than some ending up in a cul-de-sac wondering how they arrived there.

Such direction might include:

- A single M&E model to be adopted across the organisation. The model to be agreed with departmental course teams.
- Details of the nature or classification of data needed to advise the management information system.
- The scope and extent of resourcing to be made available in terms of human and material resources to facilitate the work; to raise awareness at all levels of staffing; to disseminate good method and practice; and to actually embed the M&E process in those areas selected (if not throughout the provision).
- The possibility of setting up and staffing a centralised M&E unit, backed by departmental representatives and possibly linked with a student

services unit. (Much of the data captured often relates to non-teaching features, such as enrolments, inductions, information flows, fabric of buildings, classrooms and workshops, facilities and environment.)

- The needs of different sectors of the operation, such as the organisation management team, heads of department and their managers, course teams, other departmental elements and clients.

Suggestions for successful implementation

A rationalisation of the system processes and instruments to be used is recommended. This will result in an initial instrument that provides marketing data and an end-of-course instrument that monitors perceptions, shortcomings and good points of the provision. The latter must be seen as having positive features for improving the organisation and benefiting clients, rather than as a device for clients to complain.

Instruments that may be considered as important additions to those used at the beginning and end of courses could comprise:

- an employer's instrument (monitoring perceptions and satisfaction);
- a work-placement instrument (monitoring aspects of client placements and work-provider's opinions);
- an attrition instrument (monitoring clients who leave courses early).

The plan would be to build an overall profile of each course from the instruments. This would then be used to make comparisons between one year or course and the next, as well as to track progress and target problem areas. Results would be entered onto a profile and an action plan developed. This process would yield useful information about:

- resources in different subjects or occupational areas;
- the need for individual or small group tutorial support;
- the curriculum;
- how staff might evaluate their own practices.

Marketing strategies could be improved by promoting courses using methods such as making available individual leaflets to libraries, community centres and what might be termed 'unconventional locations'. Once clients have made contact and initial assessment has taken place then what is agreed at interview should be followed up with a letter offering them a place. It is appreciated that clients often forget what they are told due to nerves. An induction pack could be given out on arrival. A general one could be compiled for the organisation with perhaps separate ones for each department and in some cases divisions within departments.

Other recommendations for improvements might include:

- ensuring school and careers teachers receive provider's leaflets and brochures;
- providing staff development training on interviewing techniques, initial assessment and induction techniques;
- ensuring provider's leaflets are on display in reception and other strategic locations;
- simplifying the enrolment or joining procedures;
- improving the infrastructure (non-course factors);
- appreciating the significance of the Careers Service in terms of clients finding out about the provision.

For the continuing process to be seen to be of value by staff and clients there will need to be:

- observable commitment by management and tangible results;
- statements of intent on resourcing and responses to the various perceptions being recorded.

The introduction of systematic monitoring and evaluation of provision results in examples of good practice being captured, documented and cascaded. Cohesive teams are developed with excellent interaction and mutual support. Areas of need and shortcomings in relation to client entitlement are highlighted, thus enabling M&E team members to promote management by exception.

Everyone becomes a winner when M&E aspects of TQM are implemented and acted upon.

CHAPTER TEN

Audits and Probes

Chapter coverage

Using probes
  The business cycle
  Reviews, probes and audits
  Internal quality audits
  Consultants
Problem solving
  Brainstorming
  Pareto analysis
  Cause and effect analysis
Linking audit feedback to service provision
  Quality assurance and organisational evaluation
  Monitoring and assessing quality
  Quality records
  Management reviews and quality audits
  Annual review of performance and planning
  A team approach to audits
Administration audit
  Administrative services
  Paperwork flows
  Staffing
  Financing management
  Administrative support for trainers
  Learner documentation
  Record-keeping
  Trainer documentation
  Certification
Environment and resource audit
  Accommodation

    Resources
    Effectiveness of the provision
    Policies
    Audit – training strategies
    Physical resource inputs
    Human resource inputs
External affairs audit
    Liaising with awarding bodies
    Purchasing services
Marketing
    Design and promotion
    Publicity
    Client liaison skills

Using probes

It is likely that all activities and functions concerned with the attainment of quality will be subject to continuous review in order to assure quality of the provision. Such reviews may comprise a mix of self-evaluation and planned and documented audits that are essential components of any quality management system. Where possible a co-operative 'all-one-team' approach to internal audits and probes should be used to verify service compliance with approved procedures, rather than antagonistic interrogative appraisals.

The business cycle

Training providers, like many other enterprises, operate a business cycle. Initially, policy and objectives will be based upon recent offerings, market research forecasts, statistical predictions, herd instinct or sometimes intuitive guesses. Strategies and operational plans will be formulated and drafted, and resources allocated. Then the plans will be implemented and the service delivered.

It is at this point that the cycle ends for some providers who operate a 'take it or leave it' business. But in a quality-assured business there will be a continuous review of performance and results, and checking of outcomes against contract or specification. Processes and procedures will be controlled and corrective action will be taken in the event of non-conformance to contract. An important feature of using quality audits is the ability to establish just where the organisation is at the time of the audit. Then by using audit data it is possible to decide what needs to be done to meet the requirements of the business plan. The business cycle described above is summarised in Figure 10.1.

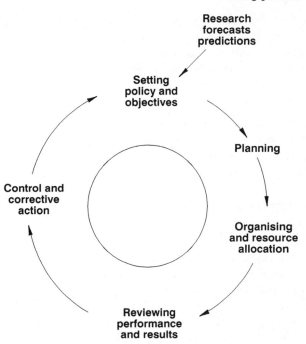

Figure 10.1 The business cycle

Reviews, probes and audits

The Further Education Unit (FEU) firmly believes that evaluation of performance of the FE service – at all levels, from course team through to national schemes – can only benefit our clients, whether these are individual students or employers. In addition, systematic and regular evaluation, which is in any case increasingly being required of us by external agencies, can not only promote the further improvement of the service but also provide important evidence of this improvement and of what factors are important for its maintenance.[1]

To **review** is to look back at part or all of the service provided. The object being to examine in some detail how effectively the service performed when compared with operational objectives, standards and customer requirements. Neither the attribution of blame to others nor the requirement to give plausible reasons when things go wrong should be encouraged. Time and ingenuity devoted to defending oneself or subordinates will neither help solve problems nor put things right. Reviewing should be a normal management routine that enables strengths and weaknesses of the provision to be identified and the efficiency of resource utilisation to be evaluated.

Reviews should be perceived as being constructive rather than as a means of attributing blame or as a device used to expose people's shortcomings.

Service audits are a means of establishing or verifying the performance of systems. It is therefore important systematically to check, analyse and address processes that are critical to effective operation. Changes and improvements will be needed where audits reveal weaknesses in systems or obsolete procedures. Feedback derived from audits must be used to restore the effectiveness of the quality system.

Audits can be expensive; it may not be useful to spend a lot of time and financial resources confirming that things that appear to be working well and meeting standards are precisely on target. Better to dig where there is most to be found – where customers are not getting value for money.

Internal quality audits

Internal audits of the provider's quality systems and documented procedures are carried out by trained and competent auditors employed by the training provider. Auditors are usually drawn from areas that are not involved in the activity being reviewed or they may have independent roles. The objective is to use people who are not concerned directly with the management or work of the department undergoing audit. This measure of independence is more likely to ensure that an even-handed and impartial approach is adopted. Where necessary, these auditors will be used to audit and review sub-contractors and work placement providers who are supplying services.

Audits will be scheduled throughout the year so that all activities are covered twice or more frequently, as appropriate. Planned audits will be necessary in order to avoid disrupting work patterns too much and activities to be audited will be prioritised according to need, work schedules or urgency.

The FEU commissioned a team of senior managers (led by Michael McAllister) to undertake a study, part of which included a literature search that suggested five possible approaches to the concept of educational effectiveness and its measurement. These approaches are reproduced in Figure 10.2.

Goal achievement	– The capability of an institution to achieve its objectives.
Resource allocation	– The capability of an institution to attract sufficient resources to ensure its survival.
Internal processes	– The means by which an institution attempts to ensure its effectiveness.
Participant satisfaction	– The degree to which an institution meets the requirements of its students, clients and staff.
Social justice	– The degree to which an institution is successful as an instrument of social policy.

Source: *Towards an educational audit*, FEU[2]

Figure 10.2 Measures of educational effectiveness

Today, many organisations are reviewing where they are at a given time and will use the approaches suggested by McAllister and his team. The results of reviews and 'DIY' quality audits can be compared with operational plans and with the TECs' (or other sponsoring agent's) quality expectations. When the provider's work is sub-contracted, audits should embrace sub-contractor's systems.

Improvements resulting from audits are often linked with total quality systems operating within the organisation.

> **Some providers prefer to have the results of audits externally assessed by external consultants and while this can be expensive, credibility and currency may be enhanced. Third-party auditing is carried out by BSI and other accredited organisations.**

Consultants

A **consultant** may be defined as:
a qualified person who provides service to industry, commerce, education or the public by identifying and investigating problems or by confirming compliance with service standards and customer requirements.

Consultants may be required to probe systems, gather and diagnose data, identify criteria and options, make recommendations and propose action for implementation designed to solve problems. Alternatively, they may be asked to conduct quality system audits.

Consultation is a voluntary relationship where two or more people meet in order to take counsel or to seek information, guidance or advice from the other or from each other, as the case may be. In an article published in *The Times* (2 December 1987) Edward Fennell described 14 different roles that consultants may be called upon to adopt. The roles are as follows:

- A catalyst and adviser – to identify the issues and potential pitfalls in a client's situation and prompt or advise on appropriate action to reach long-term goals.
- A fact finder – to gather data and identify the key implications.
- An auditor – to review a client's situation and problem areas; analyse and present the results.
- A technical expert – to provide technical information and suggestions for policy and practice decisions.
- A system specialist – to apply specific methodology involving client participation.
- A collaborator in problem solving – to operate as a team member offering alternatives and advising on options.
- An advocate – to propose guidelines and make recommendations.

- A reflector – to raise questions that should be reflected upon.
- A trainer and educator – to design learning experiences and train the client.
- A solution provider – to provide a discrete service or product specific to a client's stated needs.
- An enabler – to identify alternatives and resources for clients and help assess the consequences.
- A facilitator – to direct clients in analytical processes, challenge thinking and conclusions, and promote broader capability.
- An influencer – to seek and gain a broad commitment for specific action.
- An implementer – to assist or lead implementation of the recommendations.

Innovators will need to examine strengths and weaknesses of the existing provision and be able to perceive the need for change. They will need to introduce change and experimentation. So as to remain active in some of the now fiercely competitive areas of what was, at one time, unquestionably further and adult education territory, innovators will need to promote an entrepreneurial thrust and take other staff along with them.

Implementers will need to be competent in service development as well as being good communicators. They will need to be able to set up a teamwork approach to development work and service delivery, and be knowledgeable in relevant areas, such as validity and reliability of provision. Communicators with team-building skills will play an important part in maintaining direction and harmony by encouraging a consultative atmosphere within the team.

Quality controllers will ensure that assurance procedures are in place so that the quality and appropriateness of service resources and methods may be validated before delivery and during later M&E checks.

Monitoring staff will regularly review the provision and will report on the effectiveness of the service delivered. Information and opinion will be gathered, sifted and evaluated, to ensure that customer requirements are being met. When standards are not being met, the monitoring process will allow improvements to be made before it is too late to put things right.

Evaluators, in consultation with team members, will make decisions on the basis of data gathered during the monitoring programme. A key question that will always be in the evaluator's mind is 'Has the right quality of service been provided and has the product or experience been effective?' Other matters of concern for evaluators involve the question of cost effectiveness of the provision. This sort of question will often give rise to conflicts relating to management needs to perform within targets or efficiency ratios and those who may be committed to excellence at any cost.

The planning and delivery of future provision will be affected by outcomes of the M&E process and hence monitoring and evaluation will be a very important procedure for any provider. Meanwhile, some or all of the consultancy roles referred to by Edward Fennell, together with a selection of those listed above, will need to be fulfilled either by the provider's staff or by third-party consultants.

When initial assessment or audit is carried out by registered third parties their role may be to:

- survey, review, checklist, record and analyse all current quality processes.
- examine the quality manual, written procedures and records.
- assess each set of audit results.
- make a comparison with BS 5750, ISO 9000, EN 29000, Ford QI, TEC or other standards.
- identify weaknesses in systems.
- propose and agree corrective actions and advise on new arrangements.
- supervise rectification work.
- carry out a final review and assessment.
- follow up by conducting periodic monitoring and auditing.

Where audits of systems and procedures indicate **nonconformity**, that is, when the process or outcomes fail to comply with accepted standards or norms, logical cause and effect type analyses will need to be carried out immediately. Brainstorming can also be used to generate ideas about possible causes of a problem and to suggest possible solutions, but grabbing at straws and making panic decisions are not very effective in restoring control.

Problem solving

There are a number of techniques that may be used to aid continuous quality improvement and to identify and analyse quality problems such as causes of nonconformances. The problem-solving technique or 'quality improvement tool' selected will depend upon the nature of the problem and the time, expertise and resources available. But neither employing vast resources nor using tools and techniques will alone solve problems. It is people that solve problems and it is unlikely that solutions will be found and implemented without having their commitment, support and active involvement. Prioritising the sequence in which problems will be solved and the cost effectiveness of resources allocated will however be an important consideration.

> ## Quality probe – problem solving
>
> - Is a structured approach adopted for problem solving?
> - Are adequate facilities available for information gathering and data interpretation?
> - Are problem analysis techniques, such as brainstorming, cause and effect analysis and Pareto analysis used to help identify potential causes and suggest possible solutions?
> - Is there a logical approach to developing solutions and implementing corrective action, and monitoring the results of the innovation?

Brainstorming

Brainstorming is used to generate ideas that may be used during later stages of problem solving. This technique is widely used in quality circles as a means of drawing out from members creative thoughts about the causes of problems and their possible solutions. To be productive the method depends upon a number of key rules, such as:

- Carefully describe the quality improvement sought or specific problem to be solved.
- Encourage creativity and fluidity of expression. Promote divergent thinking.
- Ensure openness and freedom from ridicule or criticism.
- Go for a large quantity of offerings regardless of apparent quality of content.
- Record, without discussion or evaluation, each and every idea as it is generated – reject nothing at this stage.
- Allow a period of time for reflection.
- Follow up with an analysis and evaluation of ideas generated during the brainstorming session.
- Discuss the effect of implementing ideas and reach a consensus about which ideas can be used to best effect.

Pareto analysis

A **Pareto analysis** was originally carried out by Vilfredo Pareto, an Italian sociologist and economist. He used the analysis to express the frequency distribution of incomes in a society, finding that about 80 per cent of the wealth was owned by 20 per cent of the population. Pareto's 80:20 principle relates to many other facets of personal and commercial life, although the actual ratio of percentages may vary somewhat. It is a technique that can be adapted to allow people to identify the relatively few aspects of a provision that lead to the bulk of complaints or problems needing urgent attention. The outcome is to focus attention on correcting the design or provision of the relatively few product types that generate most nonconformances and adversely affect the customer service or product supplied. It could be described as a way of increasing the probability of 'digging where there is most gold' in the quest for quality improvement and meeting customer requirements.

Cause and effect analysis

This technique can be used to establish the root **cause** of a problem or nonconformance that leads to an observable **effect**. Having defined the effect, the investigating team will need to chart possible causes on a **fishbone** diagram, such as that given in Figure 10.3. The completed diagram is then used as an aid when diagnosing the actual cause or causes prior to developing and implementing a remedy.

The essential steps of a cause and effect analysis include:

- identifying the effect of nonconformance;
- constructing the fishbone diagram;
- adding appropriate causal headings;
- brainstorming potential causes;
- adding suggestions to the diagram;
- evaluating suggestions while seeking likely major causes;
- prioritising checks of probable causes and taking corrective action;
- recording corrective action and monitoring implementation;

There are many other 'tools' that may be used within the quality assurance function and these include: quality data analysis, process capability studies, quality circle implementation, quality cost reports and analysis, and statistical quality control. But there should be in place procedures for controlling nonconforming products and services. These procedures should include the means of detecting causes of quality problems arising and ways of controlling the effect. Corrective actions taken, following an analysis of the failure to meet specified customer requirements or non-compliance with procedures, should be designed to remove permanently the causes of nonconformance. In addition, there should be a continuing analysis of any revised procedure and related customer complaints to ensure that the action taken really has effected a cure.

Corrective action taken to regain control should follow without delay. Records of corrective action should be kept. The effectiveness of corrective actions should then be evaluated in order to prevent further nonconformance.

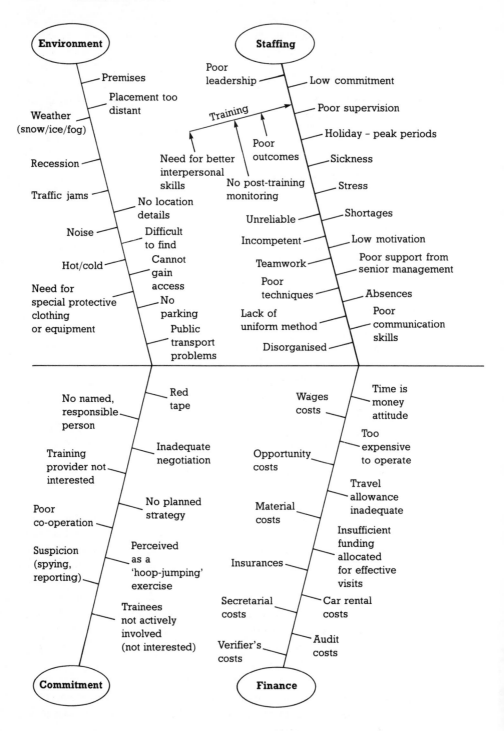

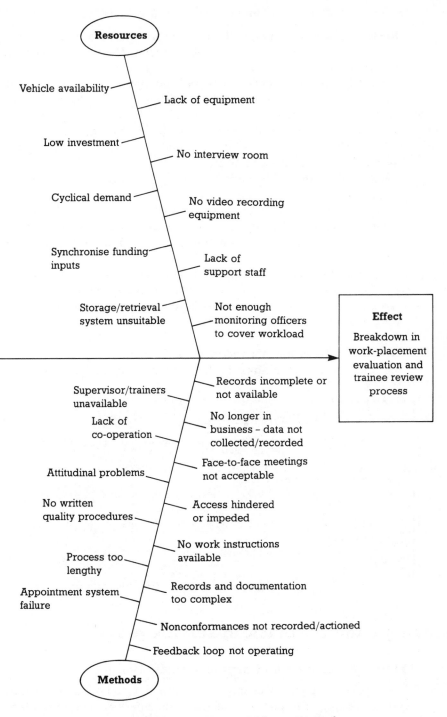

Figure 10.3 Fishbone or Ishikawa diagram[3]

Records should be kept of audit procedures and findings in respect of:

- **Reviews of systems** and **quality manual content** carried out by senior managers. The aim is to establish their relevance to current processes and procedures.
- **Departmental assessments** by an independent third party, such as the staff development officer, together with the head of department or student services manager. The business counterpart might be a department manager, together with the quality manager or representative having direct responsibility for implementing and managing the system and maintaining BS 5750 standards.
- **Sectional assessments** by an independent third party who may be an impartial course team leader drawn from another department, together with a section or division leader from the section under review. The equivalent in business is a supervisor, together with a person nominated by the quality manager or authorised management representative.
- **End-of-training audit** by the provider's M&E team. In business, a finished product audit by the inspection department and quality manager, or in the case of services by the customer services manager and an independent observer.

Where the frequency of nonconformance is relatively high it will be necessary to look again at the procedures manual.

Quality probe – service evaluation

- Is evaluation correctly targeted on the service provision?
- Do audit procedures satisfy the intended purpose?
- Is evaluation cost-effective?
- Does evaluation cover effectiveness and efficiency of the service delivered?
- Does evaluation discriminate against departments, sections or individuals?
- Will the results of evaluation lead to action planning for future improvement?

Linking audit feedback to service provision

Quality assurance and organisational evaluation

The purpose of integrating quality assurance and organisational evaluation within a training provision is to safeguard the interests of customers and continually to enhance business performance. This can be achieved by operating a system that will generate the feedback needed to support the effective, efficient and economic management of resources. Information about quality will be obtained systematically to ensure that a balanced review of performance may be undertaken. This feedback will enable managers to satisfy the control requirements of operational and strategic planning, and will also allow reporting in the context of an accountability pyramid (see Figure 10.4).

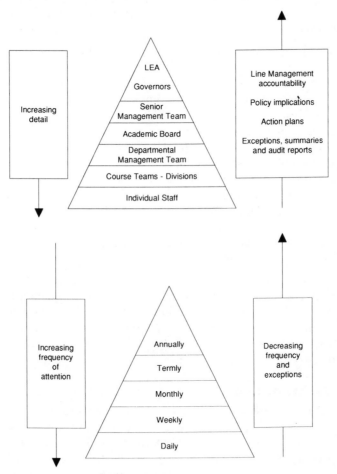

Figure 10.4 Accountability pyramid

Quality assurance

Effective training provision results in satisfied customers; this in turn contributes to staff motivation and high morale. Quality assurance will encompass the evaluation of the learning experience, customer support systems and the objective appraisal of outcomes that include – among other factors – success rates, student retention and progression to other learning opportunities or employment.

Quality assurance will form an important element in the process and reporting procedures that will capture data for use during reviews. Once implemented, the review procedure will ensure continual evaluation of the service provided and promote progressive and continuous improvement in performance.

Organisational evaluation

Organisational evaluation relies upon delegating responsibility to those managers who actually control work, resources and supplier services. Evaluation will embrace a wide range of parameters including:

- organisational arrangements relating to the area under review and the reasons for review;
- relevance to the mission statement and operational objectives;
- quality associated with customer experiences, perceptions and needs analyses;
- staff support and training;
- operational efficiency and effectiveness;
- curriculum review and development;
- systems and resource enhancement and utilisation;
- income generation;
- policy implementation, audit and review procedures.

Monitoring and assessing quality

The system and process of quality assurance will incorporate self-evaluation which is seen to be a key feature of any quality system. This will be backed up with team and line-management evaluation against specified criteria, standards of achievement and performance targets. Unacceptable variance from agreed norms will signal the need to take action to bring the system back under control. This in turn may mean that it will be necessary to carry out an urgent review of policy or reallocate resources.

Quality records

Quality records are an account, in permanent form, preserving information about facts or events relating to some aspect of a quality system. Records may be written or computerised, but should always be easily accessed, read or called up and understood by all concerned (see Figure 10.5). Records should support the achievement of required quality and may contain information about process, content, product and end user.

Information stored should be current and subject to systematic updating. Data should be available for review by management representatives seeking to take action resulting from audits or quality reviews.

Details of corrective action should be recorded whenever remedial work is undertaken to rectify a process or nonconformity of any kind.

'The supplier shall establish and maintain procedures for identification, collection, indexing, filing, storage, maintenance, retrieval and disposition of quality records.

Quality records shall be maintained to demonstrate achievement of the required quality and the effective operation of the quality system. Pertinent sub-contractor quality records shall be an element of these data.

All quality records shall be legible and identifiable to the product involved. Quality records shall be stored in such a way that they are readily retrievable in facilities that provide a suitable environment to minimise deterioration or damage and to prevent loss. Retention times of quality records shall be established and recorded. Where agreed contractually, quality records shall be made available for evaluation by the purchaser or his/her representative for an agreed period.'

Source: BS 5750: Part 1 (1987), para. 4.16.

Figure 10.5 Record keeping

Management reviews and quality audits

Management reviews are a quality system requirement that may take the form of **internal quality audits** supervised by a management representative with direct responsibility for the system. Comprehensive audit procedures should be written and presented in a form that enables reliable objective evidence of system performance to be obtained.

In order to maintain continuing operational effectiveness with quality, at the specified level, and to satisfy the requirements of BS 5750, all levels of system operation should be audited regularly. Data gathered from each of the audits should be collated and presented at an annual system review in order to assess the overall effectiveness of the quality system.

Audit sequence

A sequence for carrying out an audit based on that suggested in the FEU publication *Towards an educational audit*[4] is given in Figure 10.6.

- Establish objectives and scope.
- Establish form of reporting outcomes.
- Create audit team.
- Design audit instrument.
- Provide resources for data collection.
- Gather and record data on the audit instrument.
- Analyse data and apply performance indicators.
- Make essential management decisions and prepare an action plan.
- Review the form in which outcomes will be announced.
- Announce results and execute the action plan.

Figure 10.6 Audit sequence

Annual review of performance and planning

The purpose of an annual review is to inform strategic planning, to help shape policy and to provide reliable information that will support decision making in the allocation and management of resources.

Reviews yield information that facilitate planning and operational control of the provision. Once relevant data has been gathered, the management team can evaluate performance outcomes for the past year and, where necessary, adjust draft operational plans that will have already been prepared for the coming year. Where current plans are already operating, changes in operational targets may have to be made as a result of feedback obtained from the review.

Review meetings provide a valuable opportunity for managers to take part in the process of organisational evaluation and as a group to be accountable for the implementation of a quality-assured provision.

Stan Turner[5] suggests a tentative agenda framework for accountability, quality assurance and institutional evaluation that could take the form of that shown in Figure 10.7.

A team approach to audits

Audits conducted by teams can be used to determine the strengths and weaknesses of the provision and to assess the provider's position relative to competitors. Team members will hold common views and will co-operate, offering support to one another when needed. Individual bias will be reduced and the responsibility for results will be shared by team members so that often a more realistic picture can be obtained.

Enhanced quality and continuous product improvement brought about by a team approach to service evaluation has long been recognised as a key feature in successful businesses. Loyalty to the company and a desire to create a good corporate image is every employee's business, and the idea of operating a total quality policy within a customer-driven business is rapidly gaining ground. The Japanese have been particularly active in this area and have recognised the value of encouraging their people to work together with customers to meet user requirements. They are successful in providing the product or service at the right quality.

A team approach can be used when going through the conventional stages of auditing a service. The stages are:

- assessing one's position in the marketplace;
- assessing the provision and service delivered;
- developing a strategy that will maintain a competitive position, increase profit and otherwise improve the effectiveness and efficiency of operation.

Review of achievements and out-turns (last year)

Enrolments

Staff:student ratios (SSRs)
Average class size (ACS)
Average weekly class-contact lecturer hours (ALH)
Average student hours (ASH)

Unit cost analysis

Curriculum innovation and change:
   staff development;
   teaching schemes;
   systematic evaluation of training needs.

Resource developments

Examination results:
   analysis by numbers, percentages, grades and other indicators.

Retention and progression analysis

Quality assurance:
   oversight of teaching;
   client service agreement.

Review of departmental plans (current year)

Section by section:
   enrolment (start of current year);
   client group issues – the three Es (economy, efficiency, effectiveness).

Response to out-turns (last year's)

Organisation and staffing:
   academic;
   administrative;
   staff development;
   technical;
   morale;
   communications.

Resource management
   physical;
   revenue;
   capital.

Income generation targets and plans

Quality assurance:
   quality of teaching;
   students' perception of college (SPOC);
   employer's perception of college (EPOC).

Departmental report (last year's outcomes).

Management by exception

Identification of exceptions and related plans.

Source: M. S. Turner[6]

Figure 10.7 Annual review elements

Review team

An effective review team would comprise competent, credible and sympathetic staff headed by a person nominated to be responsible for the audit procedure and reporting. Membership of the team would include some or all of the following:

- a senior manager;
- teachers or trainers;
- support staff;
- customers (trainees, students and employers);
- sponsors;
- a LEA (local education authority) representative;
- governors;
- a finance director;
- a quality manager.

The team would report to either the Employment Department Group – Training, Enterprise and Education Directorate (TEED) representative, the Training Enterprise Council (TEC), Department of Education and Science (DES), the governing body, principal, chief executive, managing director or others who need to access audit results.

Terms of reference for audit teams would be discussed, circulated and negotiated, and responsibilities clearly defined before recording in the quality plan.

Quality probe – work groups

- Is the team allowed to function within limits negotiated with the management?
- Is the team allowed to make suggestions and take decisions?
- Is the team permitted to plan, organise and control the audit or other task allotted?
- Does senior management support and help the team leader to maintain cohesion within the team but otherwise maintain a low profile and deferring style?
- Is the team encouraged to try things out without fear of being blamed if things go wrong?
- Is the principle of interdependence and mutual support in the pursuit of individual and team goals practised?
- Do individual team members seek to understand their different points of view?
- Does the team resolve conflict quickly and constructively?
- Does a climate of openness prevail?

Administration audit

Administrative services

The **administration** is concerned with managing the affairs of the business and handling revenue, information, communication and paperwork flows. Its role is that of interacting with and supporting income-generating processes. In order to function effectively it requires a structure within which to operate.

The scope and responsibility of the administrative management function must be outlined in written quality system procedures. The documented administrative procedure will contain details of the person responsible for implementing and maintaining the systems. Additionally it will provide adequate but concise information concerning: the business structure; formulation and implementation of the policy; business objectives and plans; provision and effective use of resources; business and administrative systems; staffing; procedural manuals; and audits and reporting systems.

Paperwork flows

Overall responsibility for quality rests with the principal or senior executive and they must be kept informed of the requirements of the targeted market and how well provision is matching need. Performance against business policy, operational and quality plans and market requirements must be reported and this is a function of the administration calling for the effective communication of information.

To facilitate communication, paperwork is generated within each of the main systems used in a provider's operations, including marketing, recruiting, planning, delivering, operating, accounting, monitoring, evaluating and reporting.

Systems manuals, procedures manuals and work instructions relating to the gathering, processing, recording, storing and retrieving of information must be assessed when auditing the effectiveness of paperwork systems.

> The task of ensuring that data captured is valid and reliable must be assigned to a responsible person. The same goes for computerised inputs and outputs.

Quality probe – paperwork flows

- Is there a paperwork generation and retention policy in force?
- Is there a person responsible for systems relating to paperwork flows?
- Is there a data capture, paperwork preparation, distribution, storage and retrieval system in operation?

- Are documents securely stored when not in use and safe from potential hazards?
- Are written procedures relating to the use of the documents listed being implemented effectively with regard to the following:
    secretarial and administrative services?
    management services?
    service delivery?
    assessment?
    monitoring, review and evaluation?
    accounts, costing, pricing and cheque handling?

Staffing

Personnel records

A system for recording personal and employment details, together with details of training, disciplinary action and time off, must be in operation. Confidentiality must be maintained and users of certain personal computerised data will have to register with the Data Protection Registrar.

Recruitment, selection and interviewing

Managers and others who are responsible for the recruitment and selection of staff need to follow a systematic approach that will help ensure that the right people are selected.

Having established the staff vacancy, it is necessary to carry out a job analysis and write an accurate job description for use in recruitment and selection. It is helpful to write personnel specifications that will enable applicants to be assessed against the job requirements.

Recruitment sources can be established and these include Job Centres, employment agencies, careers services, clubs, advertisements, newsletters, house journals and word of mouth. Advertisements should be non-racist, gender-free and provide for equal opportunities.

When analysing application forms care should be taken to avoid any form of discrimination, such as sex, race, religion, marital status, disability or age.

Interviews should be planned and conducted so as to facilitate selection of the right candidate. Interviewers should recognise and take account of aspects of employment legislation and employ effective interviewing techniques.

Interview assessment sheets and interview reports should be used, and there should be procedures for taking up references and following up the interview.

Induction should be arranged so that new starters may be integrated into the department smoothly and effectively. All employees should be aware of non-pay benefits, holiday arrangements, grievance and disciplinary procedures and the importance of health, safety and welfare in the workplace.

Employment policies and procedures should be fair and effective. Administrators will deal with staff recruitment, welfare, salaries, pensions and redundancies.

Quality probe – employing staff

- Are there documented procedures for staff recruitment, selection, induction and training?
- Is a new starter really needed or can an existing employee be trained do the job?
- Are vacancies clearly defined?
- How are applicants for vacancies attracted?
- Does the personnel record form include:
     personal details?
     employment record?
     education and training details?
     disciplinary record?
     absence record?
     lateness record?
     accident record?
- Has a job analysis been conducted?
- Is there a documented job description covering:
     job title?
     main purposes of job?
     main duties?
- Is there a personnel specification covering:
     skills?
     personal qualities/desirable traits?
     abilities?
     motivation?
- Is there an appropriate application form covering:
     personal details?
     qualifications, education, training and experience?
     employment history?
- Is there an employment contract? (Refer to the Employment Protection (Consolidation) Act 1978.)
- Is there evidence that the recruitment procedure is adequately monitored, reviewed and evaluated?

Support services and technicians

In-house support services could be thought of as training subcontractors who provide technical services and back-up to the trainers delivering the programme. Each technician or other member of the support staff is a supplier to one or more delivery agents. There must be written procedures and work instructions covering their role, scope of duties, responsibilities and training requirements. In common with other systems, there should be documented procedures for contracting, controlling and reviewing their inputs to the service, and assessing the outcomes achieved.

Financial management

A management system that embraces accounting for the cost of delivering the service and measuring performance in terms of income generation, achievement of targets and quality of outcomes of the business, must be in place.

Budget and resource management

A **budget** is an itemised estimate of expected income and expenditure over a given period. Money relating to each item can be set aside for resources needed to achieve each target given in the operational plan. The budget therefore acts as a control for the resources expended.

Budgetary control is a system of managing a business by making forecasts of the various activities and applying a financial value to each item. Actual performance is then compared with the forecast.

> Budgeting can be used to aid the estimation of resource requirements and as a monitoring tool that will help managers to operate the business effectively.
>
> Pay and payment systems should satisfy the needs of the provider and the staff.

Costing procedures

Costing procedures are needed to establish the direct and indirect costs of services and products delivered. **Cost accounting** is concerned with gathering and analysing cost data and informing management decision making. Documented procedures will be needed when costing and pricing income-generating activities, such as providing fully costed training, retraining and updating services.

Management information system

A **management information system (MIS)** is a documented system that is designed to provide managers with information that will aid effective and efficient management of the provision. It comprises equipment and procedures that facilitate reviews of performance measures including: achievement and outcomes; departmental planning and control;

management accounting; resource utilisation; manpower planning; productivity; personnel and training functions; paperwork systems; and customer-related matters (degree of satisfaction, perception of service, complaints and comments etc.).

The main purpose of a MIS is to monitor the provider's internal management processes and also external parameters. Indicators of the performance of educational and training provision will include qualitative and quantitative measures of efficiency, effectiveness and quality. The indicators will be used to assist decision making at all management levels, to create a better awareness of where the provider is in terms of operational planning and to make comparisons across programmes, departments or the workplace provision.

It has been proposed that all providers should operate comprehensive, integrated, computerised management information systems that are able to generate the requirements of the Joint Efficiency Study.[7]

Administrative support for trainers

Supervisors and teachers have enough on their plates without the added responsibility of handling all the administration and paperwork that may be associated with the accreditation of prior learning and newly-acquired competence. While it has always been a role of the supervisor to carry out workplace training and staff development, the formalisation of training and accreditation of competence has added another layer to an already heavy workload.

Administrative support and organisational systems should be in place to help supervisors and workplace trainers make a success of vocational learning and training for NVQs.

Monitoring officers

Monitoring officers and **training co-ordinators** play important roles in recruitment and in planning and delivering induction sessions. During the induction, trainees are given guidance about the training programmes they will follow and information about assessment, recording achievement and relevant qualifications. The officers identify training placements and arrange for counselling and guidance support where required. They review progress during practical training, with reference to personal training plans, and they monitor arrangements for work-based projects.

Trainee achievement is recorded and filed in the NROVA (National Record of Vocational Achievement) or elsewhere by monitoring officers who liaise with employers and awarding bodies. They also establish and maintain systems for handling trainee assessment and certification.

Keeping training records

In some government-sponsored schemes, training providers are responsible for recording the achievement of competence for their own staff and also for trainees. During training, assessment records may be stored in the NROVA together with the action plan.

The NROVA is a cumulative lifelong record of credits and qualifications. Its use enables credits accumulated to be collated and recorded. Any certificates awarded or other forms of accreditation will be held by individuals in their NROVA. It is also used to hold action plans and personal training plans.

The **action plan**, stated in the form of units of competence, gives details of the qualification being pursued or training programme to be followed. It lists what needs to be done and what will be assessed in order to attain the award sought. Action planning may take place during initial assessment or induction, or as the need demands. The object is for trainee and training provider to agree a plan of activity that will provide opportunities for competences to be achieved.

The provider is normally responsible for maintaining relationships with vocational qualification awarding bodies and for arranging for the certification and issuing of certificates or units of competence to the candidate.

Learner documentation

In training circles a variety of instruments are used to record in a systematic way information about progress, achievement and competences.

Achievement records

An **achievement record** is used to express concisely the evidence collected against elements and performance criteria. The summary, in the form of a written statement, is used as an aid to assessment. The record usually contains details of:

- process skills demonstrated while carrying out an activity or performing work;
- product skills demonstrated while producing something;
- the content and circumstances that are relevant to the demonstration of competence.
- the categories and amount of evidence produced in support of a claim for accreditation.

Log-books and diaries

Claims for the accreditation of competence will be checked by the supervisor against performance criteria to ensure that the trainee has reached the required standard of skill. It is normally the provider's responsibility to ensure that details of training carried out are recorded and kept up-to-date.

Log-books may be used to:

- provide a record of the training received;
- provide a source of reference which may be of use later in the trainee's career;
- help trainees develop written communication skills and express understanding of the work performed;
- provide the training supervisor with a means of assessing the trainee's progress and achievements.

Entries should be made regularly and examined and initialled by the workplace trainer, supervisor or monitoring officer.

A **training diary** is a personal record of daily events, such as work experience, off-the-job learning, appointments, problems encountered and overcome, reviews and observations. It can also be used as a record of training activities. The diary is helpful when discussing experiences during reviews with the trainer during formative and summative assessments leading to accreditation.

When used as a basis for self-assessment the diary provides an opportunity for reflection and identification of how training skills and opportunities might be improved. It also provides a means of recording feedback. Notes of discussions and entries might include details of:

- the type of work undertaken;
- working skills learned;
- other knowledge and skills learned;
- tools, machines, equipment and other resources used;
- other workplace-related tasks where knowledge and skills gained, and tools and equipment, could be used;
- outside work uses of newly-acquired competence;
- quality of work produced and the processes involved;
- attitudes of supervisors and other workers towards the person compiling the diary;
- those who benefited from the work outcomes;
- how the type of work carried out has helped with learning and understanding of related performance criteria;
- what the next move should be.

Lead body representatives will need to examine log-books and diaries, together with completed training specifications and records of progress, before awards are recommended.

Training cards

A **training card** is a summary of training programme outcomes. When the trainee and provider agree that competence has been achieved and demonstrated, entries on the card are made. When training is completed the trainee, trainer and departmental manager discuss performance and review outcomes. Comments are written on the card and initialled. Certification is completed when the countersigning officer is satisfied that training content and performance meet relevant standards.

Record-keeping

Providers will need to maintain adequate standards of record-keeping. Records that would normally be kept by workplace trainers engaged in government-sponsored training are listed in Figure 10.8. Each of the records reflects aspects of the trainer function, such as planning, preparing, delivering or assessing. Many of the records would be used, without exception, by the trainers engaged in other forms of training and staff development.

- List of work placements
- Monitoring reports
- Work placement contracts
- COSHH assessments
- Health and safety equipment maintenance records

- Personal training programmes
- Action plans
- Trainee review sheets
- Trainee log-books and profiles
- Employer reports and work-experience diaries
- Attendance records

- NVQ units, elements and performance criteria
- Scheme of work
- Session plans
- Task analyses

- Skills tests
- Assessment records
- Records of achievement
- NROVA registration and updating

Note: The above list is not intended to be exhaustive.

Figure 10.8 Types of records

Trainer documentation

Trainers will be expected to keep records of trainees and to maintain assessment records. Trainee records are a requirement of some government-sponsored training schemes and essential to their operation.

Elsewhere, employers normally keep records of staff skills, qualifications, training and achievements, for use when carrying out **skills audits**. In each case, care should be taken to operate within the provisions of the Data Protection Act 1984. Records kept often include:

- lists of people in training;
- date of birth and sex;
- National Insurance number;
- address and phone number;
- qualifications on entry;
- start date;
- statement of any long-term health problems or disability that may affect the kind of work done;
- Standard Occupational Classification (SOC) relating to trainees' types of job and skill levels within their employment or occupation;
- location or workplace.

Providers could usefully develop a framework for monitoring, evaluating and recording training programme implementation and outcomes. Records kept vary according to providers' needs but may often include:

- action plan and training programme details;
- training start and finish dates;
- details of special training need category;
- anticipated NVQ level of achievement;
- achievements during training;
- post-training destination.

Certification

Besides the formal certification carried out by awarding bodies there are several other possibilities. These range from informal self-assessments communicated orally, to strictly objective, impersonal, computer-marked and certificated outcomes.

A **certificate** may serve as evidence that the holder meets the standards of performance needed for progressing to other studies or for employment at a level compatible with achievement. However, due to the diversity of certification in use and the varied needs of employment selection interviewers and study guidance counsellors, there will be a demand for each type of recording and certification method.

Very often, employers will need to know rather more about a person's achievements than is written on some forms of certificate. This is where continuous assessment records; initial, formative and summative assessments; profiles, diaries, records of achievement and units listing performance criteria, may be helpful.

Personal profiles

A statement in the form of a **personal profile** may be used to summarise assessed achievement. It also gives an estimate of development potential at the end of a course of training. The statement derives from learner self-evaluation of all the experience and outcomes obtained while learning, backed by a final review with the trainer/assessor. The profile builds on earlier in-course developmental reviews and takes into account the process of continuously monitoring, evaluating and recording learning achievements. In some circumstances, summary statements may be used to support bids for final awards. Features indicated on the relevant personal profile include:

- details of the learner;
- prior learning and achievement;
- details of the action plan;
- essential details of the training programme completed;
- experience gained during training;
- work-based learning provider's comments;
- attendance record;
- performance criteria and competences attained;
- vocational qualifications achieved;
- comments on reviews.

Profiling is a means of recording achievement and competence and it plays an important role in workplace accreditation and in vocational training programmes that are now offered. The profile or record of achievement produced contains details of the **formative assessments** made during training and a **summative statement of achievement** recorded on completion of the programme.

According to Garforth and Macintosh[8] the contents of profiles should contain the following three basic elements:

- A list of items forming the basis of the assessment. These may be called 'criteria' and may be in the form of a list of skills and qualities or may be embodied within a course description.
- A means of indicating the level and/or nature of performance reached for each item in this list. Almost any means can be used including marks, grades, percentages, histograms, bar graphs, statements and descriptive assessments.
- An indication of the evidence used to arrive at the description provided. This element is unfortunately often ignored, but it is vital to indicate the context in which a particular skill is assessed if the nature of its performance is to be fully understood.

Quality probe – learner documentation

Does the record keeping system contain information about:

- accreditation of prior learning and experience?
- initial assessments?
- training programmes?
- action plans?
- award body registrations, examination entries and certification?
- lead body documentation?
- national record registration, records of achievement and other documentation?
- skills tests?
- monitoring of work experience?
- reviews
- log-books and diaries?

Environment and resource audit

Accommodation

Effective utilisation, upgrading and development of premises and equipment will be a key objective for many providers. The provider will need to plan and maintain programmes designed to improve standards continuously and take full advantage of available accommodation and facilities. The needs and requirements of clients associated with the learning environment must be regularly reviewed and records kept of reviews and action taken.

Premises and equipment must be adequate for the intended purposes.

Quality probe – premises

- Is there a buildings officer or a named person responsible for signposting and maintenance of premises?
- Are premises easy to access?
- Does the temperature, humidity and lighting level meet legal requirements and customer expectations?
- Do noises interfere with concentration or performance?
- Are furnishings, fittings, equipment, tools and other resources adequate for the intended purpose?
- Are working conditions safe?

- Is security satisfactory?
- Are there cloakroom facilities and are toilets clean?
- Are refreshments available?
- Is there evidence that the premises and equipment are maintained and continuously monitored, and is action taken in order to support effectively the service delivered.

Resources

Resource identification and traceability
The ability to store and retrieve information about the provision, such as training resources, sources of training opportunities, testing and assessment materials, and trainee records, can be useful in preventing errors. When problems arise, the ability to analyse quickly the difficulty and trace the source allows rapid corrective action to be taken that will effect a cure.

Control of the training provision
In order to be able to identify benefits and faults in training provision, records should be kept of all training activities operating within the provider's delivery systems. This would apply to full-time, part-time and fully-costed course provision. Data thus recorded would then be available for analysis, should associated quality problems arise.

Handling training requests
The training provider should have an effective system of administrative support for handling enrolments and training requests. Customers are entitled to receive a quick, polite and efficient response to enquiries and bids for training places. Procedures for processing documentation should be recorded in the quality manual. A suggested approach to handling training requests is given in Figure 10.9.

Verification of resources and personnel
The establishment of the correctness of activities and human and physical resources employed in the provision and implementation of the service is known as **verification**. The process involved is that of monitoring those features essential to the implementation of quality policies.

Effectiveness of the provision

An audit could be used to evaluate the effectiveness of the provision. As can be seen in Figure 10.10 on page 220, the provision comprises three main systems:

- policies, strategies and plans;
- physical resource inputs;
- human resource inputs.

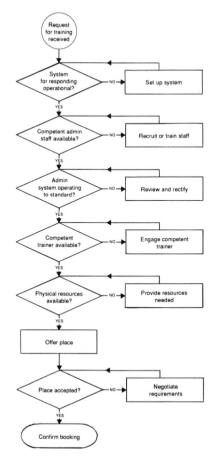

Figure 10.9 Handling training requests

Policies

When designing training programmes, providers will need to cater for the needs of trainees, placement staff, employers and sponsors. An effective programme design system would include procedures for remedial learning, adapting method and content to suit individual trainees needs and an evaluation of the outcomes.

The policy adopted should be consistent with the requirements of the different categories of customers and compatible with their individual needs.

The flow chart given in Figure 10.11 on page 221 is concerned with auditing training strategies. A suggested starting point is the **identification of training needs**. There should be a system in place that allows clients to explore their needs. Supported by a member of staff, a programme that matches clients' requirements is agreed. Outcomes are then assessed against the programme.

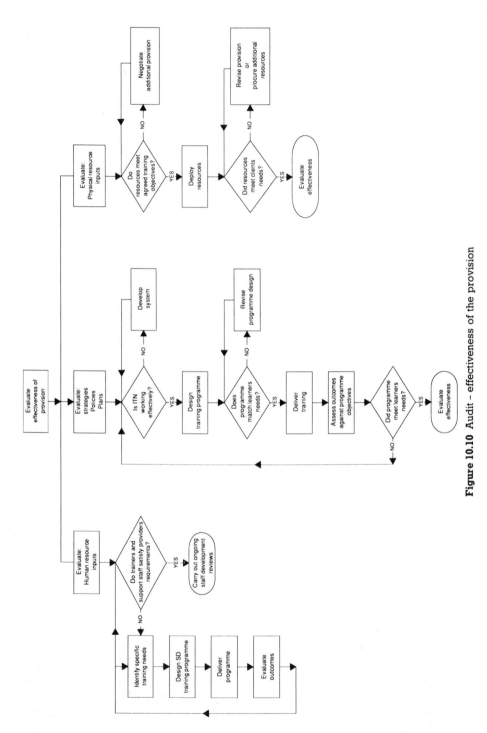

Figure 10.10 Audit – effectiveness of the provision

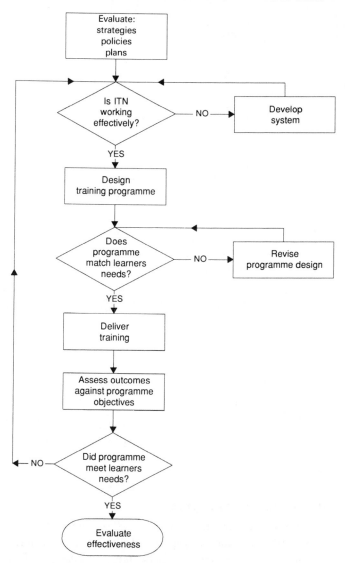

Figure 10.11 Audit – training strategies

Physical resource inputs

Resources are needed to aid and support the service offered. The training provider will need to evaluate the effectiveness of physical resource inputs against intended purpose. Additional resources may have to be provided where an audit, such as that given in Figure 10.12 overleaf, reveals that programme objectives or client requirements have not been fully met.

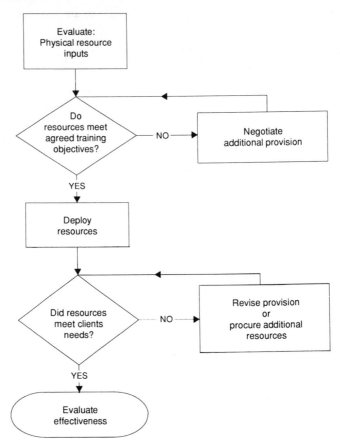

Figure 10.12 Physical resource inputs

Human resource inputs

Human resources are the sum total of all people employed by the provider. They represent **human capital** in the form of energy, effort, skills, knowledge and competence that drives the business. This human capital can be bought in or be acquired by investing in education and training. The training provider will need to operate a staff training system that is geared to managing and developing human capital to enhance service potential.

A flow diagram that may be helpful when evaluating the skills of trainers and support staff is given in Figure 10.13. It is suggested that if staff satisfy the present and predictable requirements of the service then nothing will need to be done other than to carry out ongoing training needs reviews. Where a training gap is detected, specific needs will be identified and a training programme set up to update the staff member.

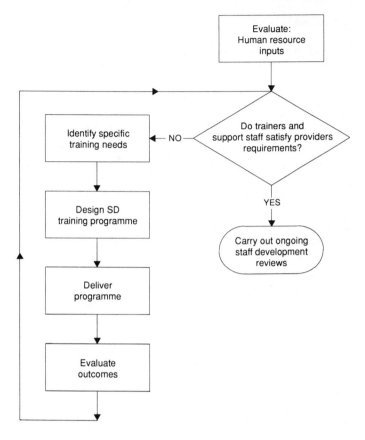

Figure 10.13 Human resource inputs

External affairs audit

Liaising with awarding bodies

A system will need to operate that enables staff to find out the requirements of awarding bodies and to produce schemes of work that will facilitate the implementation of new provision.

A liaison person needs to access the awarding body, its verifier, other members of the provider's staff, students and parents. In many cases, schools, careers and employers would be networked. Educational and training provision would need to be integrated with work-based, performance-related activities to ensure that NVQ performance criteria are met.

Purchasing services

Assessment of training sub-contractors

In the past, managing agents (MAs) for government-sponsored training, such as Youth Training and Employment Training, varied considerably in scope and size. Larger ones who were awarded contracts handled over 500 trainees, while some managed more and generated many thousands of pounds of income. Quite naturally, this kind of money was not handed over without carefully assessing the quality and effectiveness of the training and trainee support provided. The same principles applied to all MAs regardless of the size of their operation and that is why awards, such as Approved Training Organisation (ATO) status, were introduced.

Monitoring training provision

A **sub-contractor** is a person or organisation that undertakes to complete part of another's contract. For example, a subordinate contract may be entered into whereby the training provider will 'let out' work to a work-experience provider.

The training provider or main contractor will need to have in place a documented system for initially arranging a contract and then monitoring sub-contractor training placements. The flow chart given in Figure 10.14 lists a sequence of important activities and questions to be asked when initially checking out placements.

The starting point is the identification of a possible work placement. The monitoring officer arranges a visit and compares facilities and what is on offer with a documented training placement specification. If the work placement is able to meet the trainee's requirements, a training programme is negotiated and the placement is accepted. Then follows regular monitoring to assure consistent quality of training. Should a non-conformance occur that cannot be remedied, the trainee will probably have to be transferred elsewhere. Continued use of the placement will then have to be carefully considered.

The contract will cover the need for the work experience provider to provide suitable learning opportunities for trainees and to commit adequate resources to meet the contract's requirements.

> The assessment of sub-contractors and a system for continuously monitoring their performance is called for in order to meet with the 'purchasing' requirements given in BS 5750:Part 2, para. 4.6.

A **register of approved training sub-contractors** must be kept, together with details of assessments made by monitoring officers. A checklist of items to be monitored will then be drawn up.

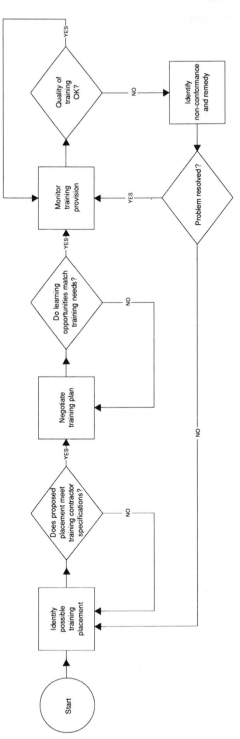

Figure 10.14 Arranging and monitoring training placements

Negotiating placement contracts

When negotiating training placement contracts, monitoring officers and work-based supervisors will be involved in discussions with training co-ordinators, trainees and other stakeholders. The contract will cover the need for the work-experience provider to provide suitable learning opportunities for trainees and to commit adequate resources to meet the contract's requirements.

Before accepting placements, the person who is awarding the contract will need to go through an approved process of monitoring practical training and other matters with employers and project managers.

The flow chart given in Figure 10.15 shows a number of additional checks that will need to be made before a placement can be accepted. Flow-charting systems may be applied to these procedures as well as to monitoring activities. As can be seen, a number of pertinent questions will be asked. The answers given, backed up by observation or examination of supporting evidence, will result in a decision being taken either to accept or reject the placement. Documented procedures concerning each stage of the check will allow valid and reliable assessments to be made.

The procedures will enlarge on, specify and clarify the concept behind each of the questions asked. This is necessary in order to confirm that the placement meets the requirements of the contract for training.

In the case of **equal opportunities** provision, the monitoring officer will check whether or not placements actually have a policy that meets the needs of the trainee to be placed and if so whether it is being implemented and continuously reviewed.

A written **health and safety** policy, together with procedures for its implementation, must be available. An audit of the work placement will reveal whether or not legislation and procedures are understood and practised. Trainees and sub-contractor's staff will be required to confirm conformance with procedures. Examination of documentation, such as emergency procedures, safe-working publications, accident books, fire-fighting equipment servicing records and availability of first aiders and adequately-stocked boxes, will supplement the evidence gathered that procedures are continuously reviewed and improved where possible.

Today, TECs and other sponsors are seeking a high-quality training provision that will result in formal qualifications, including NVQs, as an outcome of training. Many awards and training programmes are now structured in the form of units, elements and performance criteria. Monitoring officers will rigorously check placements for evidence of planned training opportunity, leading to recognised qualifications.

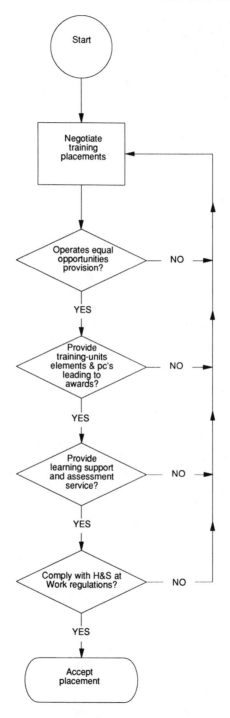

Figure 10.15 Negotiating training placements

Questions will be asked about whether or not **learning support** and **assessment** is provided for trainees, and whether health and safety regulations are complied with at the placement. There are of course many other questions that could be asked. The sample flow chart in Figure 10.15 is intended to serve only as a typical model. It may be added to depending on training plans, practical training sought and contract content.

Contractor access

When it is deemed necessary, reasonable access to the providing organisation should be afforded contractor's representatives wishing to review aspects of contracts or to inspect training resources and processes. This is not new. Her Majesty's Inspectors (HMIs), on behalf of the government as a major stakeholder of further educational establishments, have been visiting colleges over the years. Training Standards Advisory Service (TSAS) inspectors assessing providers for Approved Training Organisation (ATO) status, Department of Employment Training Enterprise and Education Directorate (TEED), TECs, employer's representatives and sponsors have also been afforded access to providers' operations.

Quality probe – sub-contractor provision

Is there a written contracting procedure for use when selecting and engaging sub-contractors?

Does the sub-contractor selected provide adequate:

- induction programmes?
- variety of teaching and learning methods?
- learning opportunities and resources?
- planned training based on the training programme, leading to occupational competence?
- systems for assessing and reviewing trainee progress towards occupational competence?
- equal opportunities provision?
- learner support?
- protection in terms of health and safety at work regulations?
- communication links with the main contractor?

Is there a documented procedure for monitoring sub-contractor provision?

Marketing

When writing operational plans, providers are now more inclined to take account of the value of adopting **public relations and marketing strategies**.

By producing and implementing a marketing plan, providers are able to inject an important aspect of modern management into the promotion of training programmes.

Marketing effort needs to be co-ordinated and market research, designed to gather data to supplement labour market intelligence, should be used to facilitate strategic planning for market penetration.

Funding will be set aside for research and development, and areas of research will be identified. Sources of external funding may be tapped for individual and team research, and arrangements made for managing expenditure.

Design and promotion

Design techniques will be applied to establishing an element of hopefulness and trust in the minds of prospective clients, backed by efficient service and satisfaction of customer expectations. The idea of selling benefits delivered by a package comprising **quality service** and **product** should be kept in mind when planning promotions. Attention should be focused on the staff expertise, experience and process skills on tap. These elements provide the service demanded and produce products that are up to the specification or end results required to bridge the training gap, need or want identified.

Publicity

The **prospectus**[9] is an important element of the marketing and recruitment strategy. It can be a very cost-effective means of informing target groups of what is on offer. Making it available to clients presents an ideal opportunity to demonstrate, by its good design, a quality approach to promoting the kind of service customers can expect.

Publicity budgets may include amounts to fund course leaflets and other publications, open nights and exhibitions, employer and school liaison, media liaison, advertising, hospitality, audio-visual programmes and the like.

> The public relations (PR) team will need to select the most appropriate advertising media that will help to maintain current recruitment levels and promote new products. Copy preparation and creative aspects of advertising will call for in-house expertise and knowledge of how to make the best use of space, visuals and words.

Effective graphic communication will be achieved by the formation of an effective corporate identity. Once the corporate logo has been agreed it should be applied to printed media, letterheads, brochures and promotional materials.

Managing exhibitions

The way a provider presents its service within the catchment area is important. Exhibitions can be useful when it comes to targeting clients and presenting what is on offer. Careers conferences are venues at which a successful image may be presented using a planned exhibition strategy and properly-staffed, well-prepared stands.

Client liaison skills

Consultancy involves providing technical and advisory services facilitated by consultants. The ability to outline effectively the advantages and benefits of buying training from a particular provider is the most important requirement of any representative.

In order to improve their ability to cope effectively with accessing clients and responding to enquiries, staff will need to become competent in using the telephone, interviewing, consulting and presenting information.

Notes

1 *Towards an educational audit,* see the Forword (p. vi) by Geoff Stanton, Chief Officer, FEU, London, 1989.

2 Ibid p. 3. Working in conjunction with the Association of Colleges of Further and Higher Education (ACFHE) and the Association of Principals of Colleges (APC), the Further Education Unit (FEU) commissioned a team of senior managers from Blackpool and the Fylde College, led by the principal, Michael McAllister, to undertake the feasibility study which included the literature search described in the text.

3 Professor Kaoru Ishikawa (1915–89) was a pioneer of quality circles and the circle with its teamwork concept greatly affected Japanese worker–management relationships after the Second World War. The outcomes and processes involving the identification, analysis and solving of work-based problems is now practised world-wide. He developed the 'fishbone' diagram, now extensively used when identifying possible causes of nonconformance and during problem-solving activities.

4 *Towards an educational audit,* p. 9, FEU, London, 1989.

5 M. S. (Stan) Turner is vice principal – planning and resources, The Bournemouth and Poole College of Further Education.

6 Ibid.

7 Joint Efficiency Study (JES) Report, *Managing colleges efficiently,* DES/Local Authority Associations, HMSO, London, 1987. (ISBN 0112706266)

8 D. Garforth and H. Macintosh, *Profiling: a user's manual,* pp. 2–4, Stanley Thornes (Publishers) Ltd, Cheltenham, 1986.

9 An account of how the provider's prospectus can be improved is given in C. N. Keen, *The College Prospectus,* HEIST, Banbury, 1987.

CHAPTER ELEVEN

The Curriculum Audit

Chapter coverage

The curriculum provision
> Developing a curriculum plan
> Curriculum development processes
> The curriculum
> Components of curriculum development
> Training needs analysis
> Curriculum design and objectives
> Course content
> Structuring the curriculum
> Assessment
> Resource planning

The curriculum audit process
> Curriculum audits
> Values and needs of adult learners
> Values and needs of trainers
> Values and needs of employers
> Marketing strategy

Design
> Recruitment and induction
> Design control
> New product design
> Design changes
> Document control – curriculum development

Implementation
> Teaching and learning strategies
> Delivery modes
> Resource development
> Guidance and support

New technology
Standards and assessment
Review and evaluation
Monitoring and evaluation (M&E)
Review and change
After sales
Servicing

The curriculum provision

Developing a curriculum plan

When developing a curriculum plan it may be useful to consider a number of parameters affecting the curriculum development process. Initially, consideration will be given to the nature of the existing business and its mission. This will enable the planners to focus on the core business and review what the provider is attempting to achieve. Once this is established attention will be focused on the environment in which the business operates and the needs, opportunities and threats that exist there. This external appraisal is necessary in order to take account of the prevalent political, social, environmental and technological climate. Account will also be taken of the views of stakeholders, such as the government, the FE Funding Council, TECs, Scottish LECs (Local Enterprise Companies), industrial agencies, the community at large, HMIs, governors, staff, shareholders, suppliers and sub-contractors; and most importantly existing and potential customers.

There will be structural forces and market competition. Having reviewed the data gathered about market forces, evaluated the present situation and estimated future trends then current provision will have to be looked at and an opinion formed about how the business is doing at present. This may be achieved by conducting a **SWOT analysis** designed to reveal the provider's strengths, weaknesses, opportunities and restrictions.

The next stage will be deciding what is to be offered to clients, what is to be done and how it is to be achieved. Having gained a clear picture of the need, the curriculum plan can be written and curriculum planners can begin to develop the curriculum.

Curriculum development processes

At one time, a commonly-held view was that the provider simply delivered training packages that happened to be on the shelf. This approach was known as **supply-led** and clients were expected to adjust their requirements so as to match provision.

In some cases, a commitment to provide just what the client needed was made but no system of design verification was available to ensure that the programme to be delivered would actually meet clients' expectations. In much the same way, design of training programmes neither fully took account of the needs of the sponsors or employers, nor of the individual trainee.

Programme content and delivery method were often fixed over long periods. Basic programme design remained intact and adaptations to meet individually-negotiated learning contracts agreed with clients were virtually unheard of. But nowadays there is a need to organise product searches and to generate new products; sometimes trading up and sometimes looking for openings where very basic technology can meet product requirements. A lot of time and effort can be spent trying to sell up-market products when there is much greater demand for more basic services.

> The time spent on evaluating routes to product introduction and associated risk management may be worthwhile.

Today, the **negotiated curriculum** is an integral part of the learner's entitlement and there is a need for providers to take account of this fact when designing the learner service and training programmes to be offered. A **demand-led** approach designed to meet the identified needs of employers and trainees calls for a wider variety of learning opportunities and greater flexibility. To facilitate this service, systems are called for that allow design change and the adaptation of standard programmes to provide mutually beneficial outcomes for clients. Providers intending to meet quality objectives relating to the design of training may wish to review continuously their existing systems for programme planning and learning design.

> Before considering aspects of curriculum audit it may be helpful to explore some of the more important aspects of design and development planning, and the means by which control of quality may be assured.

The curriculum

The curriculum may be defined as 'the planned formal and informal learning experiences offered to learners under the guidance of the training provider'. Learning opportunities may be provided in-house or elsewhere.

The curriculum provides a vehicle for planning, designing, implementing, reviewing and evaluating training provision and the diagram given in Figure 6.1 on page 111 shows how very complex the processes of curriculum development can be.[1] FEU describes the model as 'a dynamic cyclical process'. The main features of the cycle are clustered around an 'essential central hub of support services which support the other elements as appropriate'.[2]

FEU believes that the generation of quality requires a curriculum-led approach.[3]

Components of curriculum development

Curriculum development comprises eight main components:

- identifying and analysing need;
- writing curriculum aims and objectives;
- selecting course content;
- designing teaching and learning strategies;
- structuring the curriculum (teaching and learning programme);
- assessment;
- resource planning;
- monitoring and evaluating responsiveness, quality, efficiency and effectiveness of outcomes.

Each component is interrelated with the others, so the process of curriculum development should be ongoing, with continuous adjustments being made as a result of feedback from monitoring and evaluation.

Detailed procedures for setting up and assuring control of each of the eight components listed above will need to be written into the provider's quality manual.

Training needs analysis

A **needs analysis** is client-centred and may include training needs relating to an individual, group, industrial or commercial enterprise, institution or other external agency. Such needs are often classified as being demand-led.

Needs may also be anticipated by a supplier of training or education by referring to a syllabus, new legislation, market trends or otherwise predicting the likely demand for a particular learning service. Such provision is described as supply-led.

Whether demand-led or supply-led the design and implementation of the curriculum must, where feasible, satisfy clients' expectations. That is, to fulfil their needs.

Quality probe – identification and analysis of training needs

- Is there a documented procedure for identification and analysis of training needs (ITN)?
- Is there a procedure for matching identified customers' needs with the provision?
- Is there a named person responsible for developing and implementing ITN policy and procedures?
- Is the quality and effectiveness of ITN monitored?
- Is there an identified ITN team that implements ITN and carries out reviews and evaluations?
- Are there valid and reliable performance indicators relating to ITN throughout the service?
- Are outcomes of reviews widely disseminated across the provision?
- Is there staff development support for staff involved in ITN?
- Is the ITN element of curriculum development integrated with other key features of the curriculum quality plan?

Assessing needs of adult learners

Providers should recognise the purposes and benefits of operating an appraisal system and be able to identify features to be considered when planning, implementing and developing the system.

Adults may have learning needs that vary considerably from those of the young. Whereas the young will depend upon the trainer for guidance and control, and are unlikely to be self-directing, the industrial or commercial knowledge of adults and their life experience will cause them to expect different treatment.

Adults will have a wealth of experience to bring with them into the learning situation and they will be disappointed if they are not given credit for this or if their prior experience and competence are not utilised. They will expect to make use of new learning more or less immediately.

Clients will expect the provider to be in a position to help them to satisfy their learning needs. They will hope to gain from attending training sessions and will expect outcomes to make an important contribution to their career prospects or to otherwise meet their requirements.

Methods may need to be revised and access to training adjusted to suit the changing pattern of provision now being encouraged to meet adult expectations. Potential client groups, especially returners and the adult unemployed, will contain people with a wide range of abilities and attainments. It would be easy to stereotype clients on the basis of very little knowledge, but this must be avoided. Some will have a good idea of where they want to go and how they hope to get there while others will need a lot of support.

This is where a sound knowledge of confidential counselling and sources of referral becomes critical to the success of the learning proposition.

As far as the actual learning processes are concerned, there is no doubt that both younger and older adults will respond much better to methods that encourage active involvement in their own learning. However, it is likely that the older trainees will make more fuss if they do not get what they want.

Study guidance is a priority activity for successfully matching needs to training provision. Given that this is the case, both the provider and adult learner will need to be committed to a process of consultation and negotiation of content and mode of learning.

Strategies

When designing teaching and learning strategies the trainer is required to structure and organise learning opportunities that will take into account learner-related factors such as: need; ability; interest; prior learning and experience; linkages between various subjects; and learning style.

Provision should be made to involve learners actively in decisions about their learning and to recognise the value of two-way negotiation.

Study modes are changing. More training is delivered and assessed in the workplace. Training programmes tend to have greater vocational emphasis and entry to programmes is not bogged down by rigidly-set requirements. Flexible learning helps to overcome individual differences and with competence-based learning, the length of time a client spends in achieving and demonstrating competence is not fixed.

Competence is judged against a range of national standards and only the criteria for success are laid down, not the strategy by which the learner acquires the competence. There is considerable growth in distance learning so that open learning, open college, computer-based study and work-based learning now feature as important strategies for new programmes.

The possibility of providing a flexible learning environment and adequate support for learners in the form of counselling and guidance facilities needs to be considered, as does the need to co-ordinate sequences of experiences in an integrated way.

Counselling and guidance

Steps should be taken actively to involve clients in decisions about their learning. The need for joint negotiation throughout the training and accreditation programme should be agreed from the start. Study guidance would include help for clients when deciding on learning methods and resources to be used, the level of trainer support needed, the rate of learning and how this will be regulated.

> Guidance and review should be available to all clients. Giving guidance and advice is a very responsible and demanding duty. The services of someone who is able to support clients and help them to identify their individual training needs and possible learning opportunities is an essential requirement of a quality system.

Where action plans or personal training programmes have been written, it is helpful to review with clients their progress in occupational areas and in the achievement of elements of competence. This may lead to thinking about progression and transfer of training. Discussion also serves to bring into focus difficulties which hold up progress and allows possible courses of action to be considered. Advice on where and how to progress is welcomed by many, but there are cases when it is advisable to refer clients to external agencies who may be better placed to handle a particular problem.

Quality probe – flexible delivery

Does the delivery programme:

- provide for flexible access to initial assessment and subsequent ongoing study guidance?
- operate flexible timetabling that allows and encourages entry to the provision by offering attendance modes that will (as far as is reasonably possible) enable clients to choose from a range of modules and gain access at times and places of their choosing?
- provide flexible, open access to skills training and relevant underpinning knowledge leading to achievement of work-related competence?
- incorporate flexible teaching and active-learning opportunities appropriate to the needs of the clients?
- offer drop-in workshops, tutor-assisted project work and resource-based learning opportunities?
- provide flexible access to information technology resources and computer-assisted learning?
- offer off-site training provision?
- operate a 'roll-on/roll-off' facility?
- provide a year-round service?
- deliver a service that is dynamic and responsive to the changing demands of clients, sponsors and political initiatives?

Curriculum design and objectives

The design and content of the curriculum is decided by many factors including the values and needs of clients, support systems and resources for curriculum implementation and evaluation.

> Total design management is very important. Design output can be measured by cost of design and the degree to which the objectives of training deriving from a needs analysis have been met, and how well knowledge of the psychology of learning has been applied to the planning of learning experiences.

Tyler's description of the purpose of formulating objectives during the process of curriculum development explains the relevance of writing objectives for learner behaviour and the context in which these operate:

> The most useful form for stating objectives is to express them in terms which identify both the kind of behaviour to be developed in the student and the content or area in life in which this behaviour is to operate. If you consider a number of statements of objectives that seem to be clear and to provide guidance in the development of instructional programmes, you will note that each of these statements really includes both the behaviour and the content aspects of the objectives.[4]

> FEU suggest that course aims should describe not only content and delivery method, but also the range of equipment to be encountered, routes to qualifications on completion and the relationship with the occupational role.[5]

Course content

The substance of course material may be influenced by the course team (teachers or trainers in the role of curriculum developers), by powerful external influences (such as the TECs and other sponsors) or by the learner group itself.

When selecting programme content, the key concept to bear in mind is that the learning experience should be designed so as to facilitate the learners in their efforts to attain the units, elements and performance criteria comprising the award sought.

> Learning opportunities and input content should be arranged in appropriate sequential order, offered at the right level and delivered at the optimum rate. Training programme design and content should support and promote the opportunity to gain NVQs.

Structuring the curriculum

When structuring the teaching and learning programme, early communication of the purpose and value of the training content and method should be allowed for. Curiosity should be promoted and a variety of different types of activity scheduled. Options open to the learners should be built-in where possible, in order to provide flexibility and to accommodate different learning rates and adaptation of the basic programme.

Commitment to the attainment of knowledge that underpins the achievement of practical skills that are available to learners should be sought and the relevance of the learning to real-world activities assured.

The need to provide continuity and an integrated programme that embraces other subjects being studied, as well as vocational experience, should be recognised. Linkages between syllabus references, themes, concepts, and topics should be planned, and a balanced structure giving a properly-weighted allocation of resources made.

From the wide range of learning methods available, techniques should be matched to the type of learning to be applied, whether this be memorising, understanding or doing.

Recent curriculum developments require that competence be demonstrated in the writing of programmes, schemes of work and session plans, and when preparing assignments and other learning materials.

Assessment

Assessment procedures are an important consideration in curriculum development work. The purposes of assessment are diverse and many, but some commonly-used assessment processes involve:

- assessment of outcomes;
- diagnosis of strengths and weaknesses;
- evaluation of effectiveness and efficiency of teaching and learning;
- guidance in decision making;
- monitoring of work placements and the location of trainees in other learning environments;
- prediction of learner performance.

All training programmes should be designed to facilitate the development of learner competence, with provision for the assessment of achievement on demand.

A systematic audit of all training operations will need to be carried out. Every aspect of training provision – including initial assessment, induction, safe working, planning and delivering training, assessing performance and accrediting the achievement of competence – will need to be carefully monitored and evaluated.

Performance-related and competence-based trainer's and assessor's awards are being progressively developed and continuously updated. These awards and associated underlying training and developmental work provide standards that will help staff meet the challenge presented by the needs, performance criteria and targets of training functions.

The assessment of performance and competence is discussed in some depth in a recent publication by the author entitled *The Assessment of Performance and Competence*.[6]

Resource planning

The curriculum is delivered by teachers, trainers and non-teaching staff. They utilise resources, such as buildings, accommodation, space, capital equipment, consumables, information systems, finance and time.

Curriculum planning, design and methodology are all interrelated, and while at one time resources in the form of money were thrown at innovations in the curriculum development field, that scenario is fast disappearing.

The Education Reform Act changed the whole nature of the budgeting process within further education. Financial delegation and internally-devolved budgets introduced the need to carry out cost analysis at departmental level and to provide costing information.

Providers are now faced with the need to consider the effectiveness and efficiency of the provision of services in terms of resourcing implications. Using an **input/output** model, there is now a need to try to establish the efficiency of operation by measuring output against input. This is done in much the same way that the efficiency of a fuel burning is calculated. Does what you get out compare with what you put in?

> Providers will be required to calculate unit costs and units of resource, and to account in some way for the output obtained from each unit of resource input. The message for curriculum developers will therefore be 'Use your resources wisely, effectively and efficiently.'

The curriculum audit process

Curriculum audits

Regular audits of the curriculum provision, in order to assure conformance with contracted provision and to identify areas for improvement, must be conducted. The search for ways in which the service may be continuously improved should be never-ending. In order to maintain a quality service, all training inputs and curriculum processes should be controlled so that instances of nonconformances are eliminated or at least kept to the very minimum. Valid customer expectations should be met.

Quality probes and audits should be devised for every aspect of curriculum provision. The processes of curriculum development shown in the inner hub and the features of each stage in the cycle, given in Figure 6.1 on page 111, may be useful when designing probes and audits suitable for a particular training provider. The aspects of curriculum design discussed below may also serve to promote thoughts about how improved curriculum quality may be achieved.

Quality probe – curriculum audits

- Why is the information sought needed?
- What benefits will result?
- How can the information be collected?
- After gathering data, how will subsequent activity be prioritised?
- How will audit activity be monitored?
- How will the information derived be communicated?
- How will the effect of changes in curriculum planning and delivery be measured and reported?

Values and needs of adult learners

Adults like to be in control of what they do. They usually know where they want to go but may need a hand in getting there. This is where consultation and negotiation on the content and mode of learning can be the key to success. There is little doubt that adult learners tend to favour active involvement when learning.

It may be helpful for the provider to think about how adults seeking further achievements differ in their approaches to learning.

Some adults will have no study problems. Some will be highly-motivated but their expectations may be beyond their reach. They may be over-confident and not eager to apply themselves to the training. Others will have poor retention levels and will quickly forget things.

Access to facilities and resources may be a problem, as will finding the time to study and someone to lend a hand when help is needed. For these reasons provision needs to be made for the learners to work at their own pace and level using easy to follow learning materials with expert guidance on call.

> Providers will need to be able to put clients at ease by establishing a rapport and adopting a caring attitude. A customer care policy would embrace the need for providers to anticipate matters of concern to adult learners and to allay fears and apprehension.

Adult learners differ from the young in their approaches to learning. The important factors influencing learning include level of motivation and expectations, and powers of concentration. They are able to bring to the learning situation knowledge, skills, practical abilities and experience, but may be short on confidence and capacity for learning new things.

Quality probe – adults learning

- What actions will need to be taken in anticipation that some or all of the clients may need help with aspects of learning?
- What procedure is there for helping clients to cope with a return to learning and what will be needed to facilitate this?
- Have course teams identified the ways in which adult learners seeking places on their programmes may differ from young persons in their previous experience and attitudes?
- Is there a strategy for assessing a client's suitability for the training opportunity on offer? Consider in particular: the existing levels of skills, knowledge and experience; the level of qualifications or profiles or competence; how recently these have been achieved; relevance, scope and transferability of other training to the proposed.

Values and needs of trainers

Much training is now based upon NVQ performance criteria and trainers delivering programmes are required to be competent to train and assess people seeking units and elements leading to NVQ awards. In a quality-assured system, this creates a need for providers to ensure that their own staff, sub-contractors and work-placement trainers are approved by the validating body to facilitate training, leading to the award of the qualifications offered.

There should be a written procedure for monitoring contracts negotiated with those external providers who will be implementing training programmes. The procedure should include minimum standards for the supervision of trainees and training content. Reducing obstacles to learning should be an important consideration for trainers.

Adults' barriers or blockages to learning may be self-imposed or may result from past involvement with trainers. Bad experiences during previous training may have coloured attitudes towards a return to learning. Clients may have physical impairments, such as failing eyesight or hearing, that could hold them back. They may feel that they have been out of the game for too long and out of touch with modern methods. There are countless reasons for fears but whether a real problem exists or not, if the client thinks a problem exists then that client has a problem.

> **When training people with learning blocks the trainer should be aware of the fragile relationship that will initially exist and work hard at dispelling anxieties.**

Trainers can go a long way to building confidence by providing a service that is friendly and open, and avoiding getting impatient when clients appear to be slow to grasp a point. There may be a need to carry out audits of method and practice which could be focused on such matters as those listed in the following quality probe.

Quality probe – confidence building

Is there a procedure for:
- finding out whether or not special learning needs exist?
- negotiating learning objectives and agendas for action, and building on the clients' existing skills?
- integrating theory and practice?
- providing opportunity for learner-centred activities?
- allowing clients to work at their own pace?
- confirming that training is delivered in a logical sequence?
- offering information, advice and support whenever it is needed?
- encouraging self-evaluation and quality-assurance practices?
- giving advice on improving study skills and learning, when out of the workplace or formal learning environment?

Values and needs of employers

Before 1990, employers in the United Kingdom were often confused by the very wide range of qualifications in use. Award bodies gave little or no credit for prior learning that had been achieved in day-to-day working or in domestic situations. But nowadays the ability to apply skills in the workplace and to demonstrate occupational competence is valued.

The government established **The National Council for Vocational Qualifications (NCVQ)** who decided that the existing system of qualifications needed to be rationalised and made more straightforward and acceptable to employers. NCVQ also considered that the best place for the demonstration and assessment of skills and supporting knowledge is the workplace. Here performance on the job can be evaluated and accredited. National standards for each job competence or skill are being certificated in the system of **National Vocational Qualifications (NVQs)** and a NVQ framework has been created covering all occupations and significant areas of employment. The main features of NVQs are that they are **employment-led, competence-based** and **logically arranged in levels**. They are certified statements of units of competence that have been demonstrated at the right standard in a given occupation. Awards show what it is that the achiever actually can do.

> Providers may need to consider the argument that employer-led developments will lead to a restrictive view of education and training, and narrow vocational self-interest.

Lead industry bodies (LIBs)

A **lead industry body** is a group formed to represent an occupational family, a sector of industry or commerce, or a specific area of employment. It is required to work out and list acceptable competences and performance standards for those working in an assortment of jobs, firms and situations within the occupational area.

Some lead bodies, together with related training organisations, examine the skill and training requirements of a particular subdivision of industry or commerce, and monitor the provision of resources for meeting the required needs.

Community

Attitudes are changing and there is a movement toward greater involvement of the community in training matters and the management of education; and likewise greater student interaction with the community. The culture of the training provider organisation will have a significant effect on public relations. Community perception of the values and attitudes communicated will affect utilisation of the service. Positive messages transmitted will result in business and a need to provide a quality service to match user expectations. Incompetence, unsatisfactory performance and failure to meet targets and commitments will lead to a poor reputation and eventual demise.

Marketing

Successful marketing will be evidenced by winning new customers and keeping existing ones. Successful providers seek out training needs and satisfy those needs with a quality service that is valued by the client. Waiting for clients to knock on the door may not be an effective way of remaining in business. Opportunities for development have to be found and exploited.

Market research will play an important role in defining markets where opportunities exist. Relying entirely upon traditional strengths or areas of proven expertise alone may be a mistake, but utilising the competence of staff to develop a niche market could be very profitable. Finding test markets, evaluating product life-cycles, positioning products and studying customer orientation are marketing activities that may prove to be cost-effective in the end.

Marketing strategies are facilitated by staff and implementation of the curriculum marketing plan requires people who have the requisite skills, motivation and attitudes. Staff must be matched with the characteristic elements of strategy: entrepreneurial activity, organisation, delivery and administration. Keeping up-to-date records of skills audits and staff development outcomes can be useful when selecting staff that will match needs.

Giving incentives, prizes, remission, recognition or a share of the income generated from the creation of new, fully-costed business are concepts that at first may seem unthinkable, but if this leads to ways of winning new customers maybe the end will justify the means.

Giving rewards will ensure that tasks get done. Poor service may result from lack of a proper reward system.

Quality probe – marketing strategy

- Is there a documented marketing strategy in operation?
- Does the strategy complement the mission statement?
- Does the marketing policy take account of political, environmental, social and technological trends?
- Is there a nominated person responsible for marketing activities?
- Are there detailed marketing plans?
- Is market research carried out?
- Is there a system for evaluating data gathered?
- Have adequate resources been allocated?

Design

Recruitment and induction

Clients are entitled to gain access to certain aspects of a provider's service when entering the system. The provider will need to have in place documented procedures that will enable them to do so. An effective recruitment process would logically lead the client to negotiating a training programme and then to an appropriate induction programme.

Entitlement may include:

- recognition of previous experience and achievement;
- accreditation of prior learning;
- opportunities for progression and personal development;
- equality of treatment regardless of gender, race, age, ability, sexual orientation or religion;
- an effective induction;
- information, guidance, counselling and support.

An audit of the recruitment and induction could be based on asking the questions given in Figure 11.1 on page 248.

Design control

Having established a client's requirements during recruitment, initial assessment and induction to the training provision, the provider will need to be able systematically to translate the needs identified into a training programme and action plan. Where possible the outcomes should lead to NVQs or other recognised qualifications.

> Research, design and curriculum development procedures should be clearly defined and documented, and a person appointed to be responsible for design control and curriculum planning. An elementary guide for design control is given in the following quality probe.

Quality probe – design control[7]

The quality system should cover activities involved in the design of the training provision and services.

Are the requirements listed below covered by your quality system?
- Is the management of design relating to organisational structure, responsibility and authority defined?
- Do design plans include:
    the responsibility for each design and development activity?

---

the facility to allocate work to adequately-resourced and qualified staff?
an effective communication system?
a procedure for monitoring and control of design activities?
timescales relating to project plans?
systematic reviews of design activities?
systematic verification of design conformance with agreed requirements?
Is there a documented procedure that is followed when there is a need for the design process to deviate from the specification? If so, is there a procedure to adopt when permission for change is sought from the originators?

The curriculum design process needs to be systematised. A formalised design procedure, showing inputs and outputs, and all associated activities, should be in place. Each element could be logged against a timebase so that course or curriculum planners may co-ordinate progress against a training plan or proposed launch of new learning opportunities.

The system should incorporate means of controlling approval and implementation of submissions for new or updated provision, whether changes are originated in-house or by external agents (lead bodies, TECs, award bodies and the like), trainee groups, clients or other end users, such as employers.

Maintenance of contract requirements, quality, reliability, standards, safety and hygiene, and the issue and return of documentation should be formalised.

New product design

When planning and designing new training provision or devising new procedures a **flow chart** or critical path, indicating key events, could be drawn up. These devices enable critically important stages in the design programme to be highlighted and may also signal the time for a design review to take place. Changes may need to be made before the design is complete and this is often the case where providers are expected to respond quickly to new legislation and government-sponsored training initiatives. A procedure to document and record change must be maintained.

Design changes

Course design and curriculum development projects are often subject to revision, modification and change. Change in programme design occurs in all kinds of enterprise and this gives rise to the need for a documentation and control procedure.

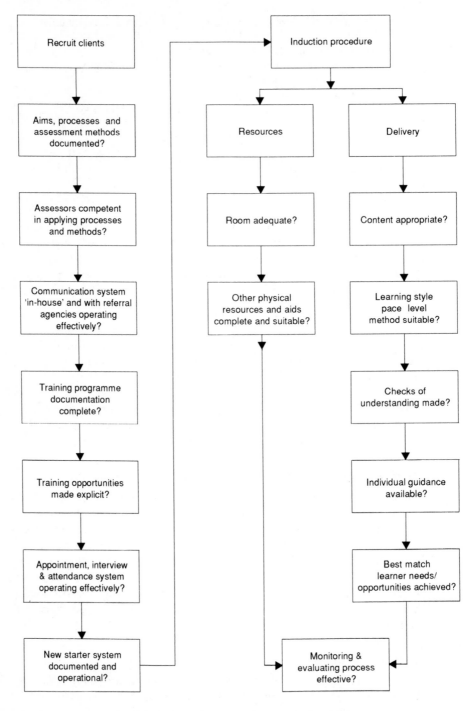

Figure 11.1 Audit – recruitment and induction process

Authorising changes

Information derived from early feedback relating to training events can benefit training providers and their clients. People will be able to learn from experiences and mistakes made, and to actuate damage-limitation contingencies.

A documented system for maintaining effective communications and feedback from training provision allows changes to be made that will promote continuous improvement.

Changes may become necessary when individual, group or organisational performance does not match the performance criteria around which the training was designed.

There should be someone nominated to initiate design changes, to approve modifications and to authorise their implementation.

Quality probe – design change[8]

Before permitting a change:

- Does the provision still conform to the design specification (or meet clients' identified needs)?
- Will the changed provision still meet requirements (such as NVQs and other performance criteria)?
- Is it possible to change the specification to meet the change sought?
- Will the proposed changes affect other work or provision?
- Will changes create problems in other parts of the provision or service, and if so are these surmountable?
- Does the provision or service still remain verifiable?
- Is the procedure for design verification documented and is the activity ongoing?

Document control – curriculum development

Responsibility for managing documentation – such as controlling and recording revisions and material generated due to course design changes, preparing and distributing updated documentation, and controlling the flow of awareness-raising paperwork – should be allocated to a member of the curriculum development team.

The person should have the authority to approve and issue documentation, to remove obsolete paperwork from the system and to retrieve non-current resources. Such items might include schemes of work, units, elements and performance criteria, assignments, assessments, records of achievement, handouts and other resources.

The items may have been issued to learning resource centres, assessment centres, teachers and work-based trainers and assessors. Some staff have a habit of hanging on to old originals for which they may have prepared session plans and notes ready for later use. They are often unaware that revised documents are available or have been issued to others. This practice can play havoc with curriculum processes and quality of provision.

Changes have to be controlled and reported to users, and hence a system for controlling the flow of documentation and changes should be maintained.

Quality probe – curriculum development

Do your curriculum aims adequately cover:

- initial assessment?
- induction?
- meeting individual's needs?
- meeting employer's needs?
- meeting examining boards and lead bodies' requirements?
- flexible learning opportunities?
- progression?
- age and aptitude range?
- equal opportunities?
- special needs and learning difficulties?
- multicultural education?
- communication, numeracy, literacy, information technology and basic skills?
- counselling and guidance?
- accreditation of prior learning and achievement?
- self-assessments and appraisals?
- assessment on demand?
- recording achievement?
- certification?
- recognising opportunities (SWOT analysis)?
- curriculum planning?
- prioritising initiatives?
- reacting to the need for change?
- matching resources to need?
- adjusting to different conditions?
- action planning
- estimating future direction?
- staff development training?
- teaching and learning methods?
- education/industry links?

Implementation

Teaching and learning strategies

Implementation is the process by which the training programme or service is delivered to the client. The effectiveness of the service in meeting curriculum objectives will depend largely upon the extent to which the delivery of training programmes meets the individual educational, career and personal development needs of clients at the right quality.

To be effective, the provider should implement strategies for facilitating a suitable induction for all newcomers, both in-house and at placements. Occupational training should be related to learners' action plans and future roles, and before the programme ends there should be a pre-release programme or adequate preparation for entry to work, or progression to higher education.

Work-based, performance-related training should reflect current developments in business and documented procedures for each NVQ element or task should be available.

Teaching of practice and theory should be integrated and supporting knowledge and understanding should be directed toward underpinning NVQ performance criteria or skills test specifications. Likewise, on-the-job and off-the-job training should be integrated with the NVQ programme or with the achievement of other positive outcomes.

The relevance and scope of training programme content and teaching and learning strategies should be matched with performance criteria. The programme should be delivered at a suitable rate and in logical sequence.

The teaching and learning strategy should contain procedures for course team meetings and regular programme review, including the examination of learning opportunities and methods.

Delivery modes

Learner participation

The need actively to involve learners during the training programme and to encourage learner independence throughout training is thought to be of paramount importance. Designing activities suitable for student-centred participative learning is a very demanding task that calls for a planning-led approach to curriculum design.

An audit of delivery modes could include checks on the use of:

- one-to-one and small group activity, with face-to-face contact between trainer and learners;
- problem solving and brainstorming;

- demonstration, coaching and practice;
- work-based projects and assignments;
- trainee-centred reviewing.

Distance learning

Open learning, distance learning and flexistudy are a means of widening and creating access to learning and the accreditation of competence. The location and timing of training sessions and other learning opportunities needs to be acceptable to clients. The provision of an all-year-round assessment service and 'roll-on/roll-off' programmes of initial assessment and training going some way to alleviating difficulties.

> Training providers may need to implement a flexible timetable adjusted to suit people with time constraints or others having difficulty in reaching the training centre.

Resource development

Training aids supplement other forms of presentation and can enhance the process of perception and retention. Learning resources and equipment relevant to the learning programme content and current practice within an occupational area tend to improve the efficiency of learning. Planned usage of audio-visual aids, computers and hands-on, practical simulations increases the scope and coverage of learning opportunities.

> An audit of training resources would include testing the applicability of learning resources in relation to specified learning objectives or performance criteria. A review and evaluation of the use of aids in the training process would provide evidence that the resources employed have resulted in improved training outcomes.

Guidance and support

Steps may be taken actively to involve people in decisions about how they will learn and other aspects of their proposed training programme. Where action plans or personal training plans have been written it is helpful to review with clients their progress in the achievement of elements of competence. Discussion during reviews serves to identify those with exceptionally high ability and may also bring to light difficulties that hold up progress.

> Review allows possible courses of action to be considered. Procedure for helping clients with special needs or learning difficulties, and the identification of problems, provision of remedial education and referral of clients with behaviour problems, may be triggered.

Quality probe – guidance and support

- Is there a documented procedure for learner guidance and support?
- Is there a personal tutor system in operation?
- Do clients receive adequate feedback on progress and outcomes of training?
- Are clients with specific learning difficulties and those with above-average ability readily identified?
- Is there a named person responsible for supervising and implementing learner support policy and procedures?
- Is the quality and effectiveness of support monitored?
- If so, is there an identified monitoring team that selects and gathers appropriate evidence and carries out reviews and evaluations?
- Are there valid and reliable performance indicators relating to the evaluation of support throughout the provision?
- Are outcomes of reviews widely disseminated across the provision?
- Are there staff-development opportunities for those involved in giving guidance and support?
- Is the guidance element of curriculum development integrated with other key features of the curriculum quality plan?

The need for careers guidance is recognised and careers staff liaise with providers and assist with interviewing, advising and supporting clients. Study guidance, personal tutoring and counselling are essential elements of a quality curriculum plan.

New technology

The provider's technology comprises curriculum processes and resources committed to the delivery of education and training. Where the technology owned is adequate to meet demands there may be little difficulty in satisfying the contract needs and wants. However, customer requirements may quickly change in response to employment trends or the introduction of new technology, and costly resource renewal may be demanded in order to remain in the race. At the same time, human resources will need to be updated to handle change.

On the plus side, computers and other modern technology may make possible more effective, supported self-study, backed by facilitators and the transfer of some work currently undertaken by trainers to administrators or support staff.

Standards and assessment

The type of assessment method used will be matched to the particular competence to be accredited. The essential feature will be the need to validate properly the candidate's claim to ownership by relating assessment methods to performance criteria.

Confirmation of competence may derive from a mix of assessed prior achievement, observation of performance and supplementary evidence. Systems should be in place for gathering, challenging and evaluating evidence to support claims for accreditation of competence. Being able to give and receive feedback on achievement is an important skill for trainees, trainers and assessors.

Modern training practice is more client-centred than in the past and self-assessment techniques backed by formative and summative assessment is now an integral part of curriculum design.

A systematic approach for ensuring that the prescribed assessment procedure is followed should be adopted. It is advisable to maintain an assessment record showing all achievement that has been accredited.

Quality probe – assessment

- Is there a documented procedure for assessment of performance and competence?
- Is there a named person responsible for developing and implementing assessment policy and procedures?
- Is the quality and effectiveness of assessment monitored?
- If so, is there an identified monitoring team that selects and gathers appropriate evidence and carries out reviews and evaluations?
- Are there valid and reliable performance indicators relating to the evaluation of assessment throughout the provision?
- Are outcomes of reviews widely disseminated across the provision?
- Is there staff development support for staff involved in assessment?
- Is the assessment element of curriculum development integrated with other key features of the curriculum quality plan?

Review and evaluation

Monitoring and evaluation (M&E)

The final stage in curriculum development is the monitoring, review and evaluation of the responsiveness of the course to the needs identified and the quality, efficiency and effectiveness of outcomes. This stage is discussed in greater depth in Chapter 9.

Another check that is normally made is that of relating learners' actual achievements to original objectives. The review and evaluation process will identify the strengths and weaknesses of the course and will give rise to modifications for future planning consideration.

The evaluators will need to make all of the course team aware of the modifications required and feed back information to all concerned in the course operation. An element of evaluation that is often overlooked is client satisfaction, that is, whether or not clients thought the training provision met their needs and expectations.

Systematic monitoring, review and evaluation of the quality of teaching and learning will need to be an integral part of a training provider's operations.

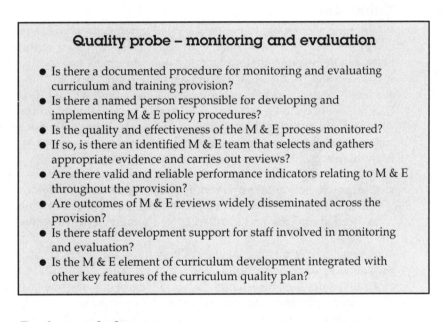

Quality probe – monitoring and evaluation

- Is there a documented procedure for monitoring and evaluating curriculum and training provision?
- Is there a named person responsible for developing and implementing M & E policy procedures?
- Is the quality and effectiveness of the M & E process monitored?
- If so, is there an identified M & E team that selects and gathers appropriate evidence and carries out reviews?
- Are there valid and reliable performance indicators relating to M & E throughout the provision?
- Are outcomes of M & E reviews widely disseminated across the provision?
- Is there staff development support for staff involved in monitoring and evaluation?
- Is the M & E element of curriculum development integrated with other key features of the curriculum quality plan?

Review and change

Monitoring and evaluating is a procedure for systematically reviewing the curriculum and training provision. Results of the review indicate the effect of programmes and help curriculum managers take action designed to ensure that completions, outcomes and client satisfaction meet internal and external requirements and expectations. The aim of the process is to raise the quality of training and service delivered.

Audits are used to inform decision makers and to justify any subsequent action taken. Audits may be based upon course team reviews, departmental programme reviews, external moderator's and assessor's reports, HMI reports and course evaluations provided by students or delegates.

A systematic approach, such as that given in Figure 11.2, could be used to handle feedback provided by delegates who have completed a M&E form. However, in practice it is often found that rating scales from one to five tempt delegates to choose a middle number for their ratings and that spaces for comments are not well utilised. Similarly, when 'happy-hour sheets' are completed half-heartedly or in a rush at the end of an event, they may not provide reliable data. This is particularly true when questions are designed to avoid negative responses and bad news.

> Before the event, it may be helpful for members of the delivery team to ask themselves the question 'Are we capable of doing the job correctly?' It will be too late to prevent failures if the question is asked during an inquest.

After sales

When things go wrong, someone will need to put matters right. A system of alerting that person will need to operate. This may entail appointing a person to be responsible for rectifying nonconformity and shortcomings whenever they occur, and preventing their recurrence. In the case of academic matters, where clients claim that training did not meet programme objectives, the facts will have to be identified and the claim reviewed. Urgent checks will be called for to establish whether or not the training programme or service offered complies with contract or award body requirements.

> Corrective action taken to rectify deficiencies in the service and associated documentation should be checked against original or revised standards and verified by the quality representative.

Clients who use an assessment-only part of the service can expect providers to operate an updating service for additional units awarded. Also, after-sales matters, such as changes in legislation, the need to top up qualifications or other factors relating to the service provided, could usefully be communicated to past users.

> Analysis of customer complaints will lead to the identification of causes of nonconformance, so that properly-documented and prompt corrective and preventive action may be taken.

Servicing

Servicing is the provision of help or assistance, and back-up materials or resources, to customers who have purchased education and training from a provider. Post-training learner support and follow up are important customer requirements. Hence, they should form part of the curriculum quality management system.

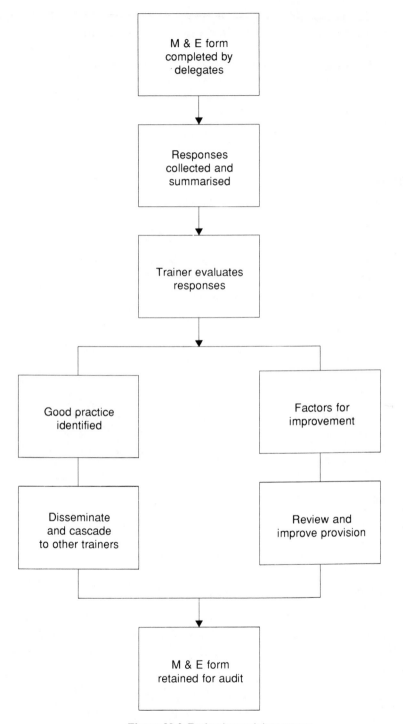

Figure 11.2 Evaluating training events

Servicing procedures should be documented in the quality manual and when required carried out effectively.

Winning customers is very rewarding for the provider, but keeping them can be even more rewarding. Giving an excellent service is to be applauded, but to be effective its utility must be perceived and valued by the end user. It is the ability of the service to satisfy the customers' wants that really counts.

Notes

1 *Strategy and Processes,* FEU, London, 1986.

2 *Quality in NAFE,* p. 6, FEU, London, 1987.

3 Ibid.

4 R. W. Tyler, *Basic Principles of Curriculum and Instruction,* pp. 46–7, University of Chicago Press, Chicago, 1949.

5 *Quality in NAFE,* p. 12, FEU, London, 1987.

6 L. Walklin, *The Assessment of Performance and Competence,* Stanley Thornes (Publishers) Ltd, Cheltenham, 1991.

7 Content based upon information given in BS 5750:Part 4 (1990), p. 5, para 4.4.

8 Ibid. p. 6, para 4.4.

Bibliography

B. J. Caldwell and J. M. Spinks, *The Self-Managing School*, The Falmer Press, Lewes, 1988.

Education and Training, July 1986, published six times a year by MCB University Press Ltd.

D. Evans and R. Ford, *Control of Manufacture*, Holt, Rinehart and Winston, London, 1984.

K. B. Everard and G. Morris, *Effective School Management*, Paul Chapman Publishing Ltd, London, 1985.

R. Fisher and W. Ury, *Getting to Yes: Negotiating Agreement without Giving In*, Hutchinson, London, 1983.

A. Foster, 'Explaining Quality Systems', published in *Training Tomorrow*, September 1990 issue, MCB University Press Ltd, 1990.

D. Garforth and H. Macintosh, *Profiling: a user's manual*, Stanley Thornes (Publishers) Ltd, Cheltenham, 1986.

P. Hanks (Editor), *The Collins English Dictionary* (Second edition), William Collins Sons and Co Ltd, London and Glasgow, 1986.

Joint Efficiency Study (JES) Report *Managing Colleges Efficiently – report of a study of efficiency in non-advanced further education for the Government and the Local Authority Associations*, Department of Education and Science and Welsh Office, HMSO, London, 1987.

C. N. Keen, *The College Prospectus*, HEIST, Banbury 1987.

J. Kenney and M. Reid, *Training Interventions*, Institute of Personnel Management, London, 1986.

M. Le Boeuf, *How to win customers and keep them for life*, Judy Piatkus (Publishers) Ltd, London, 1990.

M. H. B. McDonald and J. W. Leppard, *How to sell a service*, (second edition), published on behalf of the Institute of Marketing, Heinemann Professional Publishing Ltd, Oxford, 1988.

R. McDonald and E. Roe, *Reviewing Departments – Green Guide No. 1*, Higher Education Research and Development Society of Australasia (HERDSA), Kensington, NSW, Australia, 1984.

J. S. Oakland, *Total Quality Management*, Butterworth-Heinemann Ltd, Oxford, 1989.

R. Plant, *Managing change and making it stick*, Gower Publishing Company Ltd, Aldershot, 1987.

Scheme for Organisational Studies CGLI 771, City and Guilds of London Institute, London, 1987.

A. Spencer, N. Finlayson and S. Crabbe, *Coombe Lodge Report*, 'Women in Further and Higher Education Management', Vol. 20, No. 3, The Further Education Staff College, Coombe Lodge, Blagdon, Bristol, 1987.

The Training Provider Quality Survey Manual, Coventry and Warwickshire Training and Enterprise Council, Coventry, 1990.

Training Provider Quality Survey Manual, Dorset Training and Enterprise Council, Bournemouth, May 1991.

J. Walker and R. Hooper, *Putting the Customer First*, Lancashire County Council, Central Lancashire Business and Industrial Centre, Leyland, 1988.

L. Walklin, *Teaching and Learning in Further and Adult Education*, Stanley Thornes (Publishers) Ltd, Cheltenham, 1990.

L. Walklin, *The Assessment of Performance and Competence*, Stanley Thornes (Publishers) Ltd, Cheltenham, 1991.

Welcome to the NCVQ Database, National Council for Vocational Qualifications, London, 1990.

BSI publications

BS 3138:1979, *Glossary of terms used in work study and organization and methods (O & M)*, British Standards Institution, London.

BS 4778:Part 1 (1987), *Quality vocabulary – Part 1 International terms*, British Standards Institution, London.

BS 4778:Part 2 (1979), *Glossary of terms used in quality assurance (including reliability and maintainability terms)*, British Standards Institution, London.

BS 4891:1972, *A guide to quality assurance*, British Standards Institution, London.

BS 5750:Parts 0, 1, 2 and 3 (1987), and Part 4 (1990), *British Standard Quality Systems*, British Standards Institution, London.

BS 5781:1979, *Specification for measurement and calibration systems*, British Standards Institution, London.

BS 6143:Part 2 (1990), *Guide to the economics of quality – Part 2 Prevention, appraisal and failure model*, British Standards Institution, London.

BS 7229:1989, *British Standard Guide to Quality Systems Auditing*, British Standards Institution, London.

Guidance notes for application of BS 5750/ISO 9000/EN 29000 to education and training, BSI Quality Assurance, Milton Keynes, January 1991.

DTI publications

BS 5750/ISO 9000:1987 – A positive contribution to better business, prepared by BSI Quality Assurance for The Department of Trade and Industry, (DTI Enterprise Initiative), London, 1990.

Leadership and Quality Management – A Guide for Chief Executives, prepared by R. J. Mortiboys for the Department of Trade and Industry (DTI Enterprise Initiative), London, 1990. DTI/PUB 170/10K/11/90.

Quality Circles, prepared by Patrick Dolan, members of the National Society of Quality Circles and others for The Department of Trade and Industry, (DTI Enterprise Initiative), London, 1990. DTI/PUB 194/10K/09/90.

The Quality Gurus – What can they do for your company?, prepared by Professor Tony Bendell of Nottingham Polytechnic on behalf of Services Ltd, for The Department of Trade and Industry, (DTI Enterprise Initiative), London, 1990.

Total Quality Management – A practical approach, prepared by Professor John S. Oakland for The Department of Trade and Industry, (DTI Enterprise Initiative), London, 1990. DTI/PUB 260/20K/5/90.

FEU publications

A. Fido (project leader), *Quality assurance: summary report of a project to develop and evaluate a quality assurance package*, (DES PICKUP initiative), FEU, London, 1988.

Quality in NAFE, FEU, London, 1987.

Strategy and Processes, FEU, London, 1986.

The College Does it Better, FEU, London, 1987.

Towards a Framework for Curriculum Entitlement, Further Education Unit (FEU), London, 1989.

Towards an Educational Audit, FEU, (RP304), London, 1989.

TEED publications

Cases of good practice, Management Training and Development 'Action for Jobs' Initiative, Investing in People Booklet No. 4, Manpower Services Commission (now TEED), Moorfoot, January 1987.

Facing problems of rapid change, Management Training and Development 'Action for Jobs' Initiative, Investing in People Booklet No. 11, Manpower Services Commission (now TEED), Moorfoot, January 1987.

Literacy and Numeracy – a guide to practice, Training Agency (now the Employment Department Group – Training Enterprise and Education Directorate (TEED)), Sheffield, June 1989.

Making appraisals matter, Management Training and Development 'Action for Jobs' Initiative, Investing in People Booklet No. 3, Manpower Services Commission (now TEED), Moorfoot, January 1987.

Index

access and initial assessment   79, 115
access, contractor   228
accident procedures   35
accommodation   124, 217
accountability pyramid   201
achievement
   criteria   155
   prior   125
   records   212
action planning   112
administration   100
administrative support   122, 211
admissions   116
adults learning   235, 241
after-sales servicing   256
aims   49
analysis
   cause and effect   197
   self-   119
   strengths and weaknesses
      (SWOT)   232
annual review   204, 205
appraisal costs   56
assessing
   competence   157, 165
   needs of adult learners   120, 121, 235
assessment
   centre
      accommodation   124
      co-ordinators   123
      manager   122
      staff   122
   departmental   200
   final   156
   hardware   124
   initial   120
   learner progress   124, 155
   making initial   79, 115
   mode   157
   of sub-contractors   224
   processes   239
   recording   124
   sectional   200

standards   253
subsequent   120
test
   records   124, 160
   status   161
assessors   122
assurance, quality   28, 54, 158, 180, 200,
   201
attitudes
   formation of positive   34, 64
   towards clients   132
audio-visual aids   140
audit
   administration   207
   arranging   25
   curriculum   231-58
   defined   23
   end of training   200
   environment   217
   external affairs   223-8
   internal   192
   objectives   23, 24
   preparing for   25, 26
   provision   220
   quality   23, 56, 89
   recruitment and induction   248
   reports   169
   resource   217
   responsibilities   23
   sequence   203
   skills   119
   team approach   204
   training strategies   105, 221
auditing the quality system   89, 220
auditor responsibilities   23, 24
authorising changes   249
availability   138
awareness raising   66

benefits of TQM
   to provider   57
   for staff   57
brainstorming   196

BS 5750
  aim of 86
  certification 18, 19
  implementing 92
  in education and training 85, 86, 91
  link with TQM 89
  strengths of 90
budgetary control 210
burden of proof 32
business cycle 190-1

capital equipment 137
cascading, principles 68
cause and effect analysis 197
certification 215
change
  and product development 41, 42
  authorising 249
  challenge of 41
  introducing 38-51
  managing 44
  resistance to 40
circles, setting up 66
claiming competence 125
client
  liaison skills 229
  portfolios 125
communication skills 143
community 244
competence, claiming 125
competences, checklist of 119
complaints 81
computers 146
consultants 193-5
continuous improvement 89
contract review 93, 94, 112
contracting 93, 225
contractor access 228
control
  document 249
  quality process 131
corrective action 56, 164
costing procedures 210
counselling and guidance 237
course content 238
criterion referencing 120
culture 40
curriculum
  audits 231-58
  components of 111, 234
  design 111, 238
  development
    cycle 111
    document control 249
    processes 111, 232
  entitlement 103, 110, 112
  objectives 238
  planning 111, 232, 233
  provision 232-40
  structuring 239

customer
  care in training 71, 74
  charter 78
  destinations 168
  entitlement 110
  external 77
  internal 77
  liaison 79
  needs 87, 88
  orientation 78
  perceptions 83, 167
  relations 73
  requirements 73, 77, 88
  satisfaction 78
  services 79, 80

data processing 146
delegation 64
delivery modes 251
design
  and promotion 229
  changes 247
  control 246
  new product 247
  review 246-9
destinations 168
development 58
diagram, fishbone or Ishikawa 197-9
diaries, training 212
distance learning 252
document control 249
documentation, learner 100, 212

early leavers 168
educating the workforce 67, 94
Education Reform Act 1988
  educational aspects 21, 240
  technology 139
effectiveness
  of learning 165
  of organisation 57
  of provision 218, 220
  of teaching 165
efficiency 57
embedding
  good practice 125
  NVQs 47
employer
  perception of provision 168
  values and needs 244
entitlement 110
equal opportunities 112, 142, 226
equipment 217
evaluating training events 257
evaluation 104, 111, 178-88, 200, 202,
    254-8
evaluators 194
evidence 175
external
  affairs audit 223-8
  customers 77

failure costs   55
feedback
    giving and receiving   143
    linking audit to service provision   200
final assessment and testing   156
financial, management   151, 210
fire hazards   33
first impressions   83
fishbone or Ishikawa diagram   197-9
force field analysis   43

gathering
    data   181
    information   183
gender   113, 114
governors   82
guidance   237, 252
gurus   53

handling training requests   219
hardware
    learning   137
    teaching   137
health and safety
    basic obligations
        of employees   30
        of employers   30
    in learning environment   34, 134, 226
    policy   226
Health and Safety at Work Act 1974   29,
    102, 134
human resource inputs   9, 104, 222-3

identification of training needs   117, 118,
    135, 219, 234
image of organisation   71
implementers   194
implementing
    curriculum   111, 251-4
    recommendations   176, 187
    TQM   63
improving provision   61, 65, 76, 89
inducting clients   80, 95-103, 117, 246
information, dissemination   125
infrastructure   74
initial assessment   79, 80, 115-17
innovation   94
innovators   194
inspection   139, 149
internal
    audits   203
    customers   77
interviewing   208
investing in people   58
involving everyone   64
Ishikawa diagram   197-9

laboratory safety   32
labour   132
lead industry body   244

learners
    collaborative   142
    dependent   142
    documentation   212
    independence   142
    participation   251
learning
    assessment   228
    distance   252
    environment   150
    resources   126, 140-1
    support   109, 227
    strategies   102, 141, 236, 251
liaising
    with awarding bodies   223
    with clients   230
log-books   212, 213

machines   132
maintainability   139
maintenance schedules   139
management
    budget   210
    financial   150, 210
    information system   210
    objectives   72
    organisation   103
    representative   20
    resource   210
    responsibility   12, 28
    review   20, 203
managing
    activities   63
    change   44
    exhibitions   229
manpower (personpower)   104, 132
manual   3, 14, 15, 169, 200
marketing
    provision   72, 127, 128, 228, 245
    strategies   228, 229, 245
materials   132, 139
measurement   132, 147
method study   61, 62
methods   132, 141
milieu   132, 150
mission statements   3, 4, 105
modular programme   49
modularisation, implementation   49
monitoring
    improvements   65
    officers   211
    purpose of   180
    quality   202
    staff   194
    trainer-centred   21
    training
        placement   225, 227
        provision   224
monitoring and evaluation   149, 178-88,
    202, 254, 255

TQM
→

need
  balancing   45
  customer   87, 88, 117, 235, 241
  diagnosing   235
  for competent staff   10
  training analysis   117, 118, 135, 219,
    234
negotiating placement contracts   226
new product design   247-9
new technology   253
nonconformance   162-4
nonconformity   162
norm referencing   120
NVQs
  assessment model   160
  background to   47, 135, 165, 244
  embedding   47

objectives   3, 24, 72
open-learning packages   140, 145
operational features   183
organisation, image of   71
organisational
  aims   3
  chart   6-8
  culture   40
  evaluation   200, 202

paperwork flows   207
Pareto analysis   196
people as resources   63
performance indicators   156, 167
personal
  development   67
  profiles   216
personnel records   208
physical resource inputs   151, 221, 222
placement contracts   152, 224-8
plan
  curriculum   240
  quality   15, 16, 93
planning   22, 48, 93, 165, 240
policies   47, 99, 219
policy, quality   12-14
portfolios, client   125
premises   74, 169, 217
prevention costs   56
probes (*see also* quality probes)
    189-230
problem solving   195-200
procedural instructions   14, 17, 170-4
process
  capability   142
  control   131
  inputs   132
producing software   140
profiling   216
promotion   229
prospectus   229

provision
  audit of   220
  effectiveness of   218
  improving   76
  reviewing   61
  training   218
public relations   229
publicity   229
purchaser supplied products   125
purchasing services   224-8
putting the customer first   70-84

quality
  assessing   202
  assurance   28, 54, 180, 200, 201
  assurance aspects   158
  audits   23, 56, 105, 192, 203
  chains   54
  circles   65
  control, of training provision   218,
    221, 224
  controllers   194
  costs
    appraisal   56
    assurance   54
    failure   55
    model   55
    prevention   56
  culture   2
  documentation and records   93
  elements   106, 107
  failure costs   55
  gurus   53
  indicators   156
  management system   9
  manual   3, 14, 15, 169, 200
  market research   127
  marketing   127, 128, 228-30
  monitoring
    assessing quality   202
    of work   53
  organisation charts   6, 8
  organisational evaluation   180
  performance indicators   156
  plan   15, 21
  planning   1-37, 93
  policy   12, 13
  probes   189-230
  problem solving   196-200
  procedures   14, 16, 170-4
  product design   247
  profiles   216
  records   202, 203
  related costs   55
  service results   154-77
  surveillance   56
  survey manual   169
  system   106
quality probe covering
  accident procedures   36

adults learning   242
assessment   254
checking staff back-up   141
confidence building   243
curriculum audits   241
curriculum development   112, 250
design change   249
design control   246
diagnosing need   68
equal opportunities (gender)   115
equal opportunities policy   113
employee's responsibilities (H&S)   31
employer's responsibilities (H&S)   30
employing staff   209
evaluation, training provision   180
fires   33
flexible delivery   237
gathering information   182
guidance and support   253
health and safety policy   29
human resources   136
identification of training needs   120, 235
initial assessment staff   121
internal quality   27
introducing new resources   147
laboratory safety   33
learner documentation   217
learning environment   150
management responsibility   12
managing change   44
market research   127
marketing and access   128
marketing function   73
marketing strategy   245
monitoring
   evaluating curriculum   255
   service   179
paperwork flows   207
plant and equipment   138
premises   217
problem solving   196
promoting change   46
quality manual   15
quality planning   16
quality policy   14
responsibility and authority   20
risks and dangers   34
service design   109
service evaluation   200
service results   176
staff development   123
sub-contractor provision   228
teamwork   61
training needs   120, 235
work groups   206

record
   keeping   124, 203, 212–16
   of achievement   212
   types of   212–16

recording assessment   124
recruitment and induction   95, 208, 248
reliability   138, 159
reports   169, 175
resistance to change   40
resource
   centres   121, 151
   development   252
   financial   150
   human   9, 63, 222, 223
   identification   218
   implications   121
   learner-centred   126
   management   210
   personnel   63
   physical   151, 221, 222
   planning   240
   traceability   218
responding quickly   42
responsibility and authority   19, 65
responsiveness   88
review
   annual   204
   departmental plans   205
   outturns   205
   performance   204
   planning   204
   probes, *see quality probes*
   provision   155
   systems   191, 200
   team   206
reviewing
   curriculum   111, 254, 258
   learner progress   147–9, 170–4
   provision   61
role
   and responsibilities in TQM   65
   of central admissions   116
   of student services   79–81

safety   29–36
sectional assessments   200
selecting areas for improvement   61
selection   208
self-assessment
   audits   91
   checklist   28
   of competences   119
service
   administrative   207
   audit reports   169, 175
   delivery   130–53
   design   109–29
   evaluation   220
   model   109
   monitoring and evaluating the   178–88
   purpose and aims   151
   results   154–77
   setting up quality circles   66
   structure   165
servicing   256

skills audit   119
SOCDIM (method study)   62
software   140
staff
  accreditation   123
  competence   10
  development   105, 123
  trainers   67
  training   123
  supervisors   67
staffing   10, 74, 104, 208
standards   253
statistical techniques   161
steering groups   63
strategic
  planning   22
  service vision   4
strengths, analysis of   182, 232
student
  counsellor   79
  services   79–81
sub-contractors   224
suggestions and ideas   65
support
  administrative for trainers   211
  learner   252
  staff   133, 210
survey
  of premises   74
  quality   169
SWOT analysis   232
system
  analyst   146
  elements   106, 107, 145
  management information   210
  organisation   20
  surveys   74, 200

target groups   95
targets   87
teaching
  hardware   137
  strategies   144, 236, 251
team
  approach   64, 204
  building   59
  review   206
  work   59–61
technology   253
test
  records   160
  schedules   139
  status   139
testing   149, 156
timetabling   136
total quality management
  audits   89
  benefits   57
  concept   51, 52
  customer care   71

  defined   52
  developing   58
  education   86
  features   53
  implementing   63
  introducing   38
  link with BS 5750   89
  planning and documentation   93
  putting the customer first   71
  targets   87
  team building   59
TQM
  and BS 5750   85–107
  concept development and
    implementation   51–69
  putting the customer first   70–84
trainee
  responsibilities   99
  review   170–5, 211
  rights   99
trainer
  administrative support for   211
  competence   134
  documentation   214
  responsibilities   99
trainers   67, 133
training
  agreement factors   101
  awareness raising   66
  cards   214
  cascading principles   68
  co-ordinators   211
  cycle   134, 135
  declaration   101
  delivering   165
  diary   212, 213
  gaps   135
  need analysis   117, 118, 135, 219, 234
  personal development   67, 109
  plans and programmes   102, 118, 146, 165
  provision   218, 221, 224
  records   212
  requests   218, 219
  sub-contractors   224
  workforce   67

useful life   139

validity   159
values   241–4
verification of resources and personnel   218

weaknesses, analysis of   182, 232
work
  instructions   14, 18, 173, 174
  placement   152
working
  documents   26
  together   60
workplace, induction programme   98